GARBAGE CITIZENSHIP

ROSALIND FREDERICKS

GARBAGE CITIZENSHIP

Vital Infrastructures of Labor in Dakar, Senegal

Duke University Press   Durham and London   2018

© 2018 Duke University Press
All rights reserved
Printed in the United States of America on acid-free paper ∞
Designed by Courtney Leigh Baker
Typeset in Whitman and Knockout by Copperline Books

Library of Congress Cataloging-in-Publication Data
Names: Fredericks, Rosalind, author.
Title: Garbage citizenship : vital infrastructures of labor
in Dakar, Senegal / Rosalind Fredericks.
Description: Durham : Duke University Press, 2018. |
Includes bibliographical references and index.
Identifiers: LCCN 2018007283 (print) | LCCN 2018008409 (ebook)
ISBN 9781478002505 (ebook)
ISBN 9781478000990 (hardcover : alk. paper)
ISBN 9781478001416 (pbk. : alk. paper)
Subjects: LCSH: Political participation—Senegal—Dakar. |
Labor—Senegal—Dakar. | Working poor—Political activity—
Senegal—Dakar. | Refuse collection—Senegal—Dakar.
Classification: LCC JQ3396.A91 (ebook) |
LCC JQ3396.A91 F74 2018 (print)
DDC 322/.209663—dc23
LC record available at https://lccn.loc.gov/2018007283

COVER ART: A trash worker in Niari Tali. 2007.
Photo courtesy of the author.

FOR MOM   *for your* **grit** *and* **generosity**

CONTENTS

Acknowledgments ix

INTRODUCTION. **Trash Matters** 1

ONE. **Governing Disposability** 27

TWO. **Vital Infrastructures of Labor** 60

THREE. **Technologies of Community** 97

FOUR. **The Piety of Refusal** 123

CONCLUSION. **Garbage Citizenship** 149

Notes 155   References 171   Index 193

This book would not have been possible without the support, inspiration, collaboration, and critique of many people. I am deeply indebted to the people in Dakar who so graciously opened their homes and entrusted me with their stories. I would particularly like to thank Madany Sy and his colleagues for welcoming me with open arms into the affairs of the main trash workers union—le Syndicat National des travailleurs du nettoiement (National Cleaning Workers Union; SNTN)—and for introducing me to many of the union's leaders and delegates. I am also grateful to the leaders of the other trash unions in Dakar for their candid feedback. I am beholden to all of the trash workers who generously shared their personal histories and opinions, but especially to the sweepers and collectors of Niari Tali, Yoff, Grand Yoff, and Parcelles Assainies. I am equally indebted to the residents of HLM Fass and Tonghor who invited me into their homes and allowed me to ask difficult questions. In HLM Fass, my work would never have been possible without the time and energy of Said Gning and his family. In Tonghor, Seynabou Ndir introduced me to the neighborhood and facilitated the smooth running of my interviews. I would like to thank all of the other residents who let me interrupt their busy days, offered me food and drink, and allowed me to pry into some sticky and delicate matters.

A number of people from institutions and government agencies across Dakar helped me to piece together and document the history of trash politics. Oumar Cissé of l'Institute Africaine de gestion urbane (African Institute for Urban Management; IAGU) shared with me his trove of documents as well as his personal experience in the sector beginning with Set/Setal. I am indebted to the ex-mayor of Dakar, Mamadou Diop, for giving me access to his collection of unpublished memoirs. A huge debt is also owed to my incredible research assistants. Ndeye Bineta Laye Ndoye was more than just a partner in the day-to-day challenges of this research; she was also a great teacher. Ndeye Sophie Coly aided me immensely with the transcription of my interviews as well as the support and friendship she has offered since the project began. Abdou Mbodji was an informal research assistant for many years of this project and his friendship, boundless energy, and resourcefulness are sorely missed. My adoptive family in Yoff, especially Mbaye and Ronald, have taught me an enormous amount and have always provided support throughout my time in Dakar. Boubacar has remained a true friend and intellectual comrade since our research together many years ago.

I am deeply grateful for the years of support, guidance, and intellectual inspiration I received from Michael Watts, Gill Hart, Ananya Roy, and Mariane Ferme at UC Berkeley, where this project began as a dissertation. Mamadou Diouf has been a trusted mentor, collaborator, and friend throughout the project and it would look very different without his engagement at pivotal moments along the way. The deep engagement by members of my writing group at Berkeley, Sapana Doshi, Tracey Osborne, Mike Dwyer, Asher Ghertner, and Malini Ranganathan, were essential in early stages of the project. The intellectual community during my postdoctoral fellowship at the Committee on Global Thought at Columbia University was invaluable for beginning the revisions of the manuscript and placing the work into conversation with wider debates. The support I received as an assistant professor at NYU's Gallatin School, especially from Dean Susanne Wofford, was essential in bringing the project to completion. The conversations I have participated in with my wonderful colleagues at Gallatin have pushed me to transform the manuscript into a work that is even more valuable across disciplines. Discussions with geographical, anthropological, and Africanist colleagues over the years have helped me to hone the story and its implications for different scholarly debates. My students continue to be an inspiration, especially as they challenge me to distill the most essential lessons of this unique history.

Funding from the UC Berkeley Rocca Fellowship, National Science Foundation, Social Science Research Council, and Fulbright-Hays allowed me to carry out the original dissertation research. Funding from the Committee on Global Thought at Columbia University and NYU's Stephen Charney Vladeck

Junior Faculty Fellowship and Goddard Junior Faculty Fellowship allowed me to complete follow-up research and writing. I owe appreciation to my publisher, Duke University Press, especially Elizabeth Ault and the production team. With their help and that of two anonymous reviewers, this book has improved immensely.

Finally, my family has been an invaluable resource throughout this research. My partner, Jerome, has been a bulwark throughout the revisions and completion of this project. From careful criticism, editorial assistance, and wide-ranging discussion of relevant debates, to innumerable forms of support and encouragement as we birthed our books and babies, I couldn't have done it without him. Our girls arrived during this project and have helped to lighten the mood with smiles and giggles as well as to constantly remind me of what is most important. My father provided the original inspiration for studying discards through our forays in dumpster diving and has remained a prized intellectual and emotional interlocutor along this journey. My mother has always encouraged balance, which has kept me sane in difficult moments. This book is dedicated to her for the beacon provided by her strength of spirit.

Over the last twenty-five years, Senegal's capital city Dakar has been period-ically submerged in garbage. In 2007, seven years after winning a landmark election hailed as a signal of deepening democracy in Senegal, President Abdoulaye Wade was reelected to little fanfare. Widespread dissatisfaction was brewing over elite politics and the uneven distribution of the fruits of the city's development. Two months after the elections, the city was plunged into one of its greatest garbage crises yet, as its municipal trash workers went on strike and ordinary Dakarois, in solidarity, staged dramatic neighborhood-wide trash "revolts" through dumping their household waste into the public space. Across the city, mountains of trash choked the capital's grand boule-vards and paralyzed many of the city's functions. As the hours, sometimes days passed before the garbage was cleaned up, the quiet process of putrefac-tion slowly gripped the city in a noxious haze of filth and disgust.

The trash revolts in the working-class, central Dakar neighborhood of HLM Fass were particularly impassioned. Fed up with the state's inability to resolve the trash workers' labor dispute and with the burdens of man-aging their festering garbage, the neighborhood's youth and women were determined to publicly demand the resolution of the material inequalities of urban infrastructure. Under cover of darkness, they quietly evacuated their household trash into the Boulevard Dial Diop, blocking one of the main thoroughfares leading downtown. For weeks, garbage littered the streets alongside the remnant electoral-campaign messages (see figure 1.1), provid-ing potent testimony to the messy state of urban development and the pow-

FIGURE I.I. Remnants of the trash revolts spearheaded by Dakar residents in May 2007. Note the campaign message for Abdoulaye Wade, left over from the February 2007 presidential elections. Author's photo, 2007.

erful role played by the city's residents in the function—or *dysfunction*—of this key urban infrastructure.

Those events contrasted markedly with a different trash crisis that transpired in Dakar almost twenty years prior. In 1988–89, a now-famous social movement germinated in the streets of Dakar as youth ambushed the city's trash-clogged public spaces with brooms and buckets (see figure 1.2). Known as *Set/Setal* ("Be Clean/Make Clean" in Wolof), young men and women throughout the city set out to clean the city, buttress the failing urban waste infrastructure, and purify a polluted political sphere in a frenzied explosion of what came to be billed as *participatory citizenship* (ENDA 1991). The movement looms large in the popular imagination and has gone down in scholarly literature on Senegalese democratic politics as a pivotal juncture in germinating youth political consciousness (M. Diouf 1996). Its messages can still

FIGURE I.2. Activists from the Set/Setal movement painting neighborhood murals in 1989. ENDA, *Set Setal, des murs qui parlent*. Reprinted with permission from ENDA Tiers Monde.

be glimpsed peeking out from faded murals in unexpected corners of the city and in periodic cleanup events bearing the movement's name.

Juxtaposed, these two tales of dirt and disorder in Dakar—the Set/Setal movement and the 2007 strike—are of enormous significance. Surprisingly, most of the striking workers were actually the same young people who had spearheaded the legendary social movement years before. In a culture where cleanliness of body and soul is of deep spiritual import, their acts of dirtying or ordering public space are profoundly meaningful.

This book examines contestation surrounding Dakar's household waste infrastructure as a lens into questions of urban citizenship. Dakar's city streets have oscillated between remarkably tidy and dangerously insalubrious as the city's garbage infrastructure has become the stage for struggles over government, the value of labor, and the dignity of the working poor in Senegal's neoliberal era. As a key feature of new urban development agendas unleashed in the wake of structural adjustment, a volatile series of institutional reorganizations have reconfigured the responsibilities and rewards for doing the city's dirty work through various formulas of community participation. Differentially disciplining people through the burdens of waste disposal has become a primary mode of state power. Governing-through-disposability devolves infrastructure onto labor, reconfiguring the relations of social reproduction and mobilizing invisible burdens of stigma and disease onto specific geographies and laboring bodies. At the same time, these ordering projects have been intensely fraught. Through clogging streets with the city's rejectamenta, garbage activists have met attempts to govern through garbage with a visceral "refusal to be refuse."[1] Often framed through discourses of Islamic piety, their struggles have provided a potent language with which to critique Senegal's neoliberal trajectory and assert rights to fair labor.

This analysis bridges a cultural politics of labor with a materialist understanding of infrastructure, through an ethnography of everyday infrastructures of disposal. In doing so, it recalibrates how we understand urban infrastructure through emphasizing its material, social, and affective elements. A central contention is that infrastructure and materiality debates often miss the social and embodied parts of infrastructure, and thus fall short of fully grappling with the political implications of how lives and bodies get caught up in urban restructuring. Through focusing on labor, the analysis illuminates how urban infrastructures are composed of human as much as technical elements, and how these living elements can help make infrastructures into a vital means of political action and a tool for the formation of collective identities. On the other hand, materialist insights offer an important corrective to studies of labor and culture that elide the ways in which "things" are consequential and how bodies and things intersect. New labor arrangements for trash collection discipline specific bodies through the material power of waste. The material practice of cleaning, in turn, conditions the subjectivities and communities of affect that strive to realign the material and the moral. Waste makes clear how governing regimes and the messy possibilities for their disruption are constituted in the particularities of the matter at hand—here, discard and filth, and their obverse, cleanliness and purity.

Through fleshing out the material and social life of infrastructure in the era of austerity, the analysis bridges "old" and "new" materialist debates in order to grapple with infrastructure's political address. It brings Africanist, postcolonial, and feminist-materialist insights to bear on urban and infrastructure theory through an analysis that is at once grounded in situated knowledge and politics, and attuned to wider circuits of capital, ideas, and power. Ostensibly neutral everyday infrastructural systems are revealed to contain complex socio-technical and spiritual worlds stitched together through expert labors of salvage bricolage. These material practices of negotiation become the stage for citizenship struggles. A focus on the labors constituting these bricolage infrastructures foregrounds the ways that "people as infrastructure" render the city their laboratory through tinkering and maintenance.[2] At the same time, it reveals the corporeal and spiritual burdens of fragmented infrastructures devolved onto laboring bodies. Garbage grounds the practice of politics in the pungent, gritty material of the city. The book challenges the notion that Southern cities, especially African cities, represent exceptions to urban theories, and draws insight from Dakar's everyday urbanism toward recalibrating how we think of infrastructure, labor, and citizenship in cities anywhere.

Neoliberalism, Labor, and African Cities

Most broadly, a key contribution of the book involves reconfiguring understandings of neoliberalism. It is well recognized that urban public services have been crucibles of struggle surrounding structural adjustment and other neoliberal logics. And yet, much writing about neoliberal urban reform in the Global South privileges singular scripts of urban change viewed on a planetary scale (e.g., Davis 2004). Critiques of neoliberalism have become hegemonic in studies of African cities over the last decade, and many of these studies imagine a sort of teleological "impact model" of neoliberal globalization as a global bulldozer wreaking havoc on a passive local victim (G. Hart 2001; Parnell and Robinson 2012). Though neoliberal logics have recrafted postcolonial development trajectories in Africa in powerful ways, it is important not to portray those dynamics in reductive terms. A growing body of research emphasizes the different, often hybrid variants of processes of neoliberalization as well as "the *multiple and contradictory aspects* of neoliberal spaces, techniques, and subjects," especially in their situated expression in Southern cities (Larner 2003, 5). Building on those insights, I provide a detailed examination of the ways that such reforms get hashed out in one of the last bastions of Senegal's urban civil service. Through grappling with everyday negotiations in homes, streets, and municipal offices, my analysis rejects simplistic narratives of urban change to instead reveal the complex mix of politics unleashed by neoliberal reform, the often hybridized nature of institutional forms, and the way that people's lives and political subjectivities are restructured with important consequences.

Senegal is a rich case through which to examine the processes and consequences of neoliberal reform, as one of the first African countries to undergo structural adjustment but also a key locus around which theories of structural adjustment and critiques of the African state were articulated (Berg 1981, 1990; Van de Walle 2001). This research examines the way that logics of urban reform have manifested in political struggles around garbage infrastructure—or, more broadly, through relations of disposability, over the last three decades. It responds to the gap between the abundant literature on "the state in Africa" and the dearth of ethnographic research into new governance agendas, the ways that state power is materialized in everyday infrastructures, and how life is experienced daily by civil servants and citizens alike.[3] Recognizing that the state is an important site of neoliberal reason and that many of the recent contestations around neoliberalism in Africa have been directed at state power, this study returns state bodies to the center of political ethnography. Overall, this is a decidedly Senegalese story that is particular to the play of neoliberal ideas in the context of Dakar's urban politics. The story assembles a rich history of democratic politics, a specific political ecology of order, a fabric of religious identities and affiliations, and a complex field of globalizing relations.

In Senegal, we shall see that municipal and national state politics remain key arenas through which citizenship battles are fought. As the country's capital and the engine of the country in demographic, economic, and administrative terms, Dakar has been the heartland of postcolonial electoral politics and contestations around the nation's development. Much as the city was the seat of the French colonial administration in West Africa, today it operates as an influential center of development administration and as a key mover and shaker in regional and international politics.[4] Given that most visitors and tourists fly into Dakar, the garbage crises over the last decades have been a key challenge to aspirations of modernity. Garbage crises take on larger-than-life significance in this small country; the trashing of Dakar represents the trashing of the nation.

Examining urban labor as a grounding of citizenship is a powerful lens through which to make "theory from the South" about the neoliberal era (Comaroff and Comaroff 2012). Specifically, the book details the transformation of trash labor in contemporary Dakar. In doing so, it builds on a rich tradition of research in African studies that explores ethnographically the transformation of work and urban citizenship in the context of political economic change. Both the labor question and the city have loomed large in Africanist scholarship. An important tradition of Africanist social history and ethnography has long grappled with the ways that work in diverse contexts across the continent has transformed with the tectonic changes unleashed in African societies, as they have been integrated into global circuits of trade, development agendas, and, more recently, neoliberal globalization.[5] Foundational Africanist research in political ecology has exposed the particular ways that new political economic agendas are rooted in socio-environmental power relations and the important connections between material-environmental knowledge, labor, and landscape transformation.[6] Building on this long tradition of inquiry into contestations surrounding people's socio-natural relationships, this study focuses on urban waste infrastructure as a distinctive ecology that incorporates human labor. In so doing, it opens up new frontiers for probing intersecting material precarities and politics in the urban sphere.[7]

Though there has been a strong agenda of Africanist urban studies over the last few decades,[8] little research has explored ethnographically the way that neoliberal reforms since the 1980s have transformed labor in specific African cities. An exception is research looking at work and labor mobilization in South Africa's postapartheid neoliberal era.[9] A small but highly relevant group of geographical studies specifically examine how trash work (municipal collection and informal trash picking) has been reconfigured in South Africa over the last two decades. Like this book, these studies show how cleaning work magnifies contestations surrounding austerity, and emphasize the important role of social difference in structuring degraded labor (Beall, Crankshaw, and Parnell 2000; Miraftab 2004a, 2004b; M. Samson 2007, 2009, 2015). Faranak Miraftab, for example, details how neoliberal governance agendas forwarded in the postapartheid era were consolidated in the casualization of urban waste labor in Cape Town (Miraftab 2004a, 2004b). Her analysis of the deployment of discourses of empowerment, participation, and social capital to justify the exploitation of, especially, poor black women's labor resonates deeply with what I've observed in Dakar. My research goes a step further, however, in examining the infrastructural implications of a mode of governing-through-disposability and its grounding in the corporeal and spiritual burdens of the materiality of waste.

Beyond specific studies of urban labor, this book is deeply informed by a broader recent literature on African cities examining practices of urban citizenship. Africanist literature has driven some of the most innovative and provocative recent scholarly debates considering the urban condition.[10]

This research captures the creative innovations deployed by urban Africans while also conjuring the artifice that may be entailed in innovative forms of governing and rebellion. It has been especially generative toward reconceptualizing the spaces of belonging through which urban residents grapple with custom, imagine new rules of association, and perform civility in the city. Gender, generation, and religious affiliation come to the fore as particularly consequential shapers of sociopolitical community and citizenship practices. In the Senegalese setting, urban scholars challenge the preoccupation within Senegalese religious studies on formal religious institutions, through revealing the role of quotidian modes of religiosity in forging urban publics (Babou 2007; Diouf and Leichtman 2009). New work on gender and generation, moreover, demonstrates the complex ways that young men and women negotiate daily life and politics in Dakar (M. Diouf 2003; Foley and Drame 2013; Fouquet 2013; Fredericks 2014; Honwana 2012; Nyamnjoh 2005; Rabine 2013; Ralph 2008; Scheld 2007).

Building on this foundational Africanist research exploring the cultural politics of labor and urban practice, this book examines the communities of affect that have been animated by new material relations of disposal, focusing specifically on gender, generation, and religion. The analysis brings attention to both labor and infrastructure in a novel interrogation of urban transformation in the neoliberal era. Its concern is to cross-fertilize the Africanist research on labor and the city with the materialist literature, through attending more deeply to the materiality of labor and the city's infrastructural realm while not losing sight of the cultural references and identities through which people's labor and struggles gain meaning. It builds on a small but pioneering literature on urban infrastructural politics that brings new materialist concepts to bear on studies of urban change in Africa's contemporary era.[11] However, discussions of labor have been conspicuously absent from most of this work on political infrastructures. Through thinking about vital labors of waste infrastructure, this analysis resists the unmooring of cultural politics from the substrate on which it operates, and emphasizes the full register of meaning and material practice surrounding garbage as waste. This will allow for a deeper understanding of the full gamut of political violences, struggles, and possibilities that shape the urban condition. Before delving more deeply into this theoretical framework, the next section will overview the specific history of trash politics in Dakar.

Reforming Trash in Dakar

In 1988–89, groaning under the strains of harsh structural adjustment-induced austerity measures and disappointment in the nationalist development project, especially among the nation's youth, Dakar became the epicenter of the country's worst political crisis yet. The elections of 1988, won by the incumbent president amid widespread controversy, precipitated massive youth riots and the cancellation of a whole academic school year, including at the Cheikh Anta Diop University of Dakar. Forming the material expression of political disorder, garbage accumulated in the public space. As the municipal garbage system collapsed under the budgetary constraints of austerity, Set/Setal youth set out to clean the city on their own terms.

As I detail in chapter 1, Set/Setal was the founding moment in an era when cleanliness and the labor of urban garbage management would take center stage as a primary language of control and contestation surrounding urban citizenship. At the height of Set/Setal, Dakar's then mayor made a shrewd political calculus to mastermind the recruitment of youth activists into a citywide participatory trash-collection system. A feature of the country's new neoliberal course, the participatory trash sector brought in these young men and women as new political clients, thereby co-opting their threat to state authority through the symbolic position they were to take on as the new face of the nation and its orderly development. Their incorporation into the trash sector was facilitated by a discourse of responsibility through active participation in the cleanliness of the city and thus "a moral urban politics based on the enrolment of subjects into 'civilized' behavior" (McFarlane and Rutherford 2008, 367). They became the backbone of the municipal waste management system and remain the sector's labor force today.

Since Set/Setal, Dakar's garbagescape has become a central terrain over which the cultural and moral legitimacy of the Senegalese state has been fought. A saga of institutional reorganizations in the trash sector over the last twenty-five years manifests tumultuous struggles for power between the national and municipal state over ordering Dakar. Far from a linear trajectory of neoliberal reform, unexpected hybrid institutions were forged out of this power struggle against the backdrop of an impetus to privatize, decentralize, and shrink the public sector. Even under the banner of expressly neoliberal politics, implemented by socialists and liberals alike, formulas for managing the city have emerged that seek to centralize and nationalize control. This sheds light on the real political stakes of implementing reform in practice given the important patronage functions and performative dimensions of urban public services in Dakar. During the liberal party president Abdoulaye Wade's twelve years in office (2000–2012), the garbage sector epitomized the national government's often schizophrenic approach to managing public services and assembling urban infrastructure. Radically uneven, sporadic, and performative investments in urban infrastructure left parts of the city to rot, rust, and slowly crumble with the passage of time while others were spiffed up with elite, world-class urban aesthetics.

Spatially limited in its expansion due to its location on the Cape Verde Peninsula, and facing rapid growth rates, Dakar has sprawled out from its original colonial confines (today's downtown or Plateau *commune d'arrondissement* [district]) into its rapidly expanding *banlieue* (outskirts) (see map 1.1). Plateau is the most formally planned and serviced district, while the sprawling banlieue of Pikine and Guédiawaye represent the least formally planned and often most disfavored areas for infrastructure investments. This periphery now houses much of Dakar's population (Collignon 1984). Flooding in these neighborhoods is a perennial problem and urban public services are increasingly stretched thin as the city's population continues to climb. Though the Plateau district still hosts most of the federal government agencies as well as banking, international development, and corporate offices, much of the city's economic activity is decentralizing into more localized markets and economic hubs dispersed throughout the city. With the pull of the new industrial park and urban "pole" of Diamniadio just east of Dakar, moreover, the city's banlieue is becoming increasingly important compared with the central districts (Cohen 2007, 148). Despite this fact, these areas are still deeply disadvantaged for government services and planned infrastructure.

Though real estate values generally fall the farther one travels from downtown, historical factors and patronage politics mean that certain neighborhoods that are still quite central (for example, HLM Fass) remain disadvantaged for receiving the fruits of urban public services. Garbage regularly collects in these neighborhoods and the city's poor outskirts, and during trash strikes and collection crises they are inundated with their own waste. Elite enclaves scattered throughout the peninsula (e.g., Les Almadies), on the other hand, may take garbage management into their own hands or negotiate special privileges with the state. Shrinking funding for urban public services over the last decades has unleashed intense volatility as different

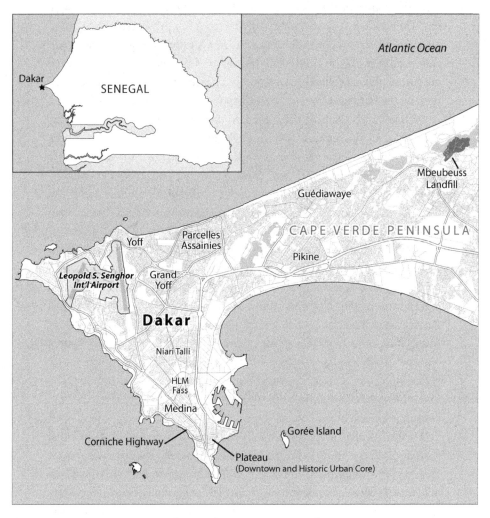

MAP I.I. Contemporary map of Dakar, 2017. The population of Dakar was estimated at 3.5 million of Senegal's 14 million inhabitants in 2015. CIA, "The World Factbook: Senegal."

governing bodies and politicians have clashed over diminishing budgets. In Dakar's garbage sector, this profoundly contested agenda evolved in fits and starts through an often confusing medley of hybridized institutional forms. Over the course of Wade's tenure in office, the garbage sector was reorganized at least ten separate times, ranging from full privatization, to nationalization, to various power-sharing arrangements between government, private, and other institutions. This instability defies quick characterization within simplistic neoliberal paradigms but has had far-reaching implications for how the burdens of waste and its disposal are shouldered in Dakar.

Chapter 2 details how these reconfigurations turned on manipulating trash labor and its remuneration through various formulas of participation. Community participation and associated empowerment discourses are a key tenet of "soft neoliberalism" (Peck 2010, xvi)—new "kinder, gentler" modes of governing austerity in the face of widespread critique and social dislocation (Mohan and Stokke 2000). In Dakar, this involved more than just participation being imposed from on high into the lexicon of Senegalese development. Originally a radical approach by Set/Setal youth to assert rights to a healthy city, the discourse of participation was transformed by key political actors into a very different set of projects concerned with disciplining certain elements of the social body through material means. Participation served as a mode of governing through reconfiguring relations of social reproduction. The greatest burdens of the municipal trash system were devolved onto labor: workers were furnished with little equipment for collection, if any at all, and existing materials were allowed to degrade. The onus of disposal work shifted onto laboring bodies as the city expanded and consumption levels rose.

Meanwhile, the periphery of the city witnessed another development that further displaced waste infrastructure onto labor, as explored in chapter 3. Linking up with participation in the "formal" municipal sector, in hard-to-access parts of the city's periphery, "informal" community-based nongovernmental organization (NGO) projects were spearheaded in the early 2000s to bring unpaid women in as "municipal housekeepers" to collect their neighborhood trash. Consistent with the wider discourse on participation and associated notions of appropriate technology and empowerment, these projects involved door-to-door horse-drawn-cart collection projects centered on the voluntary labor of neighborhood women. Across these transformations in the city and its periphery, it is possible to identify a number of different infrastructural formulas for managing the city's garbage collection that turn on flexibilizing the formal labor force and mobilizing community-based labors of collection.

In a keen demonstration of the "unruliness of infrastructure" (Larkin 2008), workers and residents in Dakar have exerted their rights to urban citizenship through tactics aimed at unsettling the "proper" function and significance of trash infrastructures. In chapter 4, I show how from 2000 to 2009, the municipal trash workers went from being disorganized, invisible, and stigmatized to being one of the most mobilized and respected labor unions in contemporary Senegal. Since the mid-2000s, the trash workers have periodically disturbed the ordering processes of governing-through-garbage by staging a series of multiday, havoc-wreaking, general trash strikes. During this time, ordinary Dakarois in neighborhoods like HLM Fass have joined in the chorus of rebellion through disorder by the concerted dumping of household garbage into public streets, squares, even in front of government buildings. Strikes by workers and public dumping by residents deploy the power of dirt to creatively subvert ordering paradigms and contest the stigma and abjection implied by living and working in filth.

The trash workers personally and publicly frame their labor as an act of Muslim piety rooted in the spiritual value of cleanliness. This refusal of disposability turns the stigma of trash work on its head. Through accompanying their strikes with a savvy public relations campaign, the trash workers have redefined their profession, earned widespread public support, and played a key role in critiquing the country's neoliberal development trajectory. With the signing of the trash union's collective bargaining agreement in 2014—which conferred formal contracts, higher salaries, and health care benefits—the garbage sector pioneered the reversal of neoliberal trends flexibilizing urban labor and signaled the possibility of a new era of urban governance in Dakar.

As can be seen from this brief history, trash in the public space in Dakar signals more than just technical failure or inadequate funding. Wrapped up with the question of trash is the negotiation of citizenship in the space of urban infrastructure. Violent neoliberal political economies congeal in the city's wastescape and are made manifest in crisis moments. I take the major trash crises of Senegal's neoliberal moment—especially 1988–89 and 2007—as key points of rupture, when political economic turmoil became materially visceral in the public space and different actors negotiated a new configuration of socio-material relations. The trash crises are thus the manifestation of the disorder of development (see Beall 2006). They are productive moments of revelation and reflection on larger political questions, when citizens renegotiate their roles in the urban labor force and, more broadly, in the orderly processes of city making. The next sections will detail the book's theoretical orientation toward a materialist ethnography of waste infrastructure.

Vital Infrastructures

In contrast to technocratic representations of solid-waste management (SWM), this book treats trash infrastructures as political matter (Braun and Whatmore 2010). It builds on a long tradition of geographical research examining the production of urban space in processes of uneven development.[12] New political economic agendas are crystallized in the space of urban infrastructure. But urban infrastructures, including housing, water, waste, and transport, are not stable edifices of power or technologies of rule. They are key sites of performative government practice as well as claim making by elite and disenfranchised citizens alike. This study is part of a growing body of ethnographic research examining urban infrastructures as key forums for negotiated processes of political contestation.[13] It builds on a recent emphasis on the urban scale as the key locus of citizenship and on everyday negotiations around access to public space and goods in the city as central to claiming citizenship.[14] It advances these discussions through emphasizing the material basis of contestations around citizenship, especially focusing on the materiality of labor.

As part of a broader field of ethnographic research on infrastructure politics, Africanist research has been particularly innovative in showing how material infrastructures such as roads, sewers, and electricity grids serve as a "political terrain for the negotiation of central ethical and political questions concerning civic virtue and the shape of citizenship."[15] Antina von Schnitzler's (2013, 2016) research on prepaid water-meter technologies in South Africa, for instance, shows how in bypassing, destroying, and tinkering with this neoliberal layer of infrastructure, township residents wage a micropolitics of innovation and subversion which contests ethical regimes of individuation and incentivization. Of particular relevance to this research, Brenda Chalfin (2014, 2016) examines citizenship practices rooted in daily engagements with sewer infrastructures in the context of modernist failure in urban Ghana. She pays special attention to how the embodied material practices through which urban residents adapt, maintain, and forge waste infrastructures renegotiate the urban social contract. Similarly, this study focuses on the embodied practices of trash collection in Senegal's neoliberal era but also on the cultural modes through which that infrastructure is organized and valued.

Waste in Dakar urges an understanding of infrastructure not as a simple, inert, technical supporting structure, but as a relational articulation of material, social, and affective elements. Infrastructures are ecologies that assemble a range of spatialized relationships between political economic imperatives, technologies, natural processes, forms of sociality, social meanings, and modes of ritual action (see Murphy 2013; Star 1999). This allows for a much broader understanding of infrastructures that can include biophysical processes, technologies of government, experiences of abjection, embodied precarities, the force of matter and machines, and aesthetic or spiritual systems of order. These relationships get articulated in and through the material form of the city, and negotiated in everyday politics specific to different urban arrangements and their attendant sociohistorical complexes. Infrastructures are not static; they are composed of fluid relations between technologies and forms of sociality. Their development, operation, maintenance, and breakdown, moreover, are imbricated with other discursive, symbolic, and religious realms. Considering these socio-technical ecologies relationally allows us to probe the intersections between human and nonhuman agencies, the concrete burdens placed on laboring bodies and communities, and the everyday meanings and practices through which infrastructures become political.

The matter at stake in infrastructures—or the materiality of relationships among people and the urban ecologies they manage—is an active agent in the political negotiations they engender. This research is informed by new materialist debates, especially the recent resurgence of materialist thinking in geography.[16] It is concerned with the force of things or, drawing on Bruce Braun and Sarah J. Whatmore's (2010, ix) important intervention, "the way that things of every imaginable kind—material objects, informed materials, bodies, machines, even media ecologies—help constitute the common worlds we share and the dense fabric of relations with others in and through which we live." This vitalist perspective emphasizes the relational nature of material and social worlds. Like other managed objects and commodities—for instance, oil, water, sewage, carbon, electricity, lead, and asbestos (Anand 2011; Fennell 2016; Gregson, Watkins, and Calestani 2010; McFarlane 2008; von Schnitzler 2016; Watts 2009; Whitington 2016)—household trash has its own unique, context-specific materiality and spatiality that conditions the social and political life of waste infrastructure. A key element of this analysis is disentangling the way that "different matters matter differently" (Gregson and Crang 2010, 1027)—or the special force of household waste in this story. We shall see how the specific materiality of Dakar's garbage, waste's connection to impurity in Islam, and the power of cleaning as a process of purification are key features of the political valence of trash in Dakar.

Extending geographical insights on materiality, this research departs from some of the new materialist thinking in how it defines and locates the political. Although the conception of vital infrastructures here shares an interest with Jane Bennett (2010, 6) in "thing-power" as "the curious ability of inanimate things to animate, to act, to produce effects dramatic and subtle," it diverges from Bennett's approach to evaluating the agency of things. Bennett's conception of politics floats in an abstract, philosophical mode that does not recognize the asymmetries of power represented by the assemblages she considers, and offers limited insight into the actual political work that nonhuman actants do in specific settings (see Braun et al. 2011). Through ethnography, this analysis goes beyond the philosophical to show how waste exerts very different power within divergent contexts, with far-reaching implications for different people in Dakar. By centering the analysis on the materiality of labor, it unpacks "the complexities, frictions, intractabilities, and conundrums of 'matter in relation'" (Abrahamsson, Bertoni, and Mol 2015, 13) to interrogate what *kinds* of politics matter has and the strategic alliances people forge with things. Reconsidering labor and infrastructure is, thus, a way to recuperate a vital politics of material infrastructures. Through drawing attention to people as infrastructure, bricolage as material work, and the material moralities of value and meaning making, I show how material geographies of trash matter to how government and citizenship are practiced.

Attention to waste in Dakar foregrounds that urban infrastructures are composed of social as much as technical elements and that waste matters in its encounter with and animation by/of human bodies. In contrast to definitions of infrastructure in much of the recent critical literature that elide the social life of infrastructure, this analysis is centered on the way that new infrastructural assemblages are situated in human labor and the crucial intersections of human and nonhuman agencies. It thus urges for a "fleshing out" of infrastructures' literal vitality (living parts) through advancing an understanding of the key role of labor and community in infrastructural systems. In this way, it builds on and extends AbdouMaliq Simone's (2004b) notion of *people as infrastructure* to examine how "infrastructure exerts a force—not simply in the materials and energies it avails, but also the way it attracts people, draws them in, coalesces and expends their capacities" (Simone 2012). Vital infrastructures are alive in all sorts of ways with the materials that compose them—including the trash and its active biological processes but also, crucially, the human labor through which they take form. This liveliness illuminates the relational precarities of infrastructure and labor—or how they are precarious in different ways that intersect in key moments.

Although there is growing attention within urban studies to how networked infrastructures are fragmenting in ways that exacerbate urban inequality all over the world, attention to human labor is especially relevant in the nonnetworked, often informal, fragmented infrastructural systems that dominate in Dakar and across the Global South.[17] Austerity and economic stagnation in recent decades have magnified the historical fragmentation of African urban infrastructures, dashing the aspirations of the nationalist era and amplifying uneven development. As we'll see in Dakar, this has bred infrastructures of salvage bricolage, even within the core of urban public services. These systems underscore that infrastructures are processual—they are constantly undergoing innovative processes of care and (re)fabrication by the bodies and systems of sociality they are built upon. On the other hand, an emphasis on labor highlights how devolved, participatory waste infrastructures have come to be a central pillar of governing practices in Senegal and of the material processes of abjection through which certain bodies become constituted as waste. Infrastructures can be seen to expend human capacities in two senses—both through disbursing them, and also through using them up. This allows for a more robust conception of the ways that people are infrastructure, which is attentive to the violences that may consolidate in the silences of infrastructure's concrete and the daily material negotiations through which those violences may be fractured.[18] Dakar's bricolage infrastructures highlight both how infrastructures may predate their human elements and the important ways that infrastructures' people may upend these systems.

Finally, infrastructures are affective worlds that give rise to a range of structures of feeling. This story draws attention to the intersections of materiality and social systems of meaning—or the generative capacity of nonhuman actants "to move us and shape our collective attachments" (Braun and Whatmore 2010, xxiv; drawing on Connolly 2010). Dakar's trash infrastructures reveal not just the social labor processes through which people stitch together livelihoods out of the fragments of stagnant economies, but also the bricolage modes of meaning making they inspire. The piety of refusal can be seen as a sort of bricolage of the self in a landscape of disrepair and pollution that serves as both a mode of piety and a collective resource. Infrastructures require belonging; they are embedded in social relations and are erected upon moral architectures. "'Modes of religiosity' forge new spaces of affiliation, movements, civic culture, and communities" (Diouf and Leichtman 2009, 3–4), but also alternative infrastructures through which new moral geographies are crafted. The focus on salvage here grounds bricolage in the material practice of dealing with ruins and waste. The qualities of waste are central not just to how these infrastructures operate, but to how they are understood and felt. As we shall see in the next section, waste's powers to disrupt and the salience of cleaning as a practice of order and piety are key features of the political valence of trash as vital matter in Dakar.

Waste Matters

Waste has special salience as vital matter on multiple registers owing to the particularities of its material properties and its role as an index of value.[19] Waste has a "gritty," coarse materiality that helps to "ground" understandings of materialism (Kirsch 2013). The high organic content, stench, and propensity for quick putrefaction in the Senegalese heat makes household trash in Dakar visceral, lively matter. Far from inert, it is a material in transition. The internal processes of decomposition endow Dakar's trash with a "toxic vitality" (P. Harvey 2016) that is a central feature of trash politics. These properties and the socio-spatial geographies of its management have important implications for a consideration of the role of discard infrastructures in formulas of governing and claims to urban citizenship.

Waste plays a key role in the cultural work of coding value. In her seminal work on pollution and taboo, Mary Douglas (1966) illustrates how symbolic associations around impurity maintain social structures. Dirt should be seen, she argues, as simply "matter out of place" or "disorder"; there is a social function behind rites and rituals defining what—and who, for that matter—is considered pure versus what is labeled a contagion. In her words, "As we know it, dirt is essentially disorder. There is no such thing as absolute dirt: it exists in the eye of the beholder. If we shun dirt, it is not because of craven fear, still less dread of holy terror. Nor do our ideas about disease account for the range of our behaviour in cleaning or avoiding dirt. Dirt offends against order. Eliminating it is not a negative moment, but a positive effort to organise the environment" (Douglas 1966, 2). Douglas exposes the powerful ways that discourses around the dangers of dirt and pollution produce social boundaries and thereby structure and spatialize social relations. However, it is important to emphasize that the meaning and thus political import of waste is not a transhistorical, -cultural, or -geographical given. Waste should be understood as a "mobile description of that which has been cast out or judged superfluous in a particular space–time. *It is a technical and political artifact* that gathers force in its performativity" within certain contexts (Gidwani and Reddy 2011, 1649; italics in original). Douglas's focus on semiotics and denial of the material force of matter beyond the cultural realm, moreover, is insufficient.[20] The power that trash comes to perform in certain contexts is constituted through its material-semiotic properties as they intersect with particular bodies. Trash matters, in other words, because its dirty associations and messy properties govern the practice of managing it and its sociopolitical power. Through pushing beyond the symbolic to grapple with the full force of waste in its material and performative dimensions, this research traces the powerful ways that government officials, municipal workers, and ordinary Dakarois harness the power of waste to different ends in specific conjunctures.

Attention to the full discursive and material import of waste draws into relief the way that "purification impulses" (Sennett 1970) have long governed modernizing missions through rigorous urban boundary making.[21] Urban space in the colonies was produced and regulated along racial lines through ideas of dirt and disease, crystallized through pivotal moments of socio-spatial reorganization like disease outbreaks. Just as urban space and its infrastructures were produced unevenly along segregationist logics in the colonial period, so do infrastructures in postcolonial cities codify government prerogatives and unequal citizenship across the urban landscape. As in the colony, the uneven provision of infrastructure for urban public services like water, sanitation, and waste management is a mechanism of abjection through which access to the rewards of the city may be extended or denied. Drawing on Julia Kristeva's formulation of how processes of abjection repel/expel the other who is deemed polluting, Nikhil Anand shows how governmental practices render abject certain residents of Mumbai through the active denial of water infrastructures.[22] Exerting control over urban development and governing urban subjects depends upon the maintenance of an aesthetic order in the city that keeps people in their proper place. Governmental techniques, which render unruly slum space unlawful, define and enforce aesthetic norms to produce specific images of modernity and legitimize the displacement of those deemed "polluting," or lacking a proper "citizen-culture," as unfit to belong in the city.[23] In this light, Vinay Gidwani (2013, 176) describes India's exclusionary urbanisms as a "century-long class war against waste."

At the base of state legitimacy, therefore, is the government's performative role in cleaning the city through managing urban waste. Waste management—or the process by which waste is rendered a "public secret" (Hawkins 2003)—is a primary vehicle of modernizing missions through ordering spaces and disciplining bodies (see Doherty, 2018; McFarlane 2008; Moore 2009; Gidwani 2013; Brownell 2014). Yet urban waste and its management is a contradictory indicator of progress and modernity. As the outcome of consumption and production, waste represents the excess of modernity (Moore 2009). Thus the challenge of managing it escalates with the pursuit of development. Because the movement of waste—its effective, proper disposal, out of sight—allows development to continue and urban order to be maintained, the blockage of that disposal process is the ultimate symbol of nonprogress and indicator of state delinquency. Without ritual practices of expulsion and elimination, the city risks being consumed by the very effluvium of its own advancement. The accumulation of urban waste in the public space exteriorizes that which is private, exposing the public secret of waste.

This book argues that practices of governing in Senegal have deployed the power of waste as impurity and disposability. This is not by any means the first consideration of the role of discourses of waste, excess, and excrement in relation to African political discourse and governing logics. An influential body of francophone political theory places excremental politics at the center of postcolonial political discourse on the continent (Bayart 1989; Mbembe 2001). Drawing on often grotesque and scatological political discourse, Achille Mbembe argues that an "aesthetics of vulgarity" is central to the exertion and derision of authority.[24] Though this analysis shares an interest in excremental languages involved in political displays of authority, it resists a tendency to characterize "the African state" in a way that ends up pathologizing African politics in blanket terms and sidestepping "the insistent materiality" of waste (Chalfin 2014, 93). I am concerned here with examining how the material power of literal waste infrastructures serves the consolidation of hegemony or its fracture in specific historical conjunctures in Senegal.

I show that governing-through-garbage is a material practice of power that works through two modes of precarity. The first involves the dirtying of specific places. The problem of trash management is a question of boundaries. Trash marks the boundary between inside and outside: the inside is constructed as protected and safe whereas the outside—which can be "rubbished"—is figured as potentially malevolent, disorderly, and dangerous.[25] Uneven trash collection in Dakar differentiates urban space—rendering abject those spaces and people not deemed a priority for urban public services through processes of neglect and its consequence, rubbishing. Waste and dirt collect in those zones, inevitably the poorer and less well connected city neighborhoods, thereby disproportionately saddling residents with filth and its associated stigmas and dangers. Processes of urban neoliberal reform are premised upon allocating precarity through assigning disposability.

Compounding the wasting of specific spaces, the second mode of precarity is rooted in the way that particular bodies are actively enlisted into labors of disposal which render them abject through the corporeal and spiritual burdens of pollution. This second mode is especially relevant here because labor has been at the center of governing-through-garbage in Dakar. Precarious labor demands attention to the materiality of bodies—their sensuous capacities, differentiated burdens, and embodied engagements with nature (Bakker and Bridge 2006; Jackson 2000). The labor of discard, as a process of positively organizing the environment, is central to the reproduction of the social order. Garbage disposal requires not just places that are discardable, but also disposable people to accomplish the task. The work entailed in trash management repels, yet the risk and danger inscribed in the process render it a vital labor at the base of urban development. Though it is by definition dirty, polluted labor, trash work can be seen simultaneously as a process of cleaning and purification. In Senegal, cleaning takes on added meaning owing to the particular importance ascribed to purity and cleanliness as an indispensable element of Islamic faith.

Labor-intensive, "participatory" waste infrastructures have come to be a central pillar of governing practices in Senegal. By respatializing the relations of social reproduction, these new infrastructural formulas devolve the burdens of garbage infrastructure onto bodies and social systems with profoundly uneven effects.[26] Feminist insights on the gendered nature of material life bring into view questions of embodiment, corporeality, and performativity which help to explain how certain bodies become constituted as waste through the full force of the burdens they bear. As Katie Meehan and Kendra Strauss (2015) point out in their reformulation of social reproduction drawing on a tradition of feminist posthumanism, attention to embodiment illuminates the material body as a "force that shapes knowledge, but also as the material *site* in which value, politics, and meaning is produced." This underscores the importance of the "fleshy, messy" aspects of the crisis of social reproduction or the way it operates through labor's materiality (Katz 2001; Meehan and Strauss 2015). The force of waste is animated through its intersection with human labor—as it literally emplaces burdens of dirt and disease onto specific bodies through differentiated experiences of precarity and discipline.[27]

By focusing on the material precarities of trash work and the infrastructure it builds, I show that the power of trash has conditioned specific knowledges, subjectivities, and practices that threaten the hegemonic power of governing-through-disposability. The matter at stake in infrastructure— here, the flows of waste and filth—shapes political possibilities, because the meanings associated with such matter (and not just the technical vulnerabilities) can be the source of its usefulness for political mobilization. Trash strikes are effective because they demonstrate the value of workers' labor as it is withdrawn, but also because the material-semiotic resonance of trash as waste makes it a particularly powerful matter of rebellion. The public secret of waste and its associated risks rely on a multitude of everyday intersecting forms of vigilance to keep it in its proper place. Years of tinkering have evolved the collection process toward a system premised upon intimate, daily intersections between women household garbage managers and municipal garbage collectors who share a commitment to ridding the city of its collective effluvium.[28] Once those labors have been withdrawn and garbage has been discharged into the public space, the natural forces of decomposition take hold and the richly organic material begins to putrefy. With time, the resolution of the crisis becomes even more pressing as the residents' message takes on a life of its own in the waste's increasingly hazardous stench and rot.

The counterhegemonic force of trash rebellion in Dakar was thus forged out of the specific subjectivities conditioned by the material practice of discard and cleaning, and manifested in the creative deployment of the material itself in rebellion. Precarious bodies, abject and empowered by waste, are always there to trouble delicate political orders. As in other settings, waste workers in Dakar harness the power of discourses of cleaning and purity as a primary weapon in the fight for better wages and respect (see Millar 2012; Moore 2009). They unsettle the ordering paradigms implied by participatory labor arrangements to argue for a sort of "garbage citizenship" premised upon fair remuneration and benefits for garbage labor, and affordable, accessible garbage services. Their appeals to Islamic morality deploy an ethical and spiritual critique of the state's erosion of labor and establish a new language through which to value a vital infrastructure. Dakar trash workers' battle to make their labor manifest and to sculpt a vernacular understanding of its worth is thus a claim for a more ethical infrastructure. In this way, an examination of the human life of Dakar's infrastructure can lend new insight into processes of urban citizenship and related questions of justice in cities anywhere.

Making "Theory from the South"

Cities in the Global South are more often than not characterized in pathological terms, through a lexicon charged with descriptions of what they lack and how their histories diverge from that of the rest of the world. Representations of African cities are often particularly gloomy and reductionist. Essentialist understandings of the continent as rural by nature and of African urbanism as necessarily dysfunctional were foundational to the constructions of difference that have historically haunted ideas of Africa. Despite the fact that a near majority of Africans now forge their lives in cities, racialized narratives of African alterity stubbornly persist. These join with theories of "proper" urban development patterned after Western urbanism to render African cities perverted, incomplete, and dysfunctional. Now yoked to a developmentalist ethos, framings of African urbanism are all too often limited to invectives of perverse growth, crumbling infrastructure, and flagging economies that demand a series of international interventions.

Garbage often stands in as the quintessential symbol of what's wrong in African cities: the material expression of the failures of development and the chaos taking over the African continent. The challenge of managing trash, in other words, acts as a potent metaphor for the African "crisis" writ large. Indeed, Dakar's trash "crisis" is almost always rendered either a technical-financial problem or a product of corruption, plain and simple. As such, it becomes part of the depressingly familiar narrative of the "failed" African metropolis, a symbol of "the coming anarchy" that influential journalist

Robert D. Kaplan predicted would soon envelop a continent ruled by chaos and decay, sliding farther and farther off the map of global connection.[29]

Narratives of African exception that paint a picture of African cities as degrading, unfinished, or unworkable are not new or imaginative. They are consistent with a long legacy of discourse, deeply tied up with other rounds of globalization, which places Africa as the primordial other, a perverted and incomplete version of the Western whole (Mudimbe 1994). But, if waste is an index of difference—of that which should be cast out—then blanket discourses of "trashing" should be roundly suspect. Describing African cities through discourses of waste and disorder profoundly ignores the "gutted infrastructures of segregated cityscapes" inherited through sedimented layers of imperial debris (Stoler 2008, 194). In the dilapidated, salvaged garbage trucks that arrive into Dakar from distant European shores we can trace ruins of empire and their role in producing and upholding violent environments. Dakar's trash collectors, like e-waste workers, pickers, recyclers, ship dismantlers, and so forth all over the world, signify geographies of dispossession, past and present. They are potent symbols of "the colonial logic of (neo)liberal modernity" (Roy, Larner, and Peck 2012). Essentializing narratives of urbanism and waste are just some of the obstinate ruins of empire that dog Africa's present.

Characterizations that pathologize African cities are surprisingly resilient, even within some current urban scholarship and policy writing on the continent. They are a central feature of what Jennifer Robinson importantly delineated as a stark geographical division in urban theory: cities in the Global North (especially "global cities") are designated as sources of theory, and Global South cities as repositories of poor people and problems that "do not contribute to expanding the definition of city-ness" but are, rather, "drawn on to signify its obverse, what cities are not" (2002, 540). In drawing attention to this uneven geography of urban theory, Robinson forces us to consider how theories of "global cities" reify their own categories and hierarchies and are, in fact, part of the production and regulation of those cities' power through an othering of "ordinary cities" (Robinson 2006). She urges a recentering of new urban scholarship on those ordinary cities normally located "off the map."

Precisely because of its presumed otherness, the African continent is essential as a source of theory. Following Jean and John Comaroff (2012), this book uses ethnographic theorizing from Dakar as a way of making "theory from the South." In addition to lending insight into the specifics of Senegal's neoliberal present, its broader intention is to incorporate African political systems into more cosmopolitan urban and political theories. I take cities to be sites of experimentation, and privilege the daily micropolitics through which new expressions of citizenship are negotiated, without neglecting the imposition of global forces of neoliberal capitalism and development discourses or "the difficulties of putting new citizenships into practice" (Holston 2010, 9). Through a perspective ethnographically attentive to place and the sociohistorical contingency of power relations, this theorization resists one-size-fits-all models of political economy or colonial legacies and rejects essentialist framings that simplistically pathologize or celebrate African cities.[30]

By considering the continent's connection to the rest of the world, my analysis works against the naturalizing and disabling effect of depictions of Africa that simply recite a series of failures, lacks, and absences (Ferguson 2006). Relational understandings of global connection elucidate the "embeddedness in multiple elsewheres of which the continent actually speaks," and, crucially, African cities' key strategic role in empire, past and present (Mbembe and Nuttall 2004a, 348). Recognizing that "Africa" is in many ways a mythical entity—fabricated as a coherent geographic object despite great internal diversity—and considering the many ways in which the continent has been injected into the neoliberal world order, I seek to ask some questions about the material and symbolic "trashing" of the continent. Digging beneath Dakar's detritus denaturalizes representations of decay, and, in doing so, refashions the very basis of how we understand cities and urban citizenship.

Outline of the Book

Chapter 1, "Governing Disposability," intervenes in debates on infrastructure politics, Senegalese democracy, and neoliberal development through the lens of Dakar's garbage politics over the last twenty-five years. Institutional volatility in the garbage sector is the outcome of intensified competition between the national and municipal state over controlling Dakar's infrastructural order in the wake of economic and political liberalization. These forces accelerated a mode of governing-through-disposability premised upon performative, fragmented infrastructure investments and strategies to flexibilize the urban workforce.

Chapter 2, "Vital Infrastructures of Labor," takes a closer look at what the institutional transformations in the garbage sector have meant for the workers caught in their sway, through a materialist reading of the cultural politics of trash infrastructure. Tracing the sector's history from the Set/Setal youth movement, it illuminates how new formulas for garbage management reconfigured everyday lives and embodied materialities of labor and, along the way, communities, political subjectivities, and relationships to the city. The turn to participatory infrastructural formulas for garbage collection devolved technology onto labor, binding people to each other through their refuse and to machines through relations of salvage bricolage.

Chapter 3, "Technologies of Community," links the highly contested battle to flexibilize the sphere of ("formal") municipal trash labor and the turn to ("informal") participatory garbage collection, through examining a community-based trash project in a peripheral neighborhood centered on voluntary women's labor and horse-drawn carts. The chapter further examines the social and material components of fragmented infrastructure devolved onto labor, while contributing to critiques in development studies unpacking notions of community, participation, and empowerment in community-based development. The continued devolution of infrastructure onto labor extends the relations of social reproduction into the neighborhood space, rendering neighborhood women municipal housekeepers and reinforcing customary authority over local development.

Chapter 4, "The Piety of Refusal," examines the values and vernacular moralities through which these infrastructures are felt and understood by the people who make up the social systems they are built upon. It details the trash workers union movement and the waves of public dumping through which workers and ordinary Dakarois have refused conditions of precarity since the mid-2000s. Through examining workers' identities and strategies as a union, the chapter shows how the particular resonance of their labor as cleaning and their refusal to clean through striking have validated garbage work, earned them widespread public support, and, in turn, allowed them to stem the tide of labor flexibilization. The chapter engages with debates considering the relationship between citizenship and spiritual identity and highlights the intimate communities of affect that forge infrastructures, through examining the architectures of faith undergirding the workers' movement.

The conclusion, "Garbage Citizenship," brings together the key arguments of the book and draws insight for understanding urban infrastructural citizenship in the wake of neoliberal development. Drawing on Dakar's trash politics, it argues for bridging new and old materialist debates through considering the material labors of infrastructure. Values are coded in urban infrastructures but especially in the vital, living parts of the urban landscape. The provocations of Dakar's garbage citizens are used to reflect on the possibilities for building more just urban infrastructures.

From March 8 to 14, 2008, Dakar hosted the 11th Organisation de la conférence islamique (Organization of the Islamic Conference; OIC) summit of
global leaders from the Islamic world.[1] As chairman of the summit, President
Abdoulaye Wade aimed to showcase Dakar as a world-class city and Senegal
as an emerging leader on the global stage (see figure 1.1). He named his son
Karim Wade president of the national agency created to organize the event,
l'Agence Nationale de l'organisation de la conférence islamique (National
Agency for the Organization of the Islamic Conference; ANOCI). The image
of Dakar that greeted the foreign dignitaries was of paramount importance.
In the months leading up to the summit, which had already been delayed a
number of times, construction ran at breakneck speed on President Wade's
urban infrastructure projects—especially his signature roadworks and the
forty-nine-meter-tall Monument de la Renaissance africaine (African Renaissance Monument) that now towers over the city (see figure 1.2).[2] Thousands of street vendors were forcibly removed from the city to keep them
from "encumbering" urban space. But perhaps the most vexing challenge
was ensuring that the capital was spotless for the duration of the summit,
and, importantly, free of unsightly protests that might mar Dakar's order and
Senegal's reputation.

The previous two years had been rife with garbage strikes and neighborhood dumping revolts, after Wade's ejection of the international company responsible for the city's garbage had left the system in institutional
limbo and the workers without contracts. In the months leading up to the

FIGURE I.I. A welcome sign featuring President Wade's image for the 11th Organisation de la conférence islamique (Organization of the Islamic Conference; OIC) summit, held from March 8 to 14, 2008, in Dakar. Author's photo, 2008.

summit, Wade endeavored to enlist the workers in his ordering project. He emphasized that it would be "un-Islamic" to dirty the capital before such an important event and that strikes would not be tolerated. In a deeply religious country, where 95 percent of the population identifies as Muslim (CIA 2016), Islam has long been an important feature of Senegal's public sphere. The trash workers rose to the occasion, working overtime to ensure that Dakar's downtown and tourist districts, as well as any other routes that the visitors were expected to see, would be clean and orderly. In the days before the summit, Wade hired an additional fifteen hundred day laborers to aid in the herculean task of cleaning Dakar. During the conference, central districts of the city were indeed the cleanest that many had ever seen them, but a different story was evident in the poor outskirts. With the beleaguered garbage workers dedicating their energies to the city's most central and elite

FIGURE I.2. Le Monument de la Renaissance africaine (the African Renaissance Monument) in Dakar. One of Abdoulaye Wade's prestige projects, the monument was completed in 2010. Photo courtesy of J.W., 2016.

areas and the infrastructure budget directed at prestige projects, the poor, off-the-beaten-track periphery of the city was left to fend for itself. In these areas, garbage piled up in streets and public spaces.

The summit went off smoothly but the rest of Abdoulaye Wade's term did not. When Karim Wade was later tried and jailed in corruption scandals, his mismanagement of funds as head of ANOCI was front and center. President Wade's prestige infrastructure projects and institutional tinkering with key urban public services came to represent a potent symbol of his disconnect from the majority of the working Senegalese population. His politicking within the garbage sector was a particularly dramatic example: under Wade's thumb, the sector saw eight major institutional shake-ups (see table 1.1). Although the wake of structural adjustment in Senegal has seen intense volatility in the infrastructural formulas for managing the city's garbage, the tenor of that volatility reached an unprecedented pitch during Wade's presidency.

It's no accident that when the new president of Senegal, Macky Sall, took power after the highly contested elections of 2012, one of his very first acts in

TABLE I.I. The institutions responsible for managing Dakar's garbage from 1960 to 2017

Year	Institution managing Dakar's garbage	Institution type
1960–1971	Municipal Services (Commune de Dakar)	Local government
1971–1984	SOADIP	Private company
1984–1986	Municipal Services (Commune de Dakar); Army Corps of Engineers	Local government and the military
1986–1989	SIAS	Parastatal company
1989–1992	Set/Setal; SIAS	Parastatal company, youth groups, coordination by local government
1993–1995	CUD; SIAS	Local government with youth group associations, parastatal company, private local contractors
1995–2000	CUD; AGETIP	Local government with youth group associations, private local contractors
2000	HAPD; APRODAK	National agency with private local contractors
2001–2002	APRODAK	National agency with private local contractors
2002	Alcyon	Private international company (Switzerland)
2002–2006	AMA	Private international company (Italy)
2006–2009	Entente CADAK-CAR; Ministry of the Environment	Power-sharing agreement between local and national state; private contractors (local and Veolia, France)
2009–2011	Entente CADAK-CAR; Ministry of the Environment; APROSEN	Power-sharing agreement between local and national state; private contractors (local and Veolia, France)
2011	SOPROSEN	National agency with private local contractors
2012–2015	Entente CADAK-CAR	Local government with private local contractors
2015–2017	UCG	National agency with private local contractors

TABLE I.I. *Continued*

Abbreviations

AGETIP
Agence d'exécution des travaux d'intérêt public contre le sous-emploi
(Public Works and Employment Agency)

AMA
Azienda Municipalizzata per l'Ambiente
(Municipal Environment Agency)

APRODAK
Agence pour la propreté de Dakar
(Agency for the Cleanliness of Dakar)

APROSEN
Agence pour la propreté du Sénégal
(Agency for the Cleanliness of Senegal)

Entente Agreement of CADAK-CAR
Communauté d'agglomérations de Dakar–Communauté d'agglomérations
de Rufisque (The Urban Agglomerations of Dakar and Rufisque)

CUD
Communauté Urbaine de Dakar (Dakar Urban Community)

HAPD
Haute autorité pour la propreté de Dakar
(High Authority for the Cleanliness of Dakar)

SIAS
Société industrielle d'aménagement urbain du Sénégal
(Industrial Urban Planning Company of Senegal)

SOADIP
Société africaine de diffusion et de promotion
(African Distribution and Promotion Company)

SOPROSEN
Société pour la propreté du Sénégal
(Company for the Cleanliness of Senegal)

UCG
Unité de coordination et de gestion des déchets
(Garbage Coordination and Management Unit)

Source: Author's chart

office was to again reform the institutions responsible for managing Dakar's garbage. As just the latest chapter in this long saga of garbage politics, Sall's dissolution of Wade's garbage management system was a highly symbolic act aimed at purging the previous administration's failings and charting the country's new course. This chapter traces Dakar's dynamic garbage struggles from the late 1980s to the present day in order to delineate the acceleration of a mode of governing-through-disposability as a primary form of state power. As a material practice of power, governing-through-disposability devolves the burdens of infrastructure onto precarious laboring bodies—those of ordinary neighborhood women and the formal trash workers themselves. And yet, in April 2016, decades of labor flexibilization were reversed when the workers won formal contracts and higher salaries. In tracing out that history, this chapter reveals the tumultuous consolidation and contestation of state power in the neoliberal era and reconfigures how we understand the politics of infrastructure.

As one of the first African countries to undertake structural adjustment and one of the continent's oldest and most respected democracies, Senegal is a fertile case through which to examine how formulas of governing are transformed in the context of austerity and democratic competition. This chapter considers the bundle of technical, institutional, social, and political factors that constitute the garbage collection infrastructure as a lens into state power and politics. In doing so, it builds on a rich tradition of academic inquiry into the relationship between infrastructure and state power, or what Michael Mann (1984) termed *infrastructural power* in his foundational inquiry into how infrastructure territorializes social life. Whether viewed through its rollout as a symbolic manifestation of modern development, analyzed at the point of breakdown, or understood through spaces and processes of abjection, disconnection, or disrepair, infrastructure is a key site for the ordering of society by the state.[3] Infrastructure assembles political economies, processes and discourses of development, and vernacular political histories in urban space and material practice. As a public collective good, moreover, it crystallizes social-power relations and patterns of injustice in the urban landscape.

The power of infrastructure becomes keenly apparent when considering not just its technical and institutional elements, but also its social components and affective dimensions. Of key importance here are the aesthetic, material, and sensuous qualities that are central not just to how infrastructures operate, but to the structures of feeling to which they may give rise—or what Brian Larkin has called *the poetics of infrastructure*.[4] Infrastructure has a performative dimension—its political address is often conjured through event and spectacle. For instance, research into projects of eviction, demolition, or redevelopment, whether justified through singular international events or in the staging of world-class city making and bourgeois environmentalisms, starkly reveal the political content of infrastructural innovations.[5] Infrastructures have a representational logic; they are the means "by which a state proffers . . . representations to its citizens and asks them to take those representations as social facts" (Larkin 2013, 335). Their development, maintenance, or breakdown can inspire awe, fear, desire, and obedience as much as they can incite rebellion or spark imaginative practice. What Dakar's garbage saga makes clear is that it is the embodied material force of these representations that gives them power. Governing-through-disposability entails the uneven provision of trash infrastructures and the flexibilization of garbage labor—effectively bringing people more firmly into the management of their own waste.

In this chapter, I unpack the implications of different infrastructural arrangements around garbage in Dakar and their associated performative practices for state power and politics. Research on postcolonial politics, especially African politics, emphasizes the reliance on spectacle in expressions of authority (Bayart 1989; Hansen and Stepputat 2001; Mbembe 2001). The theatrical mode of politics is well recognized in Senegal (Cruise O'Brien 2007; Foucher 2007), but what has not previously been explored is how performed power is material, spatial, and embodied. Weaving together an analysis of Senegalese politics, the political economy of development, and institutional transformations in the garbage sector, the chapter details how garbage labor has become a focal point of performative urban politics in the context of economic and political liberalization. Emphasizing the materiality of struggles over hegemony, the analysis shows how governing works through the way that infrastructures organize laboring bodies. In the wake of structural adjustment, performances of governing garbage infrastructures have hollowed out infrastructure's function and value, focusing instead on the display of toiling bodies in public space and the spectacle of big institutional shake-ups with little substance.[6] Reading infrastructure through waste labor politics brings the crucially important urban labor question to bear on infrastructure politics, illuminating the risks, precarities, and burdens of new systems for organizing the city. The material power of waste renders garbage management systems particularly important performative vehicles for disciplining the urban public as well as privileged loci for democratic contestation.

Specifically, I focus on garbage politics during two key moments: the implementation of structural adjustment in the late socialist period from 1988 to 2000, and the reign of self-described liberal president Abdoulaye Wade from 2000 to 2012. The first moment is characterized by the dissolution of a more comprehensive, modernist collection system and its replacement by a cheap, participatory infrastructure based on youth labor that slashed the municipal budget, extended patronage networks to new social groups, and deployed neoliberal discourses of participatory citizenship in highly visible performances of ordering. The second period is characterized by escalating tension between the president and the mayor of Dakar, the intensification of institutional instability in the attempt to consolidate power, and the increasingly uneven distribution of order throughout the city. Across these two very different modes of governing garbage, we see three key dynamics: (1) desperate political maneuvering that reinforces patronage modes of governing in the context of scarce resources through attempts to consolidate power and outcompete political rivals; (2) the manifestation of these political responses in episodic, performative, and increasingly fragmented investments that leave the city's infrastructures highly uneven and, for most, degrading; and, most importantly, (3) the differentiated devolution of the burdens of infrastructure's politicization onto residents, laborers, and social systems—or the uneven distribution of disposability across the city. Together, this analysis provides a crucial history of the democratic politics of neoliberal reform. Before I begin the analysis of governing disposability in the neoliberal era, I will first provide a brief historical contextualization of urban politics in Senegal's colonial and nationalist periods.

Colonial Legacies of Infrastructural Politics

An analysis of contemporary politics in Dakar must necessarily be situated within Senegal's unique colonial political history and the patterns of governing-through-disposability that were introduced during that time. Senegal's coastal cities have long been theaters of democratic contestation. Founded by the French, Dakar and three other coastal settlements (Saint-Louis, Gorée, and Rufisque) grew to prominence in the late nineteenth century and were organized into *communes* (municipalities) in the nineteenth century.[7] These Quatre Communes (Four Communes), as they came to be known, represented France's oldest colonial holdings in tropical Africa as well as the clearest expression of France's policy of *assimilation*.[8] Dakar was organized as a fully empowered municipal institution in 1887 and became the capital of the Afrique Occidentale Française (French West Africa) federation in 1902, and it has grown in importance, size, and reputation since that time. Colonial authorities spearheaded major infrastructure projects—including the port facilities as well as the Dakar–Saint-Louis and Dakar–Niger railways—which consolidated Dakar's role as a major West African trading and administrative center. The city has a long history of "extraversion" on a global stage (Bayart 1999) and has served as a key locus of debate and contestation around questions of citizenship. Though the basis of the economy has shifted along with the successive "globalization projects" (M. Diouf 1998)—from the export of slaves, to peanuts, to tourism today—the city has dominated politics and power in the region for some time.

The *originaires* (the original inhabitants of the Quatre Communes) are widely recognized to have enjoyed the most political expression of the French colonies in tropical Africa during the colonial period.[9] The Quatre Communes were the locus of a unique and contradictory colonial experiment: the extension of colonial "citizenship" to the originaires.[10] This gave them special rights under French colonial code, which amounted to special legal status and participation in local as well as French elections (Conklin 1997; M. Diouf 1998; Johnson 1971). It also laid the groundwork for municipal politics in Senegal as well as Dakar's role as the country's political center. At the turn of the century, black Africans began to dominate Dakar's municipal administration, and in 1914, originaire Blaise Diagne was famously elected to serve as a deputy in the French National Assembly in Paris (Johnson 1971). Thirty-two years later, Léopold Sédar Senghor would serve as one of the last deputies to France's National Assembly, before becoming the first president of independent Senegal.

Dakar's colonial history emphasizes the roots of contemporary uneven development planted in the colonial era and the long history of discourses rendering specific populations disposable. Inequality was central to planning and infrastructure development in colonial urbanism in Senegal and elsewhere (Rabinow 1989; G. Wright 1987) but also governed the distinction made between urban and rural development.[11] In Dakar, key logics of managing urban space and infrastructure during the colonial era were spatial segregation along racial lines through cyclical patterns of displacement, and the distribution of infrastructure in "native" and "colonist" areas according to privilege. As in other colonial contexts, ideas surrounding the control of wastes were central to the way colonizers fashioned themselves and defined modernity through judging the "backwardness" of natives (Chakrabarty 1991).

Senegal's bubonic plague of 1914 illuminates a key early expression of the imperative to order public space, infrastructure, and development in the city through discourses and practices of sanitation and public hygiene—or what Maynard W. Swanson termed the *sanitation syndrome*.[12] In the context of the plague, an effort was made to move native populations—including dispossessing many from their land—from what had previously been a mixed downtown area to a sort of ghetto quarantine on the outskirts of the city called the Médina (Betts 1971; Bigon 2009; Echenberg 2002; Petrocelli 2011). The immediate justification behind the project was to upgrade what were seen as dirty, substandard living conditions and to protect the Plateau district from contagion. In practice, the resettlement project was only partially completed, stemming from the special engagement of originaires in municipal politics. Blaise Diagne played a key role in critiquing the Médina project, and lack of native compliance frustrated resettlement plans (Betts 1971). The episode highlights the long legacy of urban popular resistance to projects of social engineering employing narratives of dirt and disorder in Dakar. It also foreshadowed a much larger-scale urban resettlement and expansion into the sprawling, largely unplanned *département* (department) of Pikine (founded in 1952) and Guédiawaye (founded in 1972) in the outskirts of the city. The next sections will zero in on the context for the city's garbage crisis and detail its political stakes.

1960–1980: Governing Garbage in the Nationalist Era

In the first two decades after Independence in 1960, Senegal's development was tightly controlled by the state in its grand plan to modernize and build the nation. The nationalist era was dominated by the Parti Socialiste (Socialist Party)[13] and its strategies to steer the country's economic, social, and cultural course under the strong leadership of Léopold Sédar Senghor, who served as president from 1960 to 1980. Although the country was more open to democratic competition than many of its neighbors, the political opposition was tightly controlled until reforms began in 1976. Senghor's vision was a total reconstruction of Senegal's economy, society, and geography after colonization. His approach was rooted in a developmentalist ideology, as articulated in key plans and institutions aimed at setting the country on a modernization path that was consistent with ideas of African Socialism (M. Diouf 1997). Economic development was to be steered by long-term development planning centered on a large job-creating public sector.

During these "20 glorious years of employment" after Independence (B. Fall 2002, 50), the state was the main employer, the public sector was highly subsidized, and most urban graduates were privileged with comfortable jobs.[14] The public sector grew to serve the ideological purpose of demonstrating state legitimacy and asserting a socialist legacy. In an attempt to create a middle class and keep the social peace, public sector workers earned rates that were incommensurate with revenues and the cost of basic necessities was subsidized (Bellitto 2001). In addition to the development of the peasantry, urban infrastructure was imagined as a key tool of state-led development to bring about a modern Senegal and unleash a more equitable vision of development. Significant investments were made in such sectors as road construction, housing, industry, and the building of monuments to the new nation, but resources were extremely constrained due to the country's lack of natural resources and reliance on the rural peanut economy which began to falter with droughts in the late 1960s and 1970s. The modernist, Socialist rhetoric of development and social justice was tempered by the patronage politics honed in the colonial era, which gained steam in the hiring practices and uneven infrastructural investment of the "providential state" (M.Diouf 1997).

Following on colonial trends, in the late 1960s the postcolonial state subsidized housing programs for civil servants while systematically evicting and resettling "squatters" and other "illegal" occupants farther and farther out of the peninsula to areas with little infrastructure (Vernière 1977). As René Collignon has argued, the periodic expulsion of undesirable populations— or *déchets humains* (human garbage)—seen as "encumbering" urban space ramped up in the 1960s and 1970s.[15] Real estate investment and housing construction have continued to be "key components of a strategy to project the image of a modern Dakar as the national capital," but have been overwhelming concentrated in central districts and woefully insufficient in keeping up with urban growth.[16]

In the immediate period after Independence, from 1960 to 1971, the management of household waste in the city of Dakar was a small-scale affair directly ensured by the municipal services.[17] Horse-drawn carts were used to transport the garbage to a dump located in an old quarry in Hann, not

far from downtown Dakar, until the dry lakebed, Mbeubeuss (forty kilo-
meters from Dakar), was transformed into a new dump in the late 1960s.
This municipal service ran relatively smoothly until its first crisis in 1968—
paralleling a political crisis that took place that year—which extended until
1971 (Benrabia 2002, 261). The city had become filthy and garbage a point
of political contention, so the municipal authorities decided to privatize the
waste-management system. In 1971, the city of Dakar signed a five-year contract with the local private company la Société Africaine de diffusion et de
promotion (African Distribution and Promotion Company; SOADIP) for Dakar's household trash management. The company built two transfer stations,
introduced a fleet of modern collection vehicles, and hired more than eleven
hundred people (BCEOM 1986). It assured the fairly regular management
of garbage until the early 1980s. Faced with defaults in payments from the
municipality, however, the company was unable to maintain its equipment
and service and ceased all activities in 1984 (BCEOM 1986; M. Diouf, n.d.).

Public events were staged in the 1960s to enlist Socialist Party youth in
cleaning the city and ridding it of undesirable elements encumbering the
public space (including prostitutes and vagabonds). This precedent was to
lead to other initiatives in the 1970s and 1980s, including Operation Augias,
through which the state tried to tap local energies in the city's management.
Mamadou Diouf (2002, 268) describes Operation Augias as "the occasion,
for the ruling class, to affirm its munificence, its incontestable power and
authority over populations locked into the grid of political containment." It
was a way for the ruling party to assert its nationalist project. Not surprisingly, as that nationalist project began to splinter in the 1970s, these events
were characterized by disillusionment and even violence.

1979–1988: The Messy Onset of Structural Adjustment

Senegal's state-led, nationalist development period was to be short lived. By
the end of the 1970s, it was clear that the Senegalese economy was entering into a serious economic crisis. Rural exodus and a stagnant industrial
sector were hastening rapid urbanization and the explosion of the informal
economy. The providential state—which had become the country's main
employer—was deeply indebted and inefficient.[18] Having borrowed significantly from private banks in the 1970s, Senegal received its first structural
adjustment loan from the World Bank in 1979. As such, it became one of
the first African countries to undertake adjustment policies and pioneered

a massive wave of adjustment programs across the continent and the world. Structural Adjustment Programs (SAPs) were the primary mode through which neoliberal reforms were exported to the Global South. In Africa, SAPs were the Bretton Woods institutions' solution to a reading of the African economic crisis epitomized by the Berg Report (Berg 1981). This hugely influential paper, and the SAPs that were built around its prescriptions, offered a highly internalist reading of African economic woes. The Senegalese state and its "political management of the economy" were rendered the source of the country's problems, demanding intervention and assistance from international institutions (M. Diouf 1997, 311). It was hoped that Senegal, a longtime darling of the international community, would become a model of economic liberalization through adjustment. The neoliberal reforms promoted through SAPs rendered development technical and apolitical and chased out the "nationalist dream of economic development and social equality . . . in the name of economic efficiency" (M. Diouf 1997, 314).

Senghor's handpicked successor, Abdou Diouf, led the charge for structural adjustment with his arrival onto the political stage in 1981. Diouf's presidency ushered in the period of "technocracy," where the old barons of the Socialist Party were replaced with younger technocrats. Fashioned more as managers than as politicians, the technocrats favored administrative expertise over the mass-movement politics associated with the nationalist era. Diouf and the technocrats endeavored to use structural adjustment as a strategy to defuse the economic crisis and reestablish financial equilibrium. In the 1980s, Senegal received a total of fifteen different stabilization and adjustment loans from the World Bank and the International Monetary Fund (IMF) (Van de Walle 2001). During this period, the country fell deeper into economic crisis.[19] Rapidly losing the ability to keep up with the pace of population growth as financial resources flagged, the government made minimal new investments in urban infrastructure and existing infrastructures crumbled under poor maintenance.

Garbage infrastructure began to emerge as a central issue in urban politics with structural adjustment. With the bankruptcy of SOADIP, in 1984 the city became clogged again with its own waste. The new Socialist mayor of Dakar, Mamadou Diop, took charge of garbage management, resorting to personally organizing periodic waste management activities with the assistance of the Army Corps of Engineers. Despite these efforts, immense piles of garbage built up in Dakar. A special event, Set Wecc ("Very Clean" in Wolof), was organized in February of 1985 by the army with the help of the local residents, enabling the evacuation of tons of garbage to the dump at Mbeubeuss. A new parastatal enterprise with the state as majority shareholder was then created to manage garbage through which, it was hoped, the state could exercise more control over the system than it had with the private company. The new garbage company, sias, was given the exclusive management of Dakar's trash in 1985 under the oversight of the new municipal entity federating the region of Dakar, la Communauté Urbaine de Dakar (Dakar Urban Community; cud).[20]

In many ways, sias was emblematic of the Socialist state's vision of a modern public sector in the nationalist era: it was well paid, well equipped, and the workers were unionized and rewarded with the full privileges accorded civil servants who were understood to be the breadwinners of their families. Given the wider agenda to privatize and shrink the state, it was an example of foot dragging in the public sector, an ambitious approach to postpone real adjustment that was to prove untenable in the face of pressures to scale back public expenditures and urban public services. All of this was to shift with the crisis of 1988, which both signaled a profound reckoning with the vicissitudes of structural adjustment and ushered in a more intensive implementation of economic reforms in the face of economic stagnation and pressures for compliance.

Worsening economic conditions combined with the rollback of state services to unleash calamitous social consequences, including a dramatic backtracking on progress made in health and education in the 1960s and 1970s and an employment crisis. By the late 1980s, structural adjustment had brought the golden years of state employment to an end, deeply restructured the urban workforce, and unleashed major changes in organized labor in Dakar. As a bedrock element of adjustment, a central aim of reform packages in Senegal was the shrinking of the public sector through the withdrawal of the state from employment and the flexibilization of the labor force in order to cut the public wage bill.[21] Privatization and the withdrawal of the state from public employment joined with the decline of private Senegalese industry to precipitate the collapse of formal employment in the 1980s and 1990s.[22] Rapid rates of urban migration flooded the cities, particularly the country's sprawling macrocephalic capital, Dakar, even as formal jobs there became increasingly rare. The decline of formal labor was met with the mushrooming of the informal sector, which began to dominate the Senegalese economy in the late 1980s.

The city's young people, who comprised an increasingly large segment of the population owing to demographic trends, experienced unemployment most dramatically. Stemming from their marginality in social networks and the declining efficacy of educational degrees in securing employment, youth swamped the informal markets and became a central element of the masses of out-of-work people occupying the public space. During this time, the job crisis seriously diminished the purchasing power of the Dakarois just as food prices skyrocketed. These factors and reforms aimed at scaling back health care, education, and other social service sectors all contributed to the general impoverishment of the Dakarois and their widespread dissatisfaction with the government.

Paralleling these processes of economic liberalization were processes of political liberalization that responded to increasing demands for democratic representation from the public and opposition groups, as well as pressures from the international community through SAP conditionalities. Though President Diouf deepened political reforms in the 1980s, challenges to state legitimacy would continue to plague the Socialist Party in the devastating wake of structural adjustment.[23] The growing informalization of the Senegalese economy, furthermore, had broad impacts for state power and patronage resources. Far from the intended goal of neoliberal reforms—namely, to foster the growth of a dynamic, efficient, and productive independent bourgeoisie—Ibrahima Thioub et al. argue that a merchant-capital logic continued to dominate. What changed was the state's ability to capitalize, structure, and regulate it (Thioub, Diop, and Boone 1998). Reform eroded the capacity of the state to sustain patterns of economic activity established under colonial rule (see Boone 1990) and changed the expression of patronage away from a system that assured stability (Coulon and Cruise O'Brien 1990). As the 1980s progressed, the diminished capacity of the state brought increasing pressure to control shrinking state coffers and, thus, heightened competition between political rivals and different levels of government.

The eroding social contract with the country's *marabouts* (religious leaders) was to further challenge the state's hold on power and legitimacy during this time. Senegalese Islam is overwhelmingly Sufi, with the Tijani and Mouride orders (brotherhoods) dominating the country's Islamic tradition. In Senegalese Sufi tradition, marabouts play a central role in mediating state-society relations and, as a result, a key feature of Senegalese politics has long been the relationship between government and the Sufi brotherhoods. A social contract between the brotherhoods—particularly the Mouride brotherhood—and the colonial administration provided a source of stability and legitimacy for the colonial regime. Senghor then built the political basis of his regime on these same ties, actively seeking and obtaining the cooperation and support of the powerful Mouride leadership and its disciples (Copans 1980; Cruise O'Brien 1971, 1975). State concessions to the religious authorities were reciprocated with political support. Through the use of formal *ndigals* (religious injunctions), religious leaders mobilized their disciples to vote for the Socialist Party in the elections throughout this period. This tight interrelationship between the state and the Muslim brotherhoods was a key buttress in the face of a challenging economic environment and political instability in neighboring countries.[24]

The 1980s, however, saw key shifts in the politics of religion, involving essential reorganizations in the fundamental relationship between the brotherhoods and the state and between the marabouts and their *talibés* (disciples). A number of factors joined during this period to "liberalize" the religious playing field, including the general liberalization of the economy and politics, the diversification and informalization of the economy, and the education, urbanization, and autonomization of the citizen, as well as a weakening of the hierarchical authority of the brotherhoods.[25] Perhaps the greatest illustration of this democratization was the crumbling of the ndigal as a formula for delivering disciples' votes to the Socialist regime, starting in the 1980s.[26] All of these forces would come together to politicize Dakar's municipal garbage sector in unprecedented ways.

1988–2000: A Crisis of Order and Mayor Mamadou Diop's Battle for Dakar

Together, the forces of economic and political liberalization crystallized in a full-fledged crisis surrounding the 1988 presidential elections. The political crisis manifested in the worst garbage crisis the city had ever experienced. Widespread social unrest and mobilization by a disgruntled populace in Dakar, particularly the city's youth, met with the Socialist Party state's scramble to retain its legitimacy, hold on to power, and control the social peace. The reconfiguration of the state's role in the economy, the reformulation of the relationship between religion and politics, and the liberalization of the political playing field had politicians courting voters like never before. As the dire social consequences of structural adjustment and overall economic crisis deepened and unemployment skyrocketed, young Dakarois took to the streets in record numbers. Massive student strikes in 1985 and 1987 paralyzed the education system, leading to an *année blanche* (white year) in 1987–88, where students' work was annulled (M. Diouf 1996). The workers union of the trash company SIAS joined in the conflictual spirit of labor organizing during this period and began to strike in the late 1980s to demand better working conditions.

The shifting bases of the state-brotherhood and the talibé-marabout relationships, moreover, were dramatically expressed in the controversial 1988 elections. Despite a blunt ndigal from the Khalifa-General of the Mouride brotherhood to vote for Abdou Diouf, the opposition received a significant proportion of the vote. Not since 1988 has a top brotherhood leader pronounced a political ndigal in favor of a presidential candidate, indicating the deep "cracks in the edifice" of the mutualism provided by the original social contract between the marabouts and the ruling party (Villalon 1999, 2004). Huge numbers of Dakarois rallied their support for opposition candidate Abdoulaye Wade's electoral campaign—whose slogan promised *sopi* (change)—leading up to the elections of 1988 (Diaw and Diouf 1998; Diop and Diouf 1990; Young and Kante 1992).

Youth mobilizations turned violent with the highly contested election results, which placed incumbent Abdou Diouf as the winner. The government responded to youth riots in Dakar by declaring a state of emergency, imposing a curfew, and arresting and convicting the opposition leaders for their role in inciting the violence. The city's streets then turned violent again in the spring of 1989 with a spate of ethnically motivated murders in broad daylight during the country's diplomatic crisis with Mauritania.[27] Though the Socialist Party had retained power, the integrity of the party-state appeared threatened, as acutely symbolized in the sinister vision of the young urban rioters. The crisis ushered in, moreover, a new era of urban protest that was centered on a descent into the streets and mobilization around the management of urban order. The government's formula for hegemony was being renegotiated in the material spaces of the city. New constituencies were raising their heads, new formulas of power were emerging, and garbage was taking center stage as both a symbol of state crisis and an important terrain on which to battle for control of the city.

A social movement blossomed in the wake of the crisis of 1988 that would herald a new chapter in the city's infrastructural politics. As I consider in detail in chapter 2, the youth movement Set/Setal offered a constructive response to the general population's disillusionment with the country's economic and political state of affairs through neighborhood cleaning activities.

In both an indictment of the state's failings and a call for the citizens of Dakar to take local development into their own hands after the disappointing elections, youth set out to cleanse the city—physically and morally. These labors came to the attention of Dakar's Socialist mayor, Mamadou Diop, as he reeled from the threat to his party's hold on power and schemed to design a new vision of city politics and infrastructure in the face of austerity. The failures of the trash-management system had become an enormous liability for Diop's office. His response was to seize the fervor for cleaning among the city's youth and channel it into a wholly new garbage collection infrastructure. Dissolving the last system of municipal garbage collection and firing its employees, he instead built a new system that looked altogether different: a scaled-back, low-tech, participatory garbage sector that required not much more than the simple toil of the city's youth.

Although the state's modernist development vision had never been fully realized, Diop's new garbage sector signaled a foundational shift in the ideological and material basis of the Socialist state's approach to urban development. The exigencies of neoliberal austerity and the intensification of multiparty democratic competition ushered forth a new logic of governing through infrastructure. These forces justified, indeed required, a shift from the modernist, state-planned, comprehensive infrastructure models— however aspirational—to a community-based, participatory system that was unapologetic in its fragmentation. The transition to the more piecemeal public service turned on the construction of the citizen-laborer: it absolved the state of responsibility for providing employment in the manner of an adult male patriarch and instead conceived of youth as the primary workers of the nation—conveniently extricated from their familial obligations. In other words, the new participatory waste infrastructure allowed Diop and his compatriots in the Socialist Party to instrumentalize neoliberal discourse in their favor. Taking charge of the city's order became the responsibility of the city's communities; a clean neighborhood became one in which the people were clean. This acted to patch the cracks in the state's hegemonic project that were apparent in the physical manifestation of disorder.

Steeped in the now all-too-familiar language of participation, empowerment, and entrepreneurialism, the backbone and connective tissues of the city's new garbage infrastructure were now young people and their communitarian ties, respectively. In place of state performances of monumental infrastructural achievements, there were instead the highly visible neighborhood performances of "participatory citizenship" by those doing the state's bidding through cleaning Dakar's city spaces. Though it had been attempted before, in the form of Operation Augias and various attempts by the army to coerce the Dakarois into public cleaning, Diop's *Journées de Propreté* (Days of Cleanliness) were unprecedented. The events were characterized by bright T-shirts, dust clouds rising from the now unclogged streets, and the gyrating exhortations by Senegal's national hero, musician Youssou N'Dour, for cleanliness blaring over distorted mobile speaker systems. In these scenes, a whole new citizen was born and a whole new infrastructure for managing the city was soldered. This new infrastructure spoke to an entirely different aesthetic regime of ordering. The city's business was aired and evacuated, not by a quiet and invisible army of well-paid but anonymous professionals, but by noisy, youthful, and familiar young men and women.

Channeling Set/Setal activists into the trash system—and thereby changing the institutional form of the sector as well as the composition of its labor force—offered a financial fix to a budgetary crisis, but was also a calculated political maneuver on the part of Mayor Diop. Diop's position as mayor was, in a number of respects, highly untenable. Consistent with a long tradition of state centralization in the postcolonial period, the central state tightly controlled resources away from the municipality. Diop was, like his predecessors in the post, a "prisoner" of his dependence on the central state. Though he lacked sufficient resources to run the city and conduct politics, he was charged with the enormous challenge of managing the social peace and cultivating support for the party in the urban areas that were the base of the opposition.[28] Fashioning himself and the new recruits in his administration as urban technocrats, he aimed to distance himself from the classic patronage politics that were crippling his fellow socialists (Diop and Diouf 1992).

At the same time, however, Mamadou Diop had no choice but to develop a new approach to patronage. An accomplished politician who had his own ambitions,[29] Diop was keen to find some financial independence, shore up electoral support, and quiet the foreboding youth agitations that had taken his city hostage. The new trash sector reduced the trash bill and provided him with more control over the budget through the involvement of international funders. Moreover, it served as a direct recruitment tool for political clients in two emerging social groups—youth and women—at a moment when he was considering a bid for the presidency. Offering the trash-sector jobs to the Set/Setal activists thus represented one of the state's key strategies to deal with its shrinking capacity and legitimacy and to quiet social mobilizations through a more inclusive patronage system. The garbage system that was to last for the next ten years was small scale, heavily reliant on labor, little capitalized, and progressively more fragmented. The turn to fully off-grid community-based garbage collection projects in the city's periphery, furthermore, hastened the displacement of the responsibility for the city's order away from public services and onto the bodies of the laboring poor, and further splintered the city's waste infrastructure (see chapter 3).

As the 1990s progressed, structural adjustment moved full speed ahead and the state accelerated its withdrawal from the public sector, with no choice but to appease funders. In 1994, under pressure from international lenders, Senegal devalued its currency, the West African franc (CFA), precipitating a short-term economic crisis.[30] With the devaluation of the currency, a new package of reforms was launched that would signal a more neoliberal turn and an era of even more marked state disengagement. Whereas deregulation had occurred on a limited, sectoral basis in the 1980s, massive swaths of the public sector were privatized in the 1990s, including the electricity, telecommunications, and water sectors. As a last remaining slice of public sector jobs, the trash sector continued to represent an important pot to control through a range of institutional experiments.

2000–2006: Alternance and Abdoulaye Wade's Infrastructural Dream

The progressing decade was again to bring a tenuous state of political affairs. Although the Socialist Party's efforts to gain the support of the urban youth had at least worked to quiet youth mobilization for a while, this was just a postponement of a general reckoning with what was to come. Abdou Diouf won reelection in 1993 with an overwhelming victory, largely attributed to the successful mobilization of rural voters in contrast to an incredibly high abstention vote, particularly among the urban youth (Diop and Diouf 1992). Whereas early in the decade the state had undertaken significant political reforms aimed at power sharing with members of the opposition, subsequent years saw a striking pullback of the political reforms achieved in the early 1990s (Diop, Diouf, and Diaw 2000). As precipitous declines in public spending devastated indicators of social welfare, managing the social peace was made the state's top priority in order to ensure the proper implementation of SAPs and neutralize social resistance. At the end of the decade, despite some economic improvements at a macro scale, Senegal found itself in a situation characterized by deepening inequality, the degradation of infrastructure, the decline of the educational system, and the rising cost of living. The Socialist Party could no longer keep a lid on the grievances and social mobilizations that had been bubbling up for years.

On March 19, 2000, Abdoulaye Wade was elected to the presidency. Monitored extensively by the Senegalese media as well as foreign observers, the *Alternance* (turnover) elections were widely considered to be the most free and fair elections to date in Senegal. After hearing of his defeat, Abdou Diouf graciously stepped down in a smooth and peaceful turnover of power. Despite the Socialist Party's preelection efforts to quell social unrest and exercise its remaining patronage capacities to retain the support of the growing urban electorate, desperation on the part of a population unable to envision its future, let alone its daily survival, found voice in Wade's call for *sopi* (change). The development promises of the Socialist Party appeared bankrupt, especially to the exploding youth population born after Independence, for whom the nationalist project held little or no meaning. Wade, who had been a stalwart character on the Senegalese political scene since Senghor through his Parti Démocratique Sénégalais (Senegalese Democratic Party, PDS), deftly targeted those disenfranchised and frustrated urban dwellers through dramatic theatrics of public support called *marches bleues* (blue marches) (Foucher 2007), and finally convinced the Senegalese people that he would represent a new direction in Senegalese politics and right the wrongs of the last difficult decades.

Alternance indicated to many the advent of true, substantive, multiparty democracy in Senegal. Many observers also highlighted how Wade's victory represented a dramatic collapse of the ndigal as a political tool (Audrain 2004; F. Samson 2000). Although the Mouride leader did not pronounce a formal electoral ndigal to vote for the incumbent party, there was widespread rejection of the lower-ranking marabouts' ndigals, leading many intellectuals to applaud the election as a "victory of citizenship" (Mbow 2003, quoted in Villalon 2004, 66). Ironically, these youth sought change through voting for one of the last great Independence-era politicians—and a self-declared liberal (neoliberal in the English parlance), at that.

The political economy of development under Abdoulaye Wade was to signal a departure from the previous era in a number of important respects, particularly with regard to infrastructure. When Wade arrived into office, he set out, first and foremost, to consolidate the economic base of his political power (M.-C. Diop 2013a). To his favor, he faced an economic context that was slightly improved from that facing his predecessor. From a macro-economic perspective, the second half of the 1990s had shown considerable improvement owing to the benefits of deregulation and of debt relief.[31] With the Bretton Woods funders loosening some of their control over spending, Wade set out to exert as much autonomy as possible in crafting the country's new development trajectory. Through restructuring diplomatic relations, he sought to mobilize new sources of international finance through courting South-South investment partnerships with countries such as China, Brazil, India, and South Africa, as well as nations from the Middle East. Armed with this diversified finance portfolio, he embarked upon a number of Grands Projets du chef de l'état (Major Projects of the Head of State), centered on infrastructural modernization in telecommunications, a new airport for Dakar, development of the port, new national monuments, and, especially, huge investments in road construction in and around Dakar. It was a promising period in which the great hope that people had carried for Alternance seemed to be materializing in the infrastructural transformations Wade was charting across the city. As Caroline Melly (2013, 399) argues, the personal hardship faced by Dakarois during the construction stage appeared a sacrifice worth the wait for "spectacular expectations for the future."

Wade's transformation of the garbage sector was an element of his ambitions to make his mark through infrastructure as well as to centralize control over his infrastructural visions. Just months after the 2000 elections, he set out to eviscerate the fief of Mayor Mamadou Diop through dissolving his municipal organization (the CUD) and its most important element, the participatory trash sector. After serving eighteen years as mayor, Mamadou Diop lost in the local elections on May 12, 2002, to liberal candidate Pape Diop, a close ally of Abdoulaye Wade. A new national government agency was created in 2000 to take over the management of the trash sector,[32] and a call for bids was put out on the international market for a major private waste management company. A private subsidiary of an Italian waste management company, Azienda Municipalizzata per l'Ambiente (Municipal Environment Agency; AMA), was awarded the contract for managing Dakar's household garbage from 2002 until 2006.[33] The trash workers who had entered the system with Set/Setal were officially hired by AMA with formal contracts, set salaries (65,000 CFA, or about US$120 per month), and regular benefits, temporarily closing out the insecure and informal institutional arrangements under which they had labored for more than ten years in Mayor Mamadou Diop's participatory system. The workers had new uniforms, new collection equipment, and finally felt that their labor was being valued. They had formed a union in 2000, in anticipation of the need to defend their jobs and working conditions in the turbulent restructuring that was to come, and the union was formally integrated into the company's operations.

Though at first Wade's attempts to modernize Dakar's infrastructure seemed reminiscent of the state-led modernization approach of the Senghor era and its grand aspirations for stimulating broad-based development and social equity, it was soon clear that Wade's infrastructural visions were more volatile and less principled than originally hoped. In the garbage sector, the dream of stable, protected labor began to slip within a couple of years of the new system. After some severe scandals—most notably that the company had been found to supply used trucks from Europe instead of new ones—AMA's deficiencies were apparent by 2003 and the system appeared in crisis again by 2005.[34] Garbage piled up across the city and outraged residents voiced their critiques. The first cases of cholera in many years were registered in Dakar that rainy season. President Wade definitively cancelled the contract in July of 2006, plunging Dakar into a garbage crisis characterized by nebulous institutional arrangements, frequent mobilization by the union, and extensive public dumping.[35] In the lead-up to the elections of 2006, Dakar was drowning in its refuse as workers and residents protested the institutional vacuum. Though Wade was reelected that year, instability in the garbage sector served as the material manifestation of his governing challenges. In the second half of his presidency, the garbage sector would foreground the downward slide of his legitimacy and his increasingly desperate attempts to consolidate power.

2006–2012: Infrastructural Fragmentation and Elitism

The institutional arrangements for waste management following the cancellation of AMA's contract can be inscribed within an intensification of competition between the national and local state and Wade's attempt to mitigate the power of the local state. The dissolution of the CUD as one of Wade's first actions as president represented a strategy not only to disembowel the powerbase of one of his main rivals from the Socialist Party (Mamadou Diop), but also to recentralize political power away from a powerful local government entity and into the national executive. After severing AMA's contract, he founded an intermunicipal organization federating the Dakar region, the CADAK-CAR.[36] Though seemingly patterned after the CUD, the CADAK-CAR was described as being "less political" and more "technocratic" than its precedent organization and was, in practice, just a skeleton of the CUD's power and capacity.[37] It can be seen as a thinly veiled attempt to mask centralization efforts within a façade of decentralization. After the departure of AMA, a "transitional" power-sharing agreement was set up between the national Ministry of the Environment and CADAK-CAR. Though garbage is a *compétence transférée* (responsibility of the local state), as consistent with Senegal's 1996 decentralization laws, the special arrangement with the Ministry of the Environment rests on an addendum to the law on decentralization passed in 2002 under Wade's thumb.[38] Citing Dakar's exceptionalism, this addendum specifies that decisions regarding Dakar's trash be determined by central state decree.

In this power-sharing agreement, the Ministry of the Environment contracted with the eighteen private *concessionaires* (contractors) who supplied the collection trucks and managed the collection and the dump, while the mayor of Dakar, via CADAK-CAR, managed the funds coming in from the state and oversaw the paychecks. During this time, the main problems stemmed from controversy surrounding the one international concessionaire (the rest were local), Veolia Propreté, and the increasingly fierce labor disputes between the state and the trash workers (see chapter 4). A subsidiary of the French company Vivendi, Veolia was hired in late 2006 on a "test" period to coordinate all aspects of the collection for the two downtown districts of Dakar: Plateau and Médina. The conditions under which the contract was awarded to Veolia were shady as they did not stem from a competitive public bid and were rumored to have emerged from personal connections with Wade's son Karim.[39] Even more significantly, for just these two central districts—out of the Dakar region's forty-three—at the heart of the financial and administrative operations of the city, the company received a wildly disproportionate share of the budget. In each year, at least 25 percent of the total garbage budget was paid to Veolia to serve just 6.5 percent of Dakar's population and what were, in many respects, the easiest areas to service (Cissé and Wone 2013, 744). Although the Veolia workers received no special protections and were considered temp workers,[40] this codified a sharp segregation between the poorer and more populous parts of the city—which were served by struggling, underpaid, and under-equipped contractors—and two of the richest downtown districts, serviced by state-of-the-art French equipment.

The power-sharing agreement ran relatively smoothly at the level of government owing to the fact that the mayor of Dakar, Pape Diop (head of

CADAK-CAR), and the minister of the environment both hailed from Abdoulaye Wade's party. However, resistance to the arrangement escalated from 2006 to 2009 as the trash workers mounted increasingly significant strikes and Dakarois voiced their discontent through public dumping. Garbage accumulating in Dakar's public spaces in 2007 rivaled that of 1988. Trash crisis and disorder symbolized increasing public discontentment with Wade's government and mobilization of disgruntled citizens as the decade progressed. Things were to change dramatically in 2009 as support for Wade and his party began to slip in the polls. In March 2009, in a turning of the political tide that followed on the heels of a particularly acerbic spate of trash strikes, Socialist candidate Khalifa Sall was elected to be mayor of Dakar, signaling an end to PDS control over the mayor's office.[41] From that moment until 2012, the institutional and labor arrangements in the trash sector took center stage in the political battle between Abdoulaye Wade's central government and the City of Dakar.

Immediately after taking office in July 2009, Mayor Sall acted decisively on the part of the trash workers through formally hiring them on as employees of CADAK-CAR, regularizing their payments, and providing them with social security and health services.[42] Then, under firm pressure from the trash-workers union, Mayor Sall let the final short-term contract with Veolia expire in December 2009, declaring publicly that he intended to regularize the sector for good by ending closed-door agreements and putting out a public call for bids for the company to replace Veolia. Sall aimed one more blow at Veolia in November 2010, in response to the trash workers' planned strike during the Muslim holiday Tabaski, by ordering that union delegates who had been fired by Veolia be reinstated and that a section of the union be created within that enterprise. At the same time, Mayor Sall convened a commission to study the garbage sector, propose a strategic plan for its organization, and explore pay raises for the workers.[43] Then, in January 2011, the mayor led the charge for an agreement signed between CADAK-CAR and the bank BICIS,[44] to provide accounts for all Dakar public workers, most notably starting with the garbage sector. The union vociferously declared its support for the mayor and CADAK-CAR.

In reaction to Mayor Sall's efforts to consolidate authority over the garbage sector, President Wade reshuffled Dakar's trash management again just a few months later. By April 2011, the mayor and the president had all but declared war over the sector. In a heated set of newspaper interviews that month, the mayor is quoted as saying: "It's a political battle that we will fight until the end . . . The surface technicians [trash collectors] are right to refuse to be the sacrificial lamb" (quoted in Soleil 2011). For his part, the president declared: "We must tell the truth. Today's Mayors are unable to manage garbage" (quoted in Cissokho 2011). Wade retaliated by making plans to transfer the budget and authority for garbage management away from CADAK-CAR, back to the newly resuscitated national garbage agency. A street cleanup operation with fifteen hundred youth was organized, circumventing the formal trash workers and prompting them to go on strike. Wade continued to refuse to meet with the trash-workers union and community residents expressed their dismay at the situation through periodic public dumping. A few months later, the story heated up even more when Wade created yet another new national trash-management agency that would take garbage even further out of the hands of the city.[45] Mayor Sall vociferously protested, contesting that it directly contradicted the decentralization laws of 1996 and pointing out the paradox of a (neo)liberal president who in fact seeks to centralize and nationalize, more than deregulate.

In the final months of Wade's presidency, the garbage sector was again in legal limbo. Although the new agency was not yet in force, Wade transferred the trash budget into the hands of the Ministry of Culture, essentially gutting CADAK-CAR—an institution that he himself had created. The workers and mayor alike continued to protest the creation of the new agency, but essentially hunkered down until the presidential elections of 2012 to see what the new political climate would hold for garbage. Wade's government fell back on the now hackneyed performance of public cleaning in an attempt to shore up political support. Again sidelining the formal trash workers, the Ministry of Culture organized a series of highly visible Days of Cleanliness leading up to the elections in Dakar, where over a thousand young people were paid as day laborers to conduct periodic sweeps of the city.

From these performances of state power through garbage infrastructure, we can read a wider insight into Wade's mode of governing. Volatility in the garbage sector exemplified the mismanagement of public funds and political manipulation of government agencies in the face of the flagging legitimacy that characterized the Wade era overall (Dahou and Foucher 2004; M.-C. Diop 2013b, 2013c; Mbow 2008). Wade endeavored to concentrate power in the executive, fashioning himself the supreme executor of his "major projects" across many sectors, and mutating government ministries at will in the periodic reorganization of the form and function of his patronage systems (see M.-C. Diop 2013a). This meant jealously guarding control from other political figures, even in his own government, and, sometimes, battling tooth and nail against rival politicians to control specific turf. The institutions of government were often casualties of these political agendas and personalistic logics (Mbow 2008).

Overall, Wade's governance of trash and other sectors defied consistent political economic logics or development goals. The schizophrenic approach to liberalizing the public sector is a case in point. Though privatization was key on Wade's agenda in principle, as we can see in the trash sector, Wade privatized in fits and starts. With the arrival of AMA came a more forceful move toward privatization, but with the repeal of that contract and the long transitional phase to follow, the system languished in a hybrid arrangement that defied logic outside of the urge to exert control over the sector and its vast budget. The creation of a national trash management company in the twilight hours of his presidency further marked a final desperate effort to manipulate the sector for power and prestige. Intervening sporadically in diverse sectors, Wade's style demonstrated a rationality of political maneuvering more than one of long-term development planning (see Ndoye 2013). Far from a classic reform agenda, his neoliberal experiment was a nonlinear, messy process anchored in an autocratic approach to combat his waning legitimacy.

The technical and institutional fragmentation and degradation of garbage infrastructure, especially after 2006, was part and parcel of an overall pattern of infrastructure investment and development that was profoundly uneven and, at its base, elitist. Health and education suffered enormously during this period due to low investments, and Wade's most famous investment, his roadworks, overwhelmingly benefited the rich, connecting elite parts of the city through fancy overpasses and the now famous Corniche coastal highway peppered with fancy shopping malls (M.-C. Diop 2013a; Foley 2010; Melly 2013). The mega-highway project linking the peninsula of Dakar to its sprawling suburbs is a toll road that has eased the commuting burdens for precious few working-class people. The systematic disinvestment in garbage infrastructure after 2006, except in the two downtown zones serviced by Veolia, rendered street sweeping and access to disposal deeply unequal across the city. Garbage played a central role in Wade's aesthetic dream to project a certain image of the city, especially to its elite visitors. The rich neighborhoods and fancy roads had to be clean, but a look inside the poor and working-class neighborhoods revealed an altogether different reality. This is consistent with wider trends toward splintering urban-

FIGURE I.3. A run-down garbage truck being repaired in Yoff.
Author's photo, 2006.

ism that entail the differential development of city infrastructures charted by Stephen Graham and Simon Marvin (2001), but emphasizes the political nature of such fragmentation and its deepening reliance on the body as infrastructure. Degradation of equipment (see figure 1.3) and the devaluation of trash labor worked to devolve the strains and burdens of cleaning—and thus filth and disposability—onto the bodies of the workers and the city's poorest households.

In garbage and other sectors, including roadworks, Wade's policies did not, on the whole, grow stable employment, but, rather, relied on flexibilized labor formulas (especially contract labor) which exacerbated the growing disparity between social classes and the strains of social dislocation in a city that was becoming evermore inaccessible to average working people (Ndiaye 2010, 2013). Wade's investment in work was about image and performance more than ensuring long-term stable employment. The armies of people he hired for his building projects seemed impressive, but in reality these were often day laborers making only meager salaries. Wearing tunics with slogans related to his various projects, these laboring bodies were the visible vital infrastructure of Wade's grand projects, allowing him to claim space and responsibility for the transformations taking place, to display the power and promise of the new city to come. But his forced removal of Dakar's thousands of *marchands ambulants* (street vendors)[46] and extensive efforts to ramp up street cleaning in order to cleanse and sanitize the city for the OIC summit told a different story. Street vendors encumbered urban space in ways that were messy and unmodern, and striking garbage workers betrayed the rising tide of dissent bubbling up in Dakar. Both were contrary to the image of order that Wade was trying to project to the world. Although it wasn't completed in time for the OIC, the African Renaissance Monument (see figure 1.2), on the other hand, perhaps most clearly represents Wade's vision. As the most striking of Wade's attempts to mark public space, the huge statue depicting an African nuclear family gesturing to the West sought to conjure Dakar's emergence as a world-class city in the making. Instead, it has not ceased to be the butt of jokes, and served as the site of protests when it was unveiled and during his failed bid to retain power in 2012.[47]

Trash Politics after Abdoulaye Wade

On March 25, 2012, a new era of trash management was ushered in with the election of Macky Sall as president after what turned out to be Senegal's most violent and contentious elections yet. Upon taking office, Sall announced his intention to dissolve Abdoulaye Wade's new national trash management agency and relocate Dakar's garbage management back into the hands of local government.[48] By summer 2012, Veolia had finally left Senegal and a number of steps were being taken toward regularizing the sector. Although the mayor of Dakar, Khalifa Sall, and the president, Macky Sall (no relation), hail from different parties, from 2012 to 2014 they demonstrated their willingness to work together with regard to Dakar's trash management. The CADAK-CAR organization was officially resuscitated and garbage was placed fully under its tutelage. At a trash conference hosted by the trash-workers union that took place in June 2012, representatives from both offices and other implicated institutions all indicated that they were committed to working together with the union to ensure that the sector's perpetual "transitional" phase would come to an end with a final, effective, and just management system. After years of lobbying, the trash workers' collective bargaining agreement was finally signed by the trash-workers union, the mayor of Dakar, and the director general of CADAK-CAR on June 24,

2014 (République du Sénégal 2014). This signaled an important reversal of austerity-era management trends and a major gain by a prominent social movement. Although implementation was slow, the collective convention signaled a reversal of the flexibilization of labor in the sector and carried the trash workers' hope for an end to a long period of instability and insecure legal protections.

Unfortunately, the workers' hopes that the sector would be stabilized and depoliticized once and for all were dashed as garbage continues to be thrown back into the spotlight of political maneuvering. Further reconfigurations in the sector stemmed out of an escalation of tension between President Macky Sall and Mayor Khalifa Sall. In October 2015, the president reneged on previous commitments and removed garbage from under CADAK-CAR to instead place it under the control of an agency titled l'Unité de coordination et de gestion des déchets (Garbage Coordination and Management Unit; UCG),[49] which is managed by the (national) Ministry of Local Governments. The trash-workers union, which was not consulted before this change, harshly critiqued the transfer, underlining that its key objective is safeguarding the gains it has worked so hard to obtain. Although there have been a few small issues of noncompliance with the collective bargaining agreement by UCG, most advances in the sector have been protected, and new equipment and uniforms were furnished to the workers in April 2016. The union continues to complain about salary levels and late payments, and periodically warns that it will do what it must to protect healthy working conditions in the sector.[50] The continuing saga indicates that, though the sector has pioneered a reversal of austerity trends, ongoing competition over scarce resources and power will continue to politicize Dakar's trash collection.

Conclusions

Dakar's garbagescape has become a central terrain of contestation over the legitimacy of the Senegalese state. This chapter has analyzed modes of governing in Senegal in the wake of structural adjustment, through considering battles over Dakar's garbage infrastructure at the end of the socialist era and throughout the liberal era to follow. Across both periods, we see the primary importance of infrastructure as a theater for political debate and shifting contours of state-society relations. Just as Mayor Mamadou Diop knew all too well that the garbage sector was of ultimate importance in his ability to manage the city, urban populations, and the rising tide of youth dissent in that era, President Abdoulaye Wade and Mayor Khalifa Sall also found themselves entangled—like it or not—in the delicate task of governing trash. Controlling garbage infrastructure means controlling the image and ordering processes of the city. If dirt and disorder are metaphors for corruption and vice, then a clean and orderly city signifies the proper functioning of government and the virtues of its leaders. Controlling garbage infrastructure, moreover, means capturing specific people to do the dirty work with different material burdens and rewards. As a highly visible and arduous labor, cleaning work functions as an important space for the performance of state legitimacy and a form of material power.

The first lesson to be drawn from governing garbage across these two moments concerns an anxious pattern of political maneuvering over limited resources. Politicking at the heart of the garbage sector reinforces patronage modes of governing and compromises state legitimacy, coherence, and accountability. The exigencies of austerity in both periods precipitated desperate attempts to consolidate power and outcompete political rivals, and the unraveling of a cohesive urban development vision. A long-term logic of doing politics by doling out favors through the public sector and increasingly constraining resources has bred incessant meddling and squeezing of the public sector for what little power can be gleaned. This history of institutional volatility in the garbage sector illuminates, moreover, how the governing work of different infrastructural formulas has primarily turned on the question of labor. Courting the trash workers has become imperative given their role as one of the last remaining bastions of the civil service over which the state can exert direct control, and because of the extraordinary power they hold through the general trash strike and their close contact with the Dakarois. Across both periods, a central feature of garbage politicking has been the flexibilization of trash work in cheap infrastructural solutions that simultaneously curry favor while they discipline and control.

Second, the manifestation of these political responses in episodic, performative, and increasingly fragmented investments leaves the city's infrastructures highly uneven and dilapidated in many areas. In this way, this story highlights how neoliberal development works through the governance of disposability—determining which spaces and people can be discarded, degraded, and devalued. At the same time, it shows how governing infrastructure works through a hollow, performative mode centered on mobilizing and ordering bodies in public space. The continual reinvention of infrastructure's institutional design frustrates its coherence, functional capacities, and equal access across the urban landscape. Specifically, however, we can see very different approaches to grappling with waste and disposability, especially between Mayor Mamadou Diop and President Wade. Put simply, Diop seems to have understood garbage in a way that Wade simply never did. With few other resources at his disposal, Diop embraced garbage—despite its negative connotations—as a core feature of his new political approach, and he benefited in the long run from this savvy calculus. For his part, Wade never really got his hands dirty. He ignored or sidelined the trash workers for years, trying instead to manipulate the sector through high-level institutional changes, but underestimating the power of the trash workers and neglecting trash itself as a kind of political matter. The force of discard in Dakar politics depended upon the specificity of these distinct conjunctures and their associated personalities.

Third, and as we shall explore more fully in the next chapter, the consequence of this politicization and fragmentation is that the social, material, and symbolic burdens of infrastructure are devolved onto ordinary people (residents and laborers) and social systems that are rendered disposable. New management regimes in both periods have reconfigured the relations of social reproduction, placing responsibility for cleaning the city more firmly onto the precarious laboring bodies of youth and women. In this way, garbage illuminates the material and symbolic power of governing disposability. However, this devolution precipitated its own response in the rising tide of protests and social contestation witnessed after 2006 in Dakar. Garbage politics from Set/Setal to the union strikes in 2007 illuminate how formulas for hegemony are unstable and comprise a messy dialectic of contestation that threatens to bring about radical reconfigurations. Wade losing his grip on Dakar in the late 2000s and then definitively in the elections of 2012 signaled a new era in Senegal's garbage politics and stirred hopes for stemming the practice of politicking through infrastructure. The full import of the shift to Macky Sall's governing formula remains to be seen.

Overall, this history of governing through garbage offers insight into how neoliberal reform is negotiated and managed within the state in the context of a fiercely democratic urban landscape. Senegal is a revealing case through which to examine these processes, given its rich urban democratic history as well as its role as a test case of adjustment. From the implementation of structural adjustment by the Socialists to Wade's pursuit of a new neoliberal formula to more recent battles between the mayor and the president, we see the different strategies employed by ambitious politicians to carve out their political agendas within these political economic constraints. The result is a checkered history of institutional tinkering and dramatic performativity in the space of public infrastructure. In the face of limited resources and populist demands for accountability, infrastructural labor comes to the fore as the key thing to be manipulated, often at the expense of a coherent development vision and eventually to these politicians' own political demise. In this context, austerity breeds political rationalities characterized by excessive competition within the state, perpetual processes of political reinvention, and a confusing medley of experimental institutional forms. Far from a singular script of urban change, then, neoliberal reform is consolidated and contested through unruly negotiations around everyday infrastructures in place.

The mobilizations in Dakar leading up to and following the contentious elections of 1988 hurtled Senegalese youth onto the political radar as key losers in structural adjustment, as an important new electorate, and as the greatest potential threat to the urban peace. Although they had been a visible force in the Independence struggle and then in the crisis of 1968 (Zeilig and Ansell 2008), youth had not previously been seen as the force for opposition politics that they became in 1988. The so-called *casseurs* (breakers)—Senegal's version of the "lost boys"—who rioted after the 1988 elections inspired great fear amongst the Dakarois (Cruise O'Brien 1996). Overall, these events, and then the violence surrounding the Mauritanian crisis in 1989, served as potent testimony to the sinister possibilities of youth agitation and contributed to the political crisis that closed out the difficult decade. The old social contract between the state, religious authorities, and Senegalese citizens was crumbling and the problem of youth was front and center. Economic crisis and its disproportionate impacts combined with the impasse in the education system to give young Dakarois a sense of hopelessness and abandonment by the state. Students—who had formerly been special beneficiaries of the employer state—began to "face an astonishingly bleak set of circumstances" (Zeilig 2007, 2).

In this context, the now-famous Set/Setal social movement was spawned, inspiring a new chapter in the relationship between the Dakarois and their city. Part of a wave of grassroots movements across the continent aimed at taming and managing the urban decay from structural adjustment and its uneven impacts (see Bond 2005), Set/Setal earned youth in Dakar a prominent place in studies of African social movements and democratic change (see Mamdani and Wamba-dia-Wamba 1995). The movement retains a special, almost fetishized place in the memories of the Dakarois—"rather in the way that Parisians remember May 1968" (Cruise O'Brien 1996, 62). A key missing piece of this legacy, however, is the way Set/Setal came to be instrumentalized by the state and international funders in the city's new, more intimate, low-tech community-based trash infrastructure.

In the early 1990s, Dakar's mayor replaced the city's garbage sector with a participatory infrastructure built upon the Set/Setal movement and, in doing so, devolved infrastructure onto labor. Drawing on the analysis in chapter 1 of the institutional arrangements that have emerged out of the volatile politics of garbage since Set/Setal, this chapter takes a closer look at what these transformations have meant for the young people caught in their sway. The analysis is concerned with how new arrangements for garbage management reconfigure everyday lives and embodied materialities of labor and, along the way, communities, political subjectivities, and relationships to the city. Specifically, it unpacks how the turn to participatory infrastructural formulas for garbage collection resculpted the spaces, values, and material burdens of labor for young men and women from the early 1990s up through the precarious Abdoulaye Wade years in the 2000s. In this way, the chief intervention of the chapter is in literally *fleshing out* the vital ecology of trash infrastructures through foregrounding social and bodily technologies in relation to the wider political-economic, discursive, and material worlds they compose. Vital infrastructures emphasize the junctions between material technologies and human bodies and the intersecting precarities they engender.

Austerity works through reconfiguring the relationship between the body, infrastructure, and the city. The first section of the chapter chronicles the emergence of participatory trash infrastructures as a key element of urban reform in the first major wave of structural adjustment. New infrastructural formulas for trash collection, through the formalization of the youth movement Set/Setal in the early 1990s, entailed novel configurations of sociotechnical and material relations. As new relations of social reproduction, these participatory infrastructures subjected young men and women to new forms of state discipline. This analysis shares concerns with notions of "people as infrastructure" (Simone 2004b), in conceptualizing infrastructure as a distinctive ecology that incorporates human labor. This places people at the heart of infrastructural systems and foregrounds the everyday negotiations and bonds that form the scaffolding for building the city. However, the analysis counters overly optimistic and immaterial portrayals of participatory infrastructures with a more nuanced analysis that is attentive to the symbolic and material burdens invoked by infrastructures built upon precarious socio-technical relations of disposability. As AbdouMaliq Simone (2012) points out, infrastructures expend people's capacities. Drawing on the specific force of waste and decay, this analysis emphasizes how this works in two senses—both through disbursing human capacities, and also through using them up.

The second section delves deeper into the social technologies animated by the new participatory trash-collection system, through examining how infrastructure emerges from and reshapes urban social systems and relations of belonging and sociality. Youth and women were differentially enrolled in the displacement of social reproduction into the public sphere through participatory cleaning. Gendered discourses of waste and cleaning in Senegal facilitated women's entrance into the municipal cleaning sector for the first time and conditioned the particularity of men's and women's experiences of embodied precarity. Cheap waste work provided contradictory spaces that at once instrumentalized gendered stigmas in the service of disposable labor, and also afforded strategic openings for political participation, new economic roles, and claims to authority and expertise.

As a space of formalized bricolage, trash work requires incessant maintenance and improvisation that conditions creative but dangerous relationships between workers and the decrepit machines they depend on. The third section of this chapter characterizes the precarity precipitated by continued flexibilization of labor and degradation in working conditions and equipment, as the sector was brought into the fold of (neo)liberal president Wade's institutional politicking in the mid-2000s. Here I focus on the way that residents' and workers' bodies are enrolled into new infrastructural formulas by considering questions of embodiment, corporeality, and performativity in the space of dirty labor. The devolvement of infrastructure onto labor works to constitute certain bodies as waste. Together, the sections of this chapter locate laboring bodies and the communities that bind them at the core of new infrastructural formulas, illuminating the ways that new political economic conjunctures recompose socio-material relations, political subjectivities, and spaces of citizenship.

Told from the vantage point of my fieldwork in 2007–8, much of the chapter takes on the feeling of that moment—both in a sense of nostalgia for Set/Setal and the hopeful period immediately following on its heels; and in the deep disappointment and insecurity felt by the Wade years.

People as Infrastructure

Set/Setal

In the late 1980s, garbage piled up and putrefied in city streets and public spaces, forming a barometer of political crisis. After the garbage workers' strikes fell on deaf ears and the government stopped paying the bill, the parastatal trash company SIAS ceased full operations in the late 1980s and was fully bankrupt and nonoperational by the early 1990s. Set/Setal emerged in sharp contrast to the violent events of 1988–89, as youth from many walks of life united to clean the city. Building on the cultural and sporting activities organized during the *navétanes* (summer vacation months), and incubated within the formal youth groups (ASCS, GIES, and GPFS)[1] that were expanding beyond their original focus on sports, the movement involved an unprecedented level of popular mobilization. Young people began to organize their own systems for cleaning across diverse spaces of the city. In Mamadou Diouf's (1992, 42; my translation) words: "Since July 1990, the juvenile violence has transitioned into a kind of intense madness that remains an enigma. Under the dumbfounded gaze of the adults, these former hunters of Mauritanians, groups of young people put into action their new creed: order and cleanliness."

Through painting elaborate murals, organizing local events, and cleaning up their neighborhoods, youth aimed to cleanse the city in a literal sense—in terms of sanitation and hygiene—but also morally in a fight against corruption, prostitution, and general delinquency. They drew from both meanings of the Set/Setal expression: *set*, which means "clean," "the state of being clean," and *setal*, which is the act of rendering something clean. Stemming from its roots in the neighborhood youth groups, Set/Setal assembled a cosmopolitan community of youngsters who were more or less representative of their own community demographics. Because young people generally participate in neighborhood associations regardless of their educational status, ethnic group, religion, class, or gender, the key feature of the movement was belonging to a neighborhood, regardless of other societal divisions.[2] Given the continuing educational crisis, students were key activists behind the movement.

In the context of political paralysis and, for many, feelings of economic and social powerlessness, Set/Setal was defined by mobility, action, and potency. Animated by popular music and bubbling into the streets in organic bursts of activity, the movement was generally fun, sometimes frenetic, and, more often than not, purposeful. As one participant explained, "It was exciting to be busy, to know what we had to do and do it."[3] Often, whole neighborhoods joined in. High unemployment, the growing informal economy, and school closures had only enhanced the vibrancy of Dakar's already busy street life. Whether cooling off on a street bench in the shade, trying to make a buck selling food or wares on a street corner, or simply passing the day chatting and drinking tea with neighbors, Dakarois spend much of the day outside of their homes. Where the insides of homes are often stuffy and overcrowded, and household courtyards get squeezed out by new construction for growing families, the street offers space, opportunity, and social connection. This vibrant public street life made for easy recruitment into Set/Setal.

Just like their brothers, young women left their houses on the days scheduled for cleanup events and set out to reorder space with their own hands. One key lacuna in the research on Set/Setal to date concerns the important role of young women as eager participants and, in some cases, leaders in the movement. Their participation stemmed from two major factors: women's increasing involvement in neighborhood management, whether through "female" sections of youth groups or through their own associations (GIES or GPFS), and their connection to the work of cleaning in the home. Sweeping, cleaning, and dealing with household wastes are key elements of women's duties as managers of domestic space in Senegal.[4] Waste work in the home is thus naturalized as intrinsically women's work. Women at the lower end of the household social hierarchy—according to age, ethnicity, and marital status[5]— are usually reserved the dirtiest and most onerous waste duties.[6] For this reason, young women were not only well equipped to help with cleaning the neighborhood, but also keenly motivated to be part of the solution to the garbage crisis that precipitated Set/Setal. The fact that they were seen as the "cleaners" in their households legitimized their place out and about cleaning with their male compatriots (see figure 2.1).

The elaborate Set/Setal murals painted all over Dakar—of which remnants can still be seen today—tell of a youth imaginary that strove to deconstruct the nationalist imaginary that had dominated since Independence (M. Diouf 1992; Roberts et al. 2003). Carefully documented in the book *Set Setal*, published by the NGO Environnement et développement du tiers

FIGURE 2.1. A cartoon depicting the Set/Setal activists dumping "corruption," "crisis," "unemployment," "scamming," and "April 1989" into the garbage dump. Note the participating woman (*left*). The bubble reads: "It's the 'Set Setal' of bad memories!" ENDA, *Set Setal, des murs qui parlent*. Reprinted with permission from ENDA Tiers Monde.

monde (Environment and Development Action in the Third World; ENDA),[7] and explored in probing detail by Mamadou Diouf (1992, 1996, 2003), the murals and other efforts of the movement's youth drew from continuously reformulated ethnic, religious, regional, and national identities. Celebrating such diverse political and cultural icons as Bob Marley, Nelson Mandela, Amadou Bamba, and Martin Luther King Jr.—sometimes all on the same wall—the murals signaled a departure from the Afro-pessimism gripping the times, and a move toward constructive aspirations for unity, peace, and a reorientation of values perceived as having gone astray. Through literally cleansing and writing over the space of the city—coloring it with faces, messages, and symbols, and even renaming city streets and neighborhoods—youth tried to take possession of the city, to reorder it with their own references and values (M. Diouf 1996). Their political messages elided references to the current political context and politicians, proposing a different idea of politics from that of the 1988 mobilizations. In Set/Setal, the neighborhood replaced the national territory as "the canvas for elaborating the symbolic and imaginary" (M. Diouf 1996, 248).

Youssou N'Dour's famous theme song, "Set," captures the movement's fervor for cleanliness and spirit of self-improvement:

Set, set oy. Ni set, set ci sa xel lo, ni set ci sa jëff oy . . .
Set, set, set, set, set, set. Ni bës dina ñëw . . . Seetlu naa ko . . .
Xale yaangiy jooy, ëllëg di wóorulo. Lii moy ma tiis ye . . .

Cleanliness, oh cleanliness. Be clean, pure in your spirit, clean in
   your acts . . .
Cleanliness, cleanliness, cleanliness, cleanliness, cleanliness,
   cleanliness. This [new] day will come . . . I'm watching for it
The children are crying, the future is uncertain. This is what makes
   me sad . . .[8]

Purity was an especially prominent theme. In striving to achieve purity, Set/Setal youth sought to cleanse their delinquent, even debauched reputations alongside those of their neighbors, families, and politicians. This new vision of moral urban citizenship was underpinned by a critique of the social and moral degradation that was perceived to be afflicting Dakarois society. To attack this head-on, the youth organized efforts intended to purify what they saw as a "sick" society, invaded by tobacco, alcohol, prostitution, and violence (ENDA 1991, 45). In addition to painting messages explicitly aimed at improving community behavior, they also organized activities through their associations such as school programs, vocational training, and sporting events. They even set up "vigilance" committees like the so-called Mafia Boys of Niari Tali neighborhood (ENDA 1991). The Mafia Boys and the like were groups of young locals whose job was not only to help clean up the neighborhood, but also to provide a sort of neighborhood security force to counteract social dislocation and violence. Ideas of cleanliness in Set/Setal also often drew on values of faith and piety connected to Islamic traditions.

Set/Setal's ordering efforts strove to clean up the local environment through education campaigns as well as operations aimed directly at trash and sanitation. Their educational activities were manifested in a preponderance of murals dedicated to exposing populations to the dangers of pollution and the origins of diseases like malaria and diarrhea, and outreach to *sensibiliser* (educate) local populations (see figure 2.2). Many groups also had explicitly environmental missions and framed their activities through

FIGURE 2.2. A Set/Setal mural aiming to educate about poor hygiene and disease, with a caption that reads "How we get diarrhea." ENDA, *Set Setal, des murs qui parlent.* Reprinted with permission from ENDA Tiers Monde.

discourses of sustainability that were gaining traction internationally. Dirt and trash provided both a metaphor for the general filth and degradation that the movement saw in the city, and a practical way to combat those forces with clear results. The groups' physical efforts to clean up their neighborhoods constituted an increasingly essential element of local environmental management, especially in those hard-to-reach neighborhoods with severe sanitation issues. At the same time, their educational efforts allowed them to assert their authority and expertise around the operations of the city.

Living in a world of worthless diplomas and little available work, Set/Setal youth repudiated their social impotence and rejected their superfluity in the urban labor force. In refusing their position at the bottom of the social hierarchy, they departed from the gerontocratic traditions they were supposed to have inherited from times past. No longer waiting for permission or direction from their elders, youth took ownership of their neighborhoods. "Our neighborhood is ours," stated many murals in diverse neighborhoods across Dakar. Through inhabiting new spaces and reordering the urban environment, they exercised their power and creativity and transformed their relationship to the city. In the words of Makhtar, a former Set/Setal participant and present-day trash worker: "We woke up, and we wanted to change our lives. We were tired of just sitting around, drinking tea, and waiting for things to happen. Who were we waiting for? Set/Setal was a revolution—it was the youth growing up and deciding to clean up their lives. It changed us, Dakar, and this country forever."

Reacting to the dearth of safe, unsullied, or uncorrupted public space, Set/Setal youth insisted on their rights to the city by claiming and rehabilitating public space, not just with their presence and visibility, but with their labor. Central to this message was an insistence on the value of work and a rejection of the laziness and boredom they saw as epidemic. They cleared out spaces of leisure like soccer fields and playgrounds, built monuments, and planted gardens—emphasizing not only their right to occupy the city but also their ability to mold it to their own desires. This imaginary signaled a departure from previous eras where work was something doled out by elders and politicians. For Set/Setal youth, the city became a do-it-yourself workplace, where formal labor receded into history and opportunity presented itself around every corner (see figure 2.3).

Dakar's New Trash Collectors

The participatory trash sector brought in these young men and women activists as new political clients and the fresh face of the nation and its orderly development. In a broader sense, the system responded to the exigencies of austerity through reconfiguring the relationship between labor and infrastructure. Prior to 1988, trash collection was fairly regularized. The trash workers of the parastatal company SIAS were mainly adult men from outside of Dakar who had decent salaries and were unionized. However, the system had collapsed under the financial and political constraints of austerity, and by the early 1990s Set/Setal youth's cleaning activities had become indispensable in filling the gaps. As previously mentioned, Dakar's Socialist Party mayor, Mamadou Diop, fired the sector's workers and incorporated Set/Setal volunteers (including many women) into a citywide participatory system in the early 1990s that lasted until 2001. This dramatic reconfiguration of the city's trash infrastructure represented a shrewd political calculation by Mayor Diop that helped him to cope with shrinking budgets, flexibilize the labor force, and shore up political support in the face of intensified electoral competition—especially amongst the wildcard youth electorate.

FIGURE 2.3. A Set/Setal mural depicting *emploi* (work). ENDA, *Set Setal, des murs qui parlent*. Reprinted with permission from ENDA Tiers Monde.

A key function behind the new trash sector was the escape hatch it provided for the government in the face of the emerging labor movement of the SIAS workers. The previous system was not only much more expensive; it was also organized. Dissolving SIAS and replacing the workers with youth allowed Mayor Diop to remove the nuisance of union organizing in the trash sector. Although he offered to integrate former SIAS workers into the new system, in practice only a small minority made the transition (less than two hundred). Most preferred to leave the sector altogether given the pay cut and lack of benefits, or because they did not want to work with the youth.[9] Others chose to leave or were impeded from joining because they were considered rabble rousers or were not members of the Socialist Party. In the words of a SIAS union activist regarding the workers' treatment by Mayor Diop: "Personally, I knew that [he] wanted to erase us!" The activist believed that his application to work in the new sector was rejected because he was not a socialist.

Diop wanted to use the system not only as a forum for mobilizing support for his party, but also as a reward for his political clients. As mayor of Dakar, he was keenly interested in shifting the trash sector jobs to the Dakarois. Although most of the sias workers probably spent much of their lives in Dakar, many came from non-Dakarois families or had moved to the capital for these jobs. The sias director, moreover, had shown a preference for hiring from within his family, his region outside of Dakar (Saint-Louis), or his own ethnic group (Toucouleur). The switch to hiring youth was a way of redirecting this pattern in the interest of Diop's urban constituents.

The decision to hire youth was explicitly targeted, moreover, at this newly visible constituency of Dakar youth, as illustrated in the workers' recollections. One worker looked back, stating: "Yes, there were political motivations because this was the beginning of the revolt of the youth. Because the youth wanted change. The authorities felt that these youth wanted change . . . and they really wanted to convince them that the system was still good." Similarly, the ex-president of the Coordination des associations et mouvements de la communauté urbaine de Dakar (Federation of the Associations and Movements of the Dakar Urban Community; camcud) and current department chief stated, "In 1988, there were all those troubles . . . and Mamadou Diop, when he saw all those youth, he said to them: 'Don't throw those stones.' He judged well to jump [at the opportunity]. It was he who said that if you don't occupy yourselves with the youth, they will occupy themselves with you. He was right." Urban youth had come to represent a threat that needed to be contained and brought into the state's hegemonic fold. In the context of a growing awareness of the undue burden they bore and their resultant volatility in the face of structural adjustment, Set/Setal offered the state the opportunity to channel—and thus pacify—the youth mobilizations that had been its greatest nightmare just a few years earlier. Negative associations with waste work served to discipline youth and, in so doing, diffuse the threat they might have posed to the nation. As restive, unemployed youth activists, they were dangerous, but as dirty workers on the state's payroll, they could be more easily ordered and controlled.

Through orchestrating *Journées de Propreté* (Days of Cleanliness) across the city, Diop began to tap and scale up Set/Setal youth's cleaning activities (M. Diop, n.d.). In addition to their neighborhood cleaning activities was added the job of collecting and loading garbage onto the dump truck and delivering it to the dump on the outskirts of the city. Initially volunteers, then paid day-labor rates (one to two U.S. dollars per day), the youth lacked all protections and benefits. Soon, Diop's interest in the youth dovetailed with that of a powerful international actor: the World Bank. Besieged by criticism of the dire social consequences of structural adjustment conditionalities, the World Bank was beginning to consider policies that complemented reform with more attention to social safety nets. The Dakar riots of 1988–89—a shocking event in a place considered a model of peace and development—had garnered the bank's attention and led to this policy shift. Though initially composed of volunteers and self-organized, the youth trash sector was soon managed by a new World Bank–funded public works agency modeled after Bolivia's Emergency Social Fund, centered in Dakar, and coordinated by the municipality.[10] The World Bank–funded Agence d'exécution des travaux d'intérêt public contre le sous-emploi (Public Works and Employment Agency; AGETIP) was formed in 1989 and rolled out in the 1990s in two phases, with the goal of generating a significant number of mainly manual and temporary jobs for unemployed youth.[11] Part of a global paradigm shift to a kinder, gentler, "revisionist" neoliberalism in the face of widespread social dislocation (Mohan and Stokke 2000), the agency's projects were officially aimed at improving living conditions in poor urban neighborhoods, in order to satisfy certain basic needs that had been eroded with adjustment policies and, in so doing, to keep the social peace (World Bank 1992, 1997). The context and motivation behind the AGETIP projects are laid out clearly in the following excerpt from the World Bank's Project Appraisal Report:

In 1988, Senegal faced serious economic and political problems. Despite a decade of structural adjustment, economic growth had remained weak throughout the 1980s (2.1 percent per year), and unemployment had increased (official unemployment rates rose from 16 percent in 1976 to 30 percent in 1989). Unemployment was most severe in urban areas, especially among the young (two-thirds of the officially unemployed were 25 or younger). The public blamed the structural adjustment program imposed by the World Bank, the International Monetary Fund, and France for the situation, and Senegal's political parties exploited public sentiment in order to build voter support. Then, in February 1988, the young urban unemployed took to the streets in violent riots and protest. . . . It soon became clear that existing government agencies and public enterprises would not be able to deliver such programs speedily and efficiently. Another type of agency was needed. . . . The World Bank and the government of Senegal worked closely together to find the solution that ultimately became AGETIP's trademark: delegated contract management. (World Bank 1997, 7)

The first in a wave of similar projects in Africa funded by the World Bank, AGETIP became a key partner in the youth-based trash sector in the early 1990s. A formal convention was signed in October 1995, ushering in the trash system that would replace that of SIAS (Chagnon 1996), and AGETIP was hailed as a success by the World Bank for being "lean and efficient" (1997, 16). By February 1996, the agency had executed more than 1,250 sub-projects and created more than 19,000 "person-years" of employment (World Bank 1997, 14–15). These estimates included the 1,500 trash jobs "created" by the new system. During this time, the unit of organization at the local level continued to be registered community organizations (GIES) and youth received only temporary-contract benefits and day-labor pay rates.[12] As compared with the previous system, in which the salaries often made up half of the total trash budget, the amount paid to the GIES accounted for less than 20 percent of the new budget (M. Diop, n.d., 99). The ability to minimize state expenditure, tap youth labor, and independently manage World Bank funding at the municipal level were key features of the system for Mayor Diop as he fought to enhance his power vis-à-vis the national state through the trash sector (see chapter 1).

Through its official NGO-like organization, AGETIP was intended to avoid the politicization that was seen as running rampant in the public sector. And yet, doling out new jobs was explicitly based around a political calculus. Beyond the strategy to diffuse the increasingly mobilized youth and engage them as a low-cost, flexible labor force, formalizing Set/Setal provided a direct forum for the mayor to rally political support. Participants remember the Journées de Propreté as overt Socialist Party political rallies. The youth understood that Diop was recruiting people directly for his political electorate. One current zone controller from the Niari Tali neighborhood remembered the period as follows:

> You had to do politics, by force. I remember it very well, there were celebrities, I think it was a French senator, and we were required to go to the welcome event. If not, you'd be fired that day. Because the system had become purely political. . . . It was politically motivated because if you wanted to be a part of the system, you had to be a Socialist first. . . . They gave us Socialist Party T-shirts, or else you wouldn't be paid at the end of the month. . . . So even if you were affiliated with another party, you had to follow this rule to stay in the system.

Workers had their identification cards collected by their sector leaders, who had to show them to the politicians to prove that they were filling recruitment quotas for the Socialist Party. The formalization of Set/Setal thus functioned directly to reward and recruit new Socialist Party members from the ranks of the youth.

As the previous quote suggests, however, this political calculus was not just about votes; it was also about Mayor Diop's philosophy and image, both at home and abroad. Diop was a celebrity politician who as mayor was very active in international development dialogues and networks. He mobilized the Set/Setal–based trash system as an important demonstration of his commitment to youth and to an ideal of participatory citizenship—two issues that were taking center stage in debates about African development and democracy. When interviewed for this research, Diop went so far as to repudiate the idea that the movement was at all grassroots and claimed to have invented Set/Setal himself. He said, "No, it wasn't spontaneous; it was generated, part of our plan. I was elected mayor and there was garbage everywhere in Dakar and we didn't have the financial means. After some reflection, I said to myself, why not engage the population [of Dakar]? We went down to the neighborhoods and discussed it with the youth. They each started to clean their own neighborhood. It's like that that it began. It was deliberate." He went on to pronounce the participatory system as the ideal system through which to clean the city and engage its residents. He critiqued the formalized system that followed on its heels: "[Today's workers are] simple employees! Whereas, the idea behind Set/Setal was voluntary participation. It was the people that came to participate. The new system makes it so that the workers are paid by the month and that's the spirit now. You no longer feel the engagement of the people, but before, in the neighborhoods, the people got together on Saturday and Sunday to clean. The youth now are paid . . . formalized . . . it's not good."

Mayor Mamadou Diop won some acclaim in international development circles through the new trash system. In a "best practice" case study for a prominent international NGO, the system was credited with "beginning to restore healthy and sanitary conditions . . . It has already increased garbage collection coverage by 15 percent, created approximately fifteen hundred jobs, and proven to be more efficient than systems in the past" (ICLEI 1997). It was also celebrated for its remedy of a "major weakness" of the previous system: the lack of engagement by local people (M. Diop, n.d.). The system even gained Diop and some of his most active youth notoriety in various international conferences. One trash worker from Médina looked back fondly on his experience as part of a youth delegation at the Global Forum on the theme of "Cities and Sustainable Development," held in Manchester in June 1994: "[The system] even won us medals at the national and international levels! We were knighted with the National Merit Badge. Me, I remember, I did England—Manchester—with the Global Forum . . . just to talk about the [youth-based trash] system!"[13]

In his memoir written about his experience as mayor, *My Combat for Dakar*, Diop (n.d., 70) hails the Set/Setal trash system as one of the most "exceptional and exemplary" accomplishments of the city of Dakar under his leadership. He also describes it as a key strategy toward "the construction of democratic urbanism," rooted in principles of decentralization, good governance, and community participation. In my interviews with Diop in the late 2000s, he waxed nostalgic about the system, calling it his greatest pride as mayor and insisting that the issues of youth and environment were—and remain—concerns close to his heart. He compared his Set/Setal system with the more formalized system under Wade with dismay, emphasizing the more communal approach as not just more budget savvy, but also an opportunity to draw on and foster urban civility:

> Well, now they [the Wade government] pay a lot [to clean the city]. For me, with 200 million [CFA] per month I managed to clean the city and the region [of Dakar]. And now they are almost to a billion [CFA] and it is not clean. Thus beyond even the system of management, there is the participation of the population and their cleanliness—cleaning [the city] starts there. People . . . have to do their share of cleaning, to be engaged in maintaining the communal areas. You clean your house but you throw your refuse in the street—that isn't good! It should be understood that one must be clean but also that one must also take part in management of the street. It is a whole new behavior— the education of the citizen. It is important because here it is said that the municipality has to deal with it. . . . That's not the case.

Urban infrastructure was, for Diop, to be much more than just a technical system. It was to be a social system built on an entrepreneurial moral urban politics.

Ordering Youth

Intimate Infrastructures

The advent of participation in the garbage sector was about more than budgetary constraints or a simple calculus for how to shore up party votes. The participatory trash sector aimed to foster a whole new ethic of citizenship through building a more intimate infrastructure. The intimacy of that new infrastructural system seized upon the moral urban politics that had animated Set/Setal and claimed those resources for the city. It forged a public service in which the resources previously supplied by the state were to be mobilized by workers, families, and communities. The rest of this chapter aims to flesh out how that transition was lived, experienced, and embodied by the young people caught up in that new infrastructural system—or how it was forged through social relations of belonging and their moral architectures. It begins with the transition from Set/Setal to the participatory trash system, and carries through the precarious years that followed under Abdoulaye Wade before the workers were able to reverse these trends through labor organizing.

Transitioning from cleaning up their neighborhood trash voluntarily as part of an exciting youth-driven movement to being paid low wages as the city's trash collectors was not automatic. As mentioned above, the Set/Setal activists had mobilized their communities in an explicit rebuke of the state in the wake of the political crisis of 1988. Fed up with what they saw as the neglect by politicians of the real needs of their communities and disappointed in the failure of the opposition party in the elections of 1988, these youth had rallied communal support in an exercise in self-management and autonomy from the state. Although most were relieved to have access to employment, even at day-labor rates, it took significant effort for them to reconcile the shift from activist to trash worker—especially for young men. This group of social juniors had to contend with not only poor salaries and dangerously precarious working conditions but also all of the negative associations of dirty labor.

Because the new trash collection force was built upon the Set/Setal movement, which was a cosmopolitan movement that drew from all sectors of Dakar's social sphere, this cross section of upstanding, even educated youth had never dreamed of working in garbage as their profession. The trash workers before them had been considered outsiders, not true Dakarois. As a trash-sector leader put it: "Before us this work was often done by people who were not Senegalese. In the beginning it was the Bambaras . . . then the Toukouleurs. . . . In the beginning, no one [in Dakar] wanted to do it because it was seen as unclean and unhealthy to work with trash." In his view, the SIAS workers were not even Senegalese citizens, let alone Dakarois, by virtue of the fact that they came from other regions of the country. At that time, garbage work was extremely negatively viewed, with garbage collectors described derogatorily as *buujumaan*[14] and seen as crazy, dirty, or even criminals.

Most young men I interviewed talked about being embarrassed at first when they began to work in the sector. They covered their faces to avoid being recognized and some refused to work in their own neighborhoods. These were notable differences from the time of Set/Setal when, in a spirit of patriotic civic duty, anyone and everyone contributed to cleaning their own neighborhoods. Getting paid—however little—to *be* a trash worker was altogether different, as recalled by one trash worker in the Médina neighborhood:

> It was not at all certain that the youth of Dakar would accept working in household garbage. That was the first challenge. When we signed the first contract, they asked everyone there to come work in the trash sector. Well, there were some who accepted and others who refused. Among those who accepted, there were those who hid their face in order to be able to do trash work. Because this was not a job for a youth! At that time, for youth, this was really not an acceptable job. They had girlfriends, neighbors, and everyone . . . it was out of the question to collect trash where you lived. If you lived in the Médina, you would prefer to collect trash in Grand Dakar. If you lived in Grand Dakar, you went to Pikine. This was to protect these guys. But after some time, the youth saw that this was a job like any other job and there was nothing to hide. So, there was a revolution. At a certain point, all of the youth wanted to work in garbage.

The term *youth*, in this passage, refers to young men and the particular implications of working in the new municipal trash system for the young men of Set/Setal. However, this stigma was different for women than men, due to cultural associations of domestic cleaning duties as women's work, as will be discussed in the next section.

As much as youth were, at first, suspicious of the state's involvement, it lent legitimacy to their work from the perspective of community members, and they couldn't help but be proud to be key players in the big production of the Journées de Propreté. The mayor himself made frequent personal visits to these events, and he often provided the youth with snacks, sound systems playing popular music, and T-shirts, in addition to brooms and wheelbarrows. Competitions were held and rewards given for the cleanest neighborhood at the end of the day. Mayor Diop constantly appealed to youth's responsibility toward their city and the value of their entrepreneurial spirit. In the end, the excitement surrounding the events and the sheer pressure young men felt to exploit the opportunity for work to support their families amid conditions of economic crisis outweighed the work's stigma. The opportunity to gain some political voice and connections through the sector, despite their fears from 1988, moreover, was a compelling reason to stay in the sector and watch what would unfold.

Wearing the Pants

"That day was one of my first days on the job. The mayor had brought in some trucks and we were doing the collection. I wore pants that day, so I could climb onto the truck. My family saw me leave the house and said, 'What ... ?' But I just left. That day I rode on the top of that truck all the way to Mbeubeuss [the dump]. Was I scared? Yes, but I was also proud." This quote is from a woman who was one of hundreds who, in the early 1990s, donned trousers and baseball caps and, in plain view of their shocked families and friends, climbed onto garbage trucks in order to collect their neighborhood trash. An integral element of Set/Setal, these women were transformed alongside young male activists into the city's low-paid trash collection force.

In most zones, early on in the new system, women trash workers did exactly the same tasks as men, including riding on the trash trucks for the collection. At first, the trucks were open top, not the rear-opening conventional trucks we associate with the job today. Many women were wearing pants for the first time in public, a nontraditional style of female dress that enabled them to more easily conduct the work (especially mounting the trucks), but which could have been controversial at the time. Wearing pants, baseball caps, and gloves, armed with shovels, rakes, and whatever other scant materials were provided, these women were, according to my respondents, quite a sight to see out in the public space. The following account from another trash worker who eventually became a section manager is illustrative:

At the beginning, people watched us and were surprised to see us working in the sector as women and exclaimed: "That one's a woman!" It's only because of my earrings that they recognized me, because I would wear sunglasses and a head wrap, then on top of it a baseball cap and all of that with the goal of protecting myself from the dust. With this outfit, it was difficult for people to distinguish the sex of the worker. Before, the men had a complex and were bothered about working in trash, but with the integration of women, that disappeared. Eventually, I felt proud when I climbed onto the trash-collecting truck with my work clothes on. Even more than all of that, there was a sort of unity and complicity between us, the workers of Parcelles Assainies. We didn't have a complex about the work—that really was more of a problem for the men.

A pioneering group of women in the central Dakar neighborhood of Gueule Tapée earned the nickname *Les Amazones* (The Amazons) from their colleagues for their strength and fearless dedication to their new jobs. When I spoke with these women, they recalled with intense pride the new radical spaces they had occupied and their mastery of these material practices. Contrasting trash labor with another form of stigmatized, "dirty" labor outside of the home—prostitution—they emphasized on countless occasions the upstanding moral qualities of "earning their bread with the sweat of their brow" and how much it meant to them to be able to work to support their families. Les Amazones of Gueule Tapée were often invoked many years later as key personalities in the sector's exceptional origin story. As such, women workers defended their foundational contributions toward building the new garbage system.

Despite the radical nature of some of their new labor practices, women's participation in Set/Setal and transition into the participatory trash sector was facilitated by their connections to domestic waste management and the stigma associated with dirty work. In contrast to their male compatriots, who had not previously borne the brunt of associations with waste, for women the job was not a new or mysterious one. They dealt with household garbage every day and were accustomed to the stigma of the work. In the words of a male section manager:

The people closest to this problem are women. These are the same women who sweep[15] at home so they don't have any complexes about trash. A man who sweeps, well, that's rare. In general, it's women. It was difficult [to get the men to work], but we succeeded all the same in getting rid of their complexes to have them work in the system. Now each day there are people [including men] who come to see if they can work in the trash sector.

As can be seen in this and many similar accounts, in the beginning, women were much less ashamed of working in trash publicly than men. In contrast with men's embarrassment about being recognized in their communities, women had no qualms—they were often the first to climb onto the trucks and refused to hide their identities.

One of my respondents in the Parcelles Assainies neighborhood, Aissatou, had started working in the new trash sector through her local youth group in 1992. With a small baby at home, she joined the sector in the hopes that it would help her to care for her family since she had quit school and couldn't find work. Sixteen years later on the job, she recalled how proud she had been at the beginning. Aissatou and her female colleagues, moreover, had quickly understood how important their work was to the effectiveness of the overall system. She described how their participation, alongside men, in the formalized trash system actually encouraged the men, dampening their embarrassment and enhancing community acceptance:

> At the beginning, we [women] were separated and placed as surveyors [on the ground]. . . . Then after a while, we noticed that the people acted differently toward women and men [collectors]. We decided that it was necessary to put a woman in each truck as a "security guard" to do the collection with the men. . . . Because if a woman who came to dump her garbage saw another woman in the truck, she would re-examine her behavior compared with how she would have acted with men. By this time male collectors were abused, tired. It was seen that integrating the women in the trucks was going to facilitate the work of the men. Thus, we became "security guards" and went with the trucks to Mbeubeuss [dump].

What's interesting here is the sense of moral authority extended to Aissatou and her colleagues, owing to their perceived expertise around waste and cleaning. This expertise was called upon as an important resource for the new sector, to ensure its smooth running and forge the required intimacy with the communities served. Women's "intrinsic" commitment to cleaning and authority over cleaning practices was thus constructed as a moral architecture on which to build the participatory infrastructure. Their more intimate ties to their colleagues and to household women—the key interface between the home and street collection systems—would facilitate the community collaboration that was now at the heart of the new system. Drawing directly on the moral paradigms advanced by Set/Setal, the new trash system employed community policing and collaboration as the fundamental grease to lubricate the system's gears.

Gendered subjectivities deeply shaped trash workers' perceptions and experiences of the new material labor practices and community spaces mobilized by these jobs. For men, although their participation in Set/Setal cleaning activities was legitimized because it was seen as an altruistic deed for their communities, the implications of the work changed with its professionalization. Once they were paid, they faced the stigma attached to being a trash worker and doing the dirty work—in all of its feminized connotations. As we shall see in chapter 4, men have demanded respect for their trash labors in the difficult years to follow through explicitly defending the work's value in religious terms. For women, conversely, the professionalization of Set/Setal actually enhanced their standing because of its lack of gender differentiation: they did all of the same tasks as men did and got paid for it. In this respect, their occupation of the same roles as men, and the relatively equal consideration of their labor in relation to men's, can be seen to have appreciated the value of women's cleaning labor in the period following Set/Setal. The system acted as a platform for women to occupy new roles as financial breadwinners, often for the first time, and to extend their domain of moral authority into the public sphere.

Women seized the trash jobs in order to expand their economic and political influence. By the 1990s, though there remained significant barriers to women's participation and power in the political process, they had made important headway in gaining visibility and representation.[16] In the context of increased electoral competition in the 1990s, women were becoming increasingly important as voters and political activists and their neighborhood associations had become a dynamic forum for mobilizing voters and placing specific interests on the political agenda (Beck 2003; Callaway and Creevey 1994; Creevey 1996; Gellar 2005). Through funneling the early trash-collection activities into political rallies centered on neighborhood associations and offering the trash jobs as a form of political patronage, Mayor Diop aimed to transform women activists into political clients and thereby update the image of the local state. Though some described the recruitment of women—and women's organizations—at these rallies as more for their "applause" and votes than their leadership, in other areas they were key leaders. In certain neighborhoods, women's associations were the central body around which the trash collecting activities were managed and their leaders the new sector's on-the-ground coordinators. The Set/Setal–based trash system thus enhanced women's visibility and provided them with what seemed to be a direct entrée into politics. In exchange for their participation in these political rallies, women received jobs in the shrinking public sector, a public forum for their activities, and, in theory, access to the mayor's office.

The particular history of women's emergence in the trash sector makes clear the paradoxical spaces that may be opened up by participatory infrastructural systems. On the one hand, it shows that discourses naturalizing gendered responsibility for dirty work can be deployed to further entrench women into dirty forms of labor built upon naturalized connections to waste and impurity.[17] At the same time, it shows how women's connection to waste is reconstituted in different settings, allowing them to gain some political voice within this strategic essentialism. Women's connection to cleaning in the home facilitated their role as key participants in a gender-radical movement through which they seized on new modes of engaging with the city. This challenges the historical legacy of Set/Setal as a male youth movement and raises some key questions as to where young women fit into understandings of youth politics in Senegal and beyond.[18] The trash case thus illustrates the complex implications of the simultaneous liberalization of the economic and political fields during this time and the shifting terrain on which young men and women are constituted as political subjects. The gendered implications of the crisis of social reproduction and the extension of domestic "life's work" (Meehan and Strauss 2015; Mitchell, Marston, and Katz 2004) into the public sphere through participatory labor can condition the production of new, sometimes surprising, political subjectivities.

The next section will examine what the advent of participatory waste infrastructure has meant for the bodies of laborers doing the dirty work over the long period of entrenched precarity that was to last into the mid-2000s.

Salvage *Bricolage*

The participatory trash sector instituted by Mayor Mamadou Diop continued until the early 2000s, when a new mayor came to power with the wave of gains by the opposition party that brought Abdoulaye Wade into the presidency. The trash collection system at the heart of Mayor Diop's municipal government was eliminated, beginning a long series of transformations in the institutional arrangements for garbage over the next decade. Though some improvements accrued for the workers in certain areas during this time, most continued to suffer under extremely precarious working conditions that had become even more acute as the collection equipment finally faltered in the face of increased urban growth, consumption, and discard. This period of politicking and neglect solidified trash work as a space of formalized *bricolage*[19] which conditioned new but often risky relationships between garbage *bricoleurs* (residents and workers), and the waste systems they managed.

Aside from a brief "golden era" from 2003 to 2005, when the workers were officially hired and extended benefits by the international company AMA, their labor was again rendered temporary and insecure when Wade revoked the contract in July 2006. During the early to mid-2000s, the trash workers began to organize through their union and vociferously demand better working conditions through strikes and other measures to get the state's attention. By the time I conducted the bulk of my fieldwork in 2007–8, the system's dysfunction was acute and most people were characterizing the trash sector as in crisis. Though increasingly more organized and audacious with their striking, the workers found themselves in a state of limbo as their cries fell on deaf ears. No new equipment had been provisioned for some time and no new workers were hired, despite Dakar's explosive growth. Everyone, including the workers and the residents, found themselves waiting for what would come next.

Neighborhood Disorder

Much of the burden of insufficient waste services fell onto household members, as the relations of social reproduction were respatialized and the everyday duties constituting life's work were placed more firmly on neighborhoods and, especially, household women. I spent a lot of time during this period chatting with women about how they managed with spotty collection caused by the system's insufficiencies and the workers' strikes that were becoming increasingly frequent. I found household women across Dakar to be intensely preoccupied with the vexing daily question of where their waste would go. They were eager to talk to me about garbage and the elaborate systems they had developed to mitigate the risks it could pose to their families. Managing household garbage is a thorny task in Senegal that is exacerbated by its composition, the warm Senegalese climate, and most households' inability to afford or access adequate storage and disposal materials. In contrast to the garbage of more affluent countries, which is primarily composed of paper, plastics, and other nonputrescent items, garbage in Senegal comprises a significant amount of organic matter such as fish guts, animal entrails, and plant refuse, which can get rank and dangerous fast.

The specific content of everyday garbage varies by neighborhood and by the socioeconomic profile of the community, but richer households in Dakar generally produce a greater volume of garbage overall and their garbage contains more paper and plastic. For poorer families, everything of possible value is reused. Plastic water bottles become containers in which to sell homemade juices like *bissap* and *bouye*.[20] Newspapers can be used to wrap *fattaya* (fried fish or meat fritters) or as starter for old-fashioned cooking stoves. Organics may be separated out for domestic animals or urban livestock. The cost-conscious will choose glass soda bottles over cans and return them for a deposit. Most households struggle to dispose of a few problem items like used cooking oil and ash from charcoal stoves. Big families and those butchering their own chickens and goats have particular challenges. Meticulous sweeping practices—in the daily battle to keep the encroaching Sahelian sand from dusting salons and messing neat courtyards—mean that a considerable amount of refuse is simply sand. Though sand can help to slow the stench and rate of decomposition when mixed with organics, garbage sacks can become heavy fast and damage compactors, frustrating the disposal process.

In times past, accumulating garbage could simply be kept at a distance from the house so as not to pose a nuisance, but Dakar's increasing density and vertical growth have made this a less viable means of storing trash until the next collection day. Most families cannot afford trash bags or cans and instead use materials such as baskets, rice sacks, plastic bins, or flimsy plastic grocery bags to transport the waste to its storage place or the arriving truck. In most neighborhoods, the custom is not to leave the garbage in anonymous piles for later collection by the trucks but involves the storage of garbage by households and a handoff between household members (usually young women) and collectors on pickup day (see figure 2.4). This is a key building block of the intimacy in the sector: collectors and residents know each other personally and often communicate at the moment of collection. Trucks signal their route with loud, rhythmic honking as they slowly move through the neighborhood. Breakdowns, traffic, and other unforeseen cir-

FIGURE 2.4. The point of collection in SICAP Liberté 1. Signaled by the honking of the garbage truck, household women hand over their household trash in reusable buckets or bags to collectors who deposit the waste into the truck. Photo courtesy J. W., 2017.

cumstances make their arrival time unpredictable, and so "catching" the garbage truck on its rounds becomes a key challenge of accessing disposal services. If a household misses the horn for some reason, this could mean waiting a few more days before the truck comes again. In tough times with little service, it was not unusual to see young women chasing trucks out of desperation, with garbage in tow. After periods of trash crisis and striking, the rhythmic honking offered strange relief to exhausted residents at their wits' end over what to do with their waste.

In theory, the garbage truck is supposed to make the collection rounds approximately five to six times a week. In practice, during the dysfunction of the Wade years, the truck would only pass through certain neighborhoods a couple of times a week and, in the case of workers' strikes or vehicle breakdown, sometimes not for a week or more. With reduced service, household women were forced to resort to less-than-optimal strategies to eliminate the waste and protect their families from pollution, including reducing, storing, burying, or dumping their garbage. A favorite solution from times past, burying had become less and less tenable as appropriate land diminished and, in many neighborhoods, as flooding became more frequent due to unusual rain and urban development patterns. In many cases, storing and burying in backyards precipitated intense friction between neighbors and arguments over property lines. Dumping was often people's only way to rid their homes of garbage. They had the option of finding dumping spots or paying private *charette* (horse-cart) operators to dump their garbage out of sight. Enterprising charette drivers flocked into Dakar from rural farming areas during garbage crises and charged sometimes 10,000 CFA (roughly twenty U.S. dollars) or more to a single household to cart away a load of garbage. During this time, empty lots, sewage canals, beaches, and roadsides were increasingly used as dumping grounds and the poorest neighborhoods became the most encumbered by garbage and its insidious risks. Market spaces were particularly problematic. Street markets—whether for clothing, food, or other items—are high-density refuse-generating events. The trash from street peddling and intense pedestrian traffic builds up and, by the end of market day, clogs already-hard-to-navigate sidewalks and city streets. The periodic trash crises left many spaces of the city littered and foul-smelling, periodically subjecting certain residents to the noxious consequences of waste, pollution, and disease.[21]

The infrastructural solutions developed by households were highly creative and well calibrated to the "toxic vitality" of waste (P. Harvey 2016). One woman named Mariama with whom I spoke at length about her waste-management challenges in the neighborhood of HLM Fass described herself as "obsessed with trash! I'm constantly thinking about what we'll do next, where it will go, and how we can stay clean." A fifty-five-year-old mother who ran a small vegetable stand, Mariama had three daughters who helped her to manage the household garbage. Their humble, two-bedroom home had been built in 1962 as affordable housing for civil servants. Though they were lucky enough to own the property, she and her husband had never been in the financial position to expand the house, and lived there with their six grown children and occasional other relatives. Like most of the working-class families in their increasingly dense neighborhood, the living quarters were cramped. With this many mouths to feed and progressively less and less outdoor space, trash management was a worrisome daily challenge. When I asked her what they did when the trash truck didn't come, she didn't hesitate before giving me a day-to-day rundown:

On the first day, we separate out the rice, vegetables, and banana peels and feed these to the goat. For the fish remains, we lay them out in the sun on plastic bags to dry out. The second day, we wrap up the old fish remains and bag it with the sand and plastics swept from the house. They sit out in the back, where there are no windows on the house. Day three gets harder because the bag begins to stink and we've already got many more remains piling up. Then we tie up the garbage again if we have enough plastic bags and move it out under the neighbor's tree. Usually my neighbors are doing the same by that time but we have to make sure it's OK. If we get to day four or five, then we're really in trouble and have to think about where to dump without making anyone mad. It's hard work for my girls because sometimes they have to walk far and often people yell at them. The saga begins again the next day until, finally, word gets around that the truck is coming. *Alhamdulillah* [thanks be to God].

Mariama's finely tuned strategies were aimed, in essence, at slowing, stifling, or boxing the dangerous internal processes of waste's decomposition. The longer the strike, the more unruly and difficult-to-control these ordinary waste materials became.

Neighborhood women were also well attuned to the challenges faced by the garbage workers. Since the system's founding in Set/Setal, many trash workers still collected their own neighbors' garbage. Years of dealing with insufficient materials, remuneration, and service had inspired detailed coordinating systems between households and trash collectors in many neighborhoods. Many workers would give their communities advance warning before the truck passed or warn them about breakdowns. To ease the struggle with collection delays, neighborhoods and workers would sometimes agree on collective dumping spots that the truck would pass as soon as it was up and running. Given the relationships between workers and their neighborhoods and an awareness of the difficulties faced by the workers, residents were often keen to support the workers in whatever way they could. At the least, this meant coordinating with the workers so as to smooth the collection process; at the most, it meant expressing solidarity with the workers' strike campaigns through coordinated dumping events (see chapter 4). The respatialization and devolution of life's work, in this way, can be seen to have precipitated more intimate management relations between households and their waste, as well as more intimate ties between waste workers and the families they served.

Formal Bricoleurs

The garbage workers faced profoundly precarious working conditions during this time. Years of institutional wrangling, poor salaries, and degrading equipment quickly dashed the optimism and enthusiasm they had felt at the dawn of the new system. Those who found other opportunities quickly got out, but most workers had little choice but to continue to collect garbage for what little opportunity it still represented, a professed "love of garbage," and an avowed commitment to keeping their communities clean. The period from 2005–9 was particularly grueling. In the face of rapid urbanization and, with it, a massive expansion of the city and its garbage challenges, combined with an institutional management vacuum that left the sector paralyzed, they found themselves laboring under increasingly difficult working conditions. Still without formal contracts or benefits (including health care, sick leave, and vacation), most workers cleaned streets and collected garbage with only minimal equipment, if any at all (see figure 2.5).

During the weeks in 2007 that I spent with the sweepers and collectors of the Niari Tali neighborhood, life's normal challenges combined with delays in payment to make life extremely difficult for the sector's twenty-odd workers. Many workers lost their homes as a result of payment irregularities, and many spoke of strain and dislocation in their family lives due to the stresses on the job. One street sweeper, Ahmed, was evicted from his apartment because of late rent payments. With nowhere to live, his wife had moved back to the country with her parents while Ahmed slept on the floor of his cousin's apartment. Unable to see his wife regularly and ridiculed by her family for not being a good provider, Ahmed's marriage eventually failed and he found himself lonely and disgraced. When a gastric infection left him compromised at work, he went further into debt, borrowing money from colleagues to see a doctor. He described his situation to me as "completely ordinary. We all live like this. What kind of existence is this?"

Workers' basic pay had stagnated at around 60,000 CFA per month (about US$120 per month) in 2007. Combined with steadily increasing work burdens, stigmatization, the rising cost of living in Dakar, and, for many, extensive family obligations, they found themselves struggling to survive with no

FIGURE 2.5. A trash worker in Niari Tali during one of the long periods in 2007 without pay. Author's photo, 2007.

means to envision their futures. Once celebrated as youth for their vitality, energy, and innovative citizenship practices, young men instead languished in their inability to graduate into adulthood. Unable to properly support their relatives and often powerless to establish their own homes and families, many felt trapped as social juniors, even though they may have been well into their thirties or forties.[22] Ahmed and others believed, moreover, that the designation of youth had become a disciplinary ploy by the authorities to keep the sector informal and exploitative. He explained, with frustration: "Yes we are young and that makes us proud of our energy and ideas. But they use it as an excuse not to pay us normal wages!"

Many women also left the sector as soon as they got married or had children but a good proportion stayed in the system, with no other choice than to squeeze all the opportunity they could from these rare jobs (see figure 2.6). Though they had been transferred out of the more "physical"

FIGURE 2.6. Women trash workers from the Niari Tali neighborhood at their usual hangout in the median. Author's photo, 2007.

duties—like collecting on the trucks—into street sweeping, women workers faced particular strains throughout this precarious period due to such challenges as lack of bathroom access and child care. Their positions, moreover, became increasingly insecure as the jobs became more sought after with the progressive deterioration of the job market in Dakar. Women workers' perceived inferiority as household breadwinners was sometimes invoked to legitimize replacing them with men. Quite in contrast to the legend of Les Amazones, at these moments women were described as being poorly suited to the tough demands of the work. As we shall see in chapter 3, the firing of all of the female trash workers in the neighborhood of Yoff during a round of downsizing was justified as making room for the "real" breadwinners: male heads of household. Soon after, these women were conscripted into a purely voluntary, NGO-led, horse-drawn-cart trash-collection experiment that was framed through a discourse of empowerment.

The material practices of the degraded labor process mattered profoundly for the bodies of the workers doing the dirty work. They bore the brunt of this labor-intensive infrastructure through the onerous physical demands of the work itself, associated diseases (including injury, heat exhaustion, and illness from exposure to microbes), and the stigma of laboring in filth. Most wore tattered work clothes and open-toed shoes like plastic "jelly" sandals, and many gathered garbage with their bare hands. Generally lacking protective clothing like masks and gloves and provisioned only with minimal instruments of collection like brooms and wheelbarrows, the workers stood vulnerable to an array of harms. An outbreak of tuberculosis in 2007 was but one dramatic expression of their disproportionate burdens of disease.

Both male and female workers faced the challenges of poor, degrading equipment and the incessant maintenance activities they required. The material intimacy between filth and labor actualized not just the relations between households and bodies, but also those between workers and the machines they depended on. The central pillar of the material technology was the garbage truck, but the trucks were a precariously weak link in the chain. Many, if not most, trucks arrived in Senegal from Europe used and already in disrepair, and once put to work in Senegal they faced the wear and tear caused by poor roads, lack of maintenance, and overcharged loads. One look at the collection fleet illuminated the serious challenges posed by this rickety, dilapidated material scaffolding (see figure 2.7).[23] At any point in time, at least a third of the collection fleet was broken down, and many of the trucks were used despite not being fully functional. The disintegration of the infrastructure's steel precipitated incessant expert labors of salvage bricolage.

Like *bricoleurs* all over the continent, the workers had no choice but to transform someone else's rubbish infrastructure into new utility. These material practices signaled the ingenuity required by incessant relations of maintenance, fixing, and making do—as well as their inherent dangers (see Graham and Thrift 2007; Mavhunga 2013b). From tinkering with or disabling the mechanical arms and crushers to physically maneuvering broken mechanical parts, the collectors were infrastructure hackers, navigating and manipulating the system's steel architecture through fastening their own bodies to the trucks' dysfunctional steel plates. The bodies and the machines conformed to each other's labor as the workers employed their own arms as artificial limbs for the ailing trucks. The dangers of such intimacy were cleanly written on the bodies of the collectors and their scars, bruises, even missing limbs.

FIGURE 2.7. A trash worker in Niari Tali who detailed many of the challenges he faced working with rickety equipment. Author's photo, 2007.

Amadou and Saliou had worked together as collectors in the Grand Yoff neighborhood for some time when I met them in 2007. They were experts in the particularities of the route, the "mentalities" of the people in the neighborhood, and they were no strangers to the strenuous and sometimes dangerous conditions of working with broken-down old trucks. They knew where people dumped, the homes with potentially the most-valuable materials, and the ever-present risks posed by the trash compactors. Amadou told a sobering story of one day when the compactor malfunctioned just as they had finished loading a large pile of garbage left from the weekly market. The machine jerked unexpectedly as it compressed a bag that apparently contained a broken lamp, shattering the glass and spraying it at Amadou. He turned away as soon as he could but not before a large shard embedded in his arm. The blood was everywhere. Not wanting to leave Saliou to finish the route on his own, he kept collecting but by the time the day was over, his arm was throbbing and swollen. Amadou eventually had his uncle remove the shards and bandage the arm but he couldn't afford to see a doctor. Though Amadou was back at work the next day, Saliou did all the heavy lifting and through teamwork they were able to get through the difficult period. "I was lucky," he said, when he showed me the scar. "God spared me." These conditions of salvage bricolage illuminate the intersecting precarities of labor and infrastructure. Infrastructural systems devolved onto labor can be downright hazardous for workers' bodies but can also be imperiled by their reliance on labor. The more advanced the state of decay of these steel technologies, the more precarious their intersections with working bodies.

Though much of their lives were spent contending with the difficult material practices of the actual collection, an even larger slice of workers' daily lives was spent simply waiting. When I visited workers on the job during the tumultuous 2007–8 union battle for recognition by the state, they were stuck in a state of limbo. Having been again rendered temporary laborers under the management of a confusing set of institutional power-sharing agreements, they dreamt of any change that could improve their daily lot. But in the end, nothing had happened for years. So, they waited and waited. No equipment and often no pay meant little incentive and sometimes not even the means to work, but they needed to stick around to make sure their precarious jobs didn't disappear.

When I interviewed the team in Niari Tali, the workers had not received their salary for several weeks. Each day, the team dutifully showed up for work, swept the streets, and did the household collection, but it was hard not to wonder if the work was futile. They bided their time sitting on benches and mats in the shade provided by trees in the large, sandy median between the parallel roads that are the center of the neighborhood (*niari tali* means "two roads"). Here, the workers blended in with the other human threads of this dense urban fabric. Many people walking by on their way to work, the market, or a family visit took no notice of the parked trash truck or the chatty workers as they debated the merits of union strategy or simply discussed the daily news. Other people accustomed to sharing the space with the workers—like the used-refrigerator salesman who waited patiently for someone to buy one of his old machines, the taxi drivers who washed their cars in the median, and the various vendors also taking advantage of the shade—were all too aware of the workers' plight. They checked in here and there for updates on the situation, always keen to offer their opinion.

FIGURE 2.8. Trash workers in Yoff during a strike. Author's photo, 2007.

The Yoff trash workers had been lent an old abandoned building by a neighborhood association, which they transformed into an imaginative headquarters where they bided time in between shifts and held union meetings (see figure 2.8). With all manner of reclaimed objects meticulously placed about—mats to lay on, an old radio, a fan that limped along, an old map of the United States—it struck me as a kind of secret fort, a hideaway for those who knew something mysterious and special. Making tea in the shade, they passed the time chatting about local gossip and waiting for word from the union. Other sectors had less glamorous hangouts, squeezed on the side of the road or in empty lots with little shade. And the patience at being stuck in this state of "waithood" (Honwana 2012) was not universal. Mbaye from Médina summed it up as follows: "I can't stand it anymore. What am I doing here but waiting? All I want is to do my job—to clean this city for the people who live here. Where is my dignity?" His words are a prescient commentary on the temporal violences of "killing time" (Ralph 2008), waiting for life to happen. Injury, illness, strain, and boredom are but a few of the corporeal expressions of the lived effects of disrepair.[24]

Conclusions

Labor and infrastructure have become powerfully conjoined through the turn to labor-intensive, participatory waste infrastructures as a central pillar of governing practices in Dakar. This chapter has shown how the incessant political maneuvering charted in chapter 1 worked to unevenly distribute precarious, dirty work through infrastructures devolved onto labor. A close look at the micropolitics of these infrastructures illuminates "the complex and contingent 'constructed-ness' of technological systems" (Ferguson 2012, 558). The socio-material technology at play here—community participation grounded in a moral paradigm of purity and architectures of belonging— emerged as a radical alternative to politics as usual in Set/Setal. These vernacular expressions of participatory development were then transformed and harnessed in the interest of cheap, neoliberal urban management solutions with explicit political utility for ambitious Dakar politicians. Just as new, advanced technologies reconfigure social relations, this history shows how gaps in infrastructure and the devolution to low-tech solutions also operate as means of discipline and control.

New infrastructural formulas interface with communal identities and spaces to mobilize political subjectivities in novel ways. The labor of participatory trash management illuminates the way that neoliberal rationalities of community and individual responsibility produce highly gendered and generational political subjectivities. Both young men and young women found themselves operating in new political spheres through novel material labor practices that reconfigured their positions within their communities. The formalization of Set/Setal into a participatory trash collection system diffused and domesticated the threat these young people had posed and placed them as pawns in a political battle between different politicians and echelons of government jockeying to control the urban space. In harnessing youth labor at meager rates through a moral discourse of participatory citizenship, it offloaded the burdens of austerity more firmly onto community systems. And yet, the very same reliance upon belonging and intimate community relations was what, in the end, would nurture workers' power when they were to raise their heads again in the form of the trash-workers union (see chapter 4). Participatory trash management was, thus, a contradictory infrastructural arrangement: it enabled new spaces of citizenship while producing and reinforcing other inequalities and power relations.

Beyond just trucks and the city dump, infrastructures of disposal comprise a complex ecology of material objects and human labor, tethered together through their affective registers and political actualities. The things, living bodies, and values that make up trash infrastructures operate as performative vehicles of emergent agendas of technology, discipline, and rebellion, gaining force through their animation and interaction. In this setting, the symbolic associations and material force of garbage intersect with human labor to order specific bodies and geographies. The force of garbage derives from its associations with waste, disposability, the opposite of value, and the impure, as well as its sticky material properties which vex those charged with its orderly disposal. The vitality of the decomposition process makes household garbage management especially risky during times of crisis but gives waste its power as a matter of rebellion (see chapter 4). Decaying machines, furthermore, can wreak havoc on the bodies of the bricoleurs charged with managing and disposing of garbage. Garbage illuminates the ways that material matters in its encounter with human bodies and the intersecting precarities that are bred when infrastructures rely increasingly on laboring bodies.

A materialist reading of garbage politics in Dakar lays bare the contradictions ushered forth in the era of austerity that can be deciphered in the urban landscape. In so doing, it contributes to an updated formulation of emergent geographies of "life's work in crisis" that is attentive to bodies, spaces, and material social practices (Meehan and Strauss 2015; Mitchell, Marston, and Katz 2004). Participatory garbage management represents a formula of governing the city that is premised on tapping and respatializing relations of social reproduction. A focus on waste exposes the dirty, messy burdens this imposes on workers and how different bodies come to disproportionately shoulder these burdens. It thus allows us to see how neoliberal assemblages work through disposability, highlighting the full range of their material violences. Decay in physical infrastructures has precipitated an intricate ecology of improvisational social systems and material practices premised upon intimacy between households, workers, waste, and machines of collection. The burdens of bricolage are borne—invisibly and visibly—on workers' and residents' bodies in the scars, impurities, and stigmas they carry along. Discard labor, as the animation of trash's matter, crystallizes the values manifested in structures of vulnerability. The next chapter will explore the intensification of participatory infrastructures in the city's outskirts and how this further displaced the burdens of dirty work onto gendered laboring bodies.

In the spring of 2003, the clogged transfer station for the Yoff community-based trash collection project had transformed into an enormous, unruly *dépôt sauvage* (garbage pile). The station was designed to link the project's horse-drawn-cart collection to the municipal garbage trucks, but the coordination of these two systems had failed miserably. Under the uncompromising West African sun, the stinking edifice of waste provided visceral testimony to all that had gone wrong with the neighborhood experiment in low-tech community trash collection infrastructure. It stood in dramatic contradistinction, moreover, to the celebratory representation of such projects in the NGO literature. In the end, because of its location on the road to Dakar's airport, the clogged station was a politically untenable eyesore. When flocks of birds began swarming the pile and interfering with planes' flight paths, the writing was on the wall. The national aviation authority stepped in to order the transfer station's closure, thereby signaling the end to one chapter in Yoff's participatory trash history. For the women who had been the central labor force comprising this infrastructure, its abrupt closure was bittersweet. On the one hand, it put an end to a contentious initiative that had starkly increased their dirty-labor burden and compromised their standing in the community. On the other hand, it dashed their hopes for the opportunities that might develop from their exemplary acts of "participatory citizenship."

In the mid- to late 1990s, after the city's municipal trash infrastructure had been devolved onto youth participation under Mayor Mamadou Diop's thumb, a different kind of community-based garbage collection sprang up in the city's periphery.[1] While the municipal garbage workers in Dakar were organizing to resist the devaluation of their labor at the hands of notions of participatory citizenship, one of Senegal's best-known NGOS, ENDA,[2] was spearheading new participatory experiments that devolved garbage infrastructure even more onto communities through disarticulating hard-to-reach neighborhoods from the city's collection system. Off-grid, neighborhood-based liquid- and solid-sanitation systems using small-scale alternative technologies were installed in place of the networked municipal trash and sanitation infrastructure. Consistent with global trends, the shrinking of the state with structural adjustment catalyzed an explosion of so-called third-sector initiatives aiming to fill the space in urban public services. Community-based development, led by NGOS, was seen not just as more efficient but as more democratic and empowering for community members (World Bank 1989). This new paradigm governing urban policy interventions emphasized "tapping the knowledge, resources, and capacities among the population within each city" toward bringing economic and social gains and reversing environmental degradation (UNCHS 1996, 59). The ENDA community-based waste initiatives were a front-running sector in this wave of nonstate urban-management strategies and were widely hailed as "best practices" of participatory urban governance in Africa.[3]

These NGO community waste projects represent a further adaptation of the urban labor question through infrastructure politics based on generalizing women's labor as communal, municipal labor. This chapter looks specifically at the material and sociopolitical technologies employed in the waste infrastructure built by the ENDA pilot community-based trash collection project in the Tonghor neighborhood of Dakar's Yoff district. The lens of infrastructure allows for a nuanced exploration of these projects as complex articulations that assemble multiple technologies differently in specific places and moments, paying special attention to material relationships. The analysis finds that the Yoff project produced an elitist, ethnicized image of community and that women were subjected to dirty-labor burdens as the vehicles of these new agendas. Overall, this led to a more disjointed and fragmented urban infrastructure in which garbage literally spilled out at the joints and the coherence of the local state was compromised. This chapter further examines the social and material components of infrastructure while also contributing to critiques in development studies unpacking notions of community, participation, and empowerment in community-based development.

Infrastructures are not isolated material relationships but complex ecologies of different material, social, and bodily technologies that need to work locally to be integrated. The hallmark material scaffolding of community-based infrastructural systems is their low-tech, "appropriate" technology that is supposed to be more cost effective and attuned to local conditions and traditions. Consider ENDA's technological vision for its low-tech sanitation projects in Dakar: "The new approach places technology at its proper level of human affairs; at the service of human beings, as a tool which they master, rather than a dominating alien force which they buy from other cultures at prices they cannot afford. The new approach seeks to establish a friendly, familiar technology that even poor people can afford and can control, and that can be replicated from community to community, creating new jobs, new skills, a new self-confidence and faith in the future" (Gaye and Diallo 1997, 10). Though scholars of infrastructure are often preoccupied with more advanced, high technologies, regressive technological innovations that render infrastructures more primitive also introduce new forms of subjectification. From hand water pumps to bicycles to, in this case, horse-drawn carts, these technologies embody a romanticized yearning for a more sustainable development path and a conception of developing societies as closer to nature and less technologically inclined. They also endeavor to render more "appropriate" the promise of development and assure everything from self-confidence to community control to an end to "fatalistic attitude[s] and the mentality which expects the state to provide everything" (Gaye and Diallo 1997, 21).

Community-based development builds infrastructures animated, in particular, by labor and community. Often imagined as unproblematic sites of tradition and consensus, communities are produced through systems that harness the labor of specific members as participants and mobilize the "glue" of communal solidarity. In this way, labor and community can be understood as technologies because they become the primary, innovative instruments essential to infrastructure's functionality. As a flexible technology that stems out of local histories and can adapt to the conditions at hand, labor is the key to operationalizing new infrastructures and powering their low-tech development visions. Labor, in turn, mobilizes the production of specific "images of community" (Li 1996). This chapter examines new configurations of community-based trash collection in Yoff to emphasize how labor is animated differently within distinct infrastructural systems. In comparison with chapter 2, we will see how women have come to represent a different technology within this system, in relation to the new, more "appropriate" material scaffolding of horse carts. As such, they become the vehicles driving new political agendas of community and novel political economies of development.

Shifting focus from the participatory municipal trash sector to the fully community-based waste sector exposes the further splintering of infrastructure and how it works through gendered bodies. Even more so than Dakar's participatory municipal trash sector, the low-tech, off-grid waste systems in the periphery rendered women as infrastructure through extending their social-reproductive duties into the neighborhood space. Municipal garbage trucks, the material technology of the trash collection infrastructure, were replaced by horse-drawn carts and women's laboring bodies. This anachronistic technology conjured a scaled-down, small-is-beautiful aesthetic deemed more appropriate and green than grid-based collection. But appropriate to what vision of development, and green by what terms? This chapter is concerned with unpacking the new relations between actors implicated in these innovative infrastructural visions, namely NGOs, "communities," and women participants, while grappling with the implications of rendering women's work and bodies infrastructural.

Like the flexibilization of the municipal trash sector, these new infrastructural systems produced new visions of community and reconfigured "life's work" by bringing people into the intimate management of their own and their neighbors' waste (Meehan and Strauss 2015; Mitchell, Marston, and Katz 2004). Community-based waste-management projects, including the Yoff project, further displaced the burdens of neoliberal restructuring onto marginalized neighborhoods. Relying on free labor as a replacement for municipal garbage services while requiring the participation of local households via a user fee, the projects converted neighborhood garbage management into an exclusively community-held responsibility and detached the public service from the local municipal governance structure. Consistent with the global rise of gender as a primart focus of development policy (R. Pearson 2005), the Yoff project enlisted poor women as its main participants, underpinned by a discourse of gender empowerment. But it didn't enlist just any women; some of the women selected had been fired from their jobs in Mayor Mamadou Diop's municipal trash collection system (see chapter 2). These women were enlisted to be the neighborhood's "municipal housekeepers" (Miraftab 2004b) through the instrumentalization of gendered associations with household waste management and perceptions of their diplomatic community-management skills. These new spaces subjected these women to novel forms of material discipline and stigma within their communities. This entrenchment into dirty labor and its associated violences formed a stark contrast to the project's empowerment claims.

The osmosis between "formal" and "informal" trash labor introduced through participatory management, moreover, solidified existing community hierarchies through reinforcing specific divisions and power relations. A defining feature of neoliberal rule, discourses of community mobilized by "sustainable development" often represent communities as defined by "harmony, equality, and tradition" (Li 1996, 502). However, as Michael Watts (2005b, 105) reminds us, what gets demarcated as a community is "not always warm and fuzzy" but may, in fact, comprise a sinister political life. The images of community produced in the Yoff trash-collection project turned on ethnic difference and, in the end, bolstered an exclusionary understanding of community. Municipal housekeeping was used by the ethnic elite to solidify the group's authority over the neighborhood by performing urban service provision. In this way, community-based management allowed local customary authorities to deepen their neighborhood power through seizing the opportunity to govern through garbage. The project thus reconfigured the lines of authority in the municipal district by abstracting the city even further from the provision of social-reproductive goods and reinforcing customary authority over local development.

Appropriate Technology

The ENDA community-based trash project in the Yoff district was piloted in the Lebou (one of Senegal's nine ethnic groups) neighborhood of Tonghor. Dakar's Lebou neighborhoods include some of the self-proclaimed "traditional" Lebou fishing villages that have occupied the Cape Verde Peninsula for over five hundred years but which are now absorbed into the rapidly growing capital city (Sylla 1992; UNESCO 2000). Uniquely situated as the "original" inhabitants of the area, the Cape Verde Lebou have a long tradition both of incorporation into Dakar municipal politics and of autonomy and self-determination in the face of urban development.[4] In certain areas—of which Yoff is an important example—the Lebou have retained an extremely insular and powerful customary authority base, even as their villages have been rapidly absorbed into the urban agglomeration of Dakar. This traditional political organization overlaps with the municipal authority with important effects.[5]

Despite being officially incorporated into the greater Dakar municipality, these Lebou neighborhoods are disadvantaged in receiving Dakar-based public services due to their location on the periphery of the city and their traditional village plan. Built around the family concession and spatially limited in their expansion, the neighborhoods are extremely dense and irregular, and many areas have only narrow, sandy pedestrian paths (see figure 3.1). Combined with a fierce politics of land and resistance to change by the local customary authorities, these features have posed a number of challenges to infrastructural upgrading and waste management. Whereas wastes previously were disposed of in "the bush" surrounding the villages, these neighborhoods are now often plagued with sanitation problems. These challenges were part of the justification for choosing Lebou neighborhoods as the main sites of the participatory waste-management and sanitation projects spearheaded by ENDA in the 1990s and early 2000s in the context of the wider turn towards NGO community-based strategies of urban public service provision (Abdoul 2002; Gaye and Diallo 1997; Simone 2003; Soumaré 2002). These projects have been a central thrust of ENDA's activities to improve Dakar's urban environment.[6]

Tonghor is one of the oldest of Yoff's seven traditional neighborhoods and had a population estimated at around 7,000 of Yoff's 53,200 habitants in 2002 (N. B. L. Ndoye 2005, 36). Though the majority of residents are employed in the fishing industry, declining fish stocks have contributed to widespread insecurity in that economic sector. Most of the residents of Tonghor are Lebou, though there have been waves of immigration by poor fisherman and a more recent influx of wealthier city folk. A long-term population of Geejndar fishermen of the Sereer ethnicity have relocated to Yoff from Saint-Louis for the fishing industry.[7] Unlike most Lebou, who own their own property, most of the Geejndar do not own land, and they often live in even more cramped, irregular habitations near the water. They are generally understood to be the poorest, least-educated members of the population and are still often seen as outsiders, despite having been in Yoff for generations in many cases.

In 2001, ENDA launched the pilot community-based trash project in Tonghor in collaboration with the neighborhood's main community-based organization, le Comité de gestion de Tonghor (Tonghor Management Committee;

FIGURE 3.1. The narrow pedestrian paths inside Yoff's traditional neighborhoods. Author's photo, 2007.

CGT).[8] Seed funding would come from French and Canadian development agencies, and the project was to be maintained through a revolving savings fund based on household contributions (a user fee). The local district government (commune d'arrondissement de Yoff) and Yoff's main community association—l'Association pour la promotion social, economique et culturelle de Yoff (Association for the Social, Economic and Cultural Promotion of Yoff; APECSY)—were official, noncontributing partners. The project involved a door-to-door horse-drawn-cart "precollection" system that targeted over six thousand residents and would, in principle, connect up with the Dakar-based collection system at the transfer station on the main Airport Road (ENDA 1999).

Tonghor was chosen for the pilot partly because it had long been considered one of the most garbage-challenged neighborhoods in Yoff (ENDA 1999; N. B. L. Ndoye 2005). Tonghor's garbage-management challenges were gen-

FIGURE 3.2. Garbage cluttering the Yoff beach. Author's photo, 2007.

erally attributed to the distance from most houses to the paved road where the city's trash truck passed to collect garbage. The sandy roads in the interior were often impassable for these vehicles, so most households had to walk some distance to the road when they heard the honking of the trash truck. Many women disposed of their household garbage through burying it or dumping it onto the beach (see figure 3.2).[9] During the project's tenure, the municipal garbage trucks that had previously collected the neighborhood's garbage ceased to enter the Tonghor neighborhood. The project ushered in a more intimate system in which select women would collect their neighbors' garbage using what was considered the more appropriate, "traditional" method of horse-drawn carts.

The project-feasibility study emphasized the importance of local participation (ENDA 1999). The CGT created a pilot committee and appointed a young male member as its coordinator. The most important element of community participation was the six women chosen as *animatrices* (activity lead-

FIGURE 3.3. An educational mural in Tonghor, Yoff, instructing neighborhood women on proper waste-management behavior as part of the ENDA project. Author's photo, 2007.

ers) of the project—liaisons between the households and the three (male) horse-cart drivers. Though not originally from Yoff, the horse-cart operators were locally based Sereer men who owned their own horse carts. Two animatrices accompanied each horse-cart driver to collect the garbage from the homes and load it onto the cart. Originally completely voluntary, these women received a small "reward" of 15,000 CFA per month (US$30) for a few months until community contributions waned and they received next to nothing. The drivers were hired on at 35,000 CFA per month (US$70) for their labors and the coordinator received 30,000 CFA per month (US$60) for managing the project.[10] The animatrices were also charged with educating neighborhood women on how to properly store, separate, and dispose of their garbage (see figure 3.3). A key element of the education campaign entailed discouraging women from dumping on the beach or burying their garbage. In the face of persistent recourse to the beach, an ordinance was eventually enacted which prohibited all beach dumping and fined all perpetrators. This forced residents to use the fee-based horse-cart system and placed the animatrices in the role of policing their participation. A guard was placed on the beach at night to discourage dumping, but people still attempted to surreptitiously hide their garbage in wastewater evacuated at the ocean's edge.

For the daily collection process, each animatrice would complete her household duties to start the neighborhood rounds in the morning. They walked door to door alongside the horse carts, entering their neighbors' courtyards and homes to speak with women, verifying the sorting, retrieving the garbage, and loading it onto the carts. In the beginning, they did the rounds every day, but they eventually reduced their labors to four days per week to lessen the burden. On certain days, the animatrices had to solicit each household's financial contribution (1,000 CFA per month)—a demand that was often disquieting and frequently unanswered. The cart drivers dumped the garbage at the transfer station by the main road where it was, theoretically, to be delivered to the city's dump, Mbeubeuss, by municipal trash trucks. For a couple of short months, a young male volunteer separated out the organics at the transfer station in a pilot compost project.

Producing Community

In principle, public services provide public goods equally to the whole of the city. However, we saw in chapter 1 that, in practice, people and spaces in the city are disciplined through the uneven distribution and governance of disorder. Completely devolving infrastructure down to the community introduces different possibilities for governing-through-garbage as well as potential new dangers. In spite of conceptualizations deployed within development discourse of communities as undifferentiated "sites of consensus and sustainability" (Li 1996, 501), they are as riven with power relations and social divisions as any other social body. New infrastructural formulas built by and for the "community" interface with these internal political dynamics in ways that affect not just project outcomes but also socio-spatial hierarchies and agendas.

The images of community produced through the community-based trash infrastructures in Yoff reinforced an exclusionary ethnic definition of the Yoff community as Lebou. These community discourses, moreover, advanced notions of the Lebou as traditional and inherently ecologically minded while fueling animosity toward the poor, ethnic-minority group through discourses of disorder. Because autochthonous claims in Yoff are defined by ethnicity, claims to manage Yoff "traditionally" yoke ethnicity with tradition. In their community-management and self-branding activities, the Lebou (and their historians alike [see Mbengue 1997]) are quick to emphasize their solidarity and traditional ways. The selection of the Lebou neighborhoods rather than other sanitation-challenged peri-urban communities was explicitly made on these ethnic terms. The promotional literature produced by ENDA often highlighted the historical legacy of Dakar's "traditional neighborhoods" and hailed the Lebou as a proud, independent people for whom community-driven development is a natural and long-standing truth.

In choosing Yoff and focusing on Lebou values, ENDA instrumentalized a reputation that had been honed by the Lebou in Yoff. The neighborhood had been a pioneer in the Set/Setal movement in the early 1990s and in the municipal garbage collection system that followed on its heels, and so they were no strangers to participatory garbage activities. Moreover, through Yoff's powerful community association, APECSY—which is seen by many to be the seat of Lebou power—residents had been working on a series of environmental initiatives for years and they were proud to cast themselves as deeply invested in urban sustainability. The longtime president of that association, Serigne Mbaye Diene, had become influenced by permaculture while pursuing his PhD at Cornell University in the early 1990s, and had set out to fuse these principles with vernacular notions of sustainability in Yoff through a series of green development projects. In an interview, he explained his motivations simply: "in Yoff, we had those principles and were losing them . . . we were going the other way."[11] Yoff hosted the 3rd International Ecocity and Ecovillage Network Conference in 1996, which showcased Yoff's "village wisdom" and explored strategies to foster ecological urbanism.[12] In founding the horse-cart trash-collection project in Yoff and developing it in consultation with APECSY, ENDA was building on this legacy and crafting a narrative that would have charismatic appeal to international funders and community-based-development advocates.

Centering the project on Lebou traditions and values and structuring it through Lebou leadership worked to sideline participation by the Geejndar and fed stereotypes vilifying their role in Yoff's disorder. The vast majority of Lebou household members and implicated local leaders—from the community associations to the mayor's office—were quick to blame the poor *comportement* (behavior) of the Geejndar for Yoff's garbage problems. The Geejndar neighborhood along the beach was the neighborhood's most notoriously filthy section and people were quick to invoke pejorative ethnic stereotypes. Even a Lebou university professor of Yoff history stated in an interview: "The Geejndar do not have the same standards of hygiene and cleanliness. It is a behavior issue." He went on to explain: "They are Muslims and they have integrated partially. But, the Lebou are jealous. The fisherman have this idea of liberty, of freedom. They don't respect authority, and this goes for both Lebou and Geejndar. This creates a sort of tension between freedom and solidarity." This tension and "jealousy" manifested in the complete elision of feedback or participation from the Geejndar. Blaming the Geejndar for the filthy conditions of the neighborhood and the beach justified disciplinary action toward that already disenfranchised and embattled group of residents. In this way, the Lebou elite sought to govern their adversaries through discourses of waste animated by community-based development.

None of the animatrices were Geejndar. They were, however, initially encouraged to spend extra time educating this "problem population" and endeavoring to rid their trash-clogged corners of the neighborhood of waste. The Geejndar residents bore the brunt of the ban on beach dumping since they lived next to the beach, had the least amount of available space for storing garbage, and were often the least willing and able to pay the user fee. An older Geejndar woman named Anta who had been in Yoff since 1960 described her experience as follows:

> We have a lot of garbage problems down here but not a lot of options. The garbage truck is so far away on the main road that it's difficult to catch. When the animatrices were collecting garbage, they worked hard to help out but they didn't come often enough and we couldn't afford it! A thousand francs is not nothing for me! These services should be free. It's not the fault of the animatrices—they are just women like us, trying to make a living—but really, that project did not have our interests at heart. Many of us had no choice but to dump on the beach. I used to send my daughter out at midnight to dump in the ocean when no one was looking. She would hide the garbage at the bottom of a bucket of wastewater. One day, though, she got caught and we had to pay a fine. See, I had no options!

A deep feeling of frustration at the lack of options pervaded responses like these. Anta was embarrassed to admit that she had strategized to circumvent the beach ordinance but her candor revealed the unjust constraints that were placed upon Geejndar women.

After the animatrices faced particular difficulty collecting the user fee from the Geejndar families, they were encouraged by the association's leadership to cease collecting from this part of the neighborhood. Unable to participate financially and banned from taking recourse to the beach, the Geejndar found themselves in a progressively more untenable situation. Though my respondents were reluctant to critique the project or the Lebou establishment, it was clear that the project had exacerbated internal divisions between neighborhood households. These divisions and the elision of Geejndar participation stand in direct contrast to ENDA's rhetoric of inclusivity and their supposed concern with the most marginalized members of society. Despite their being the poorest members of Tonghor society, predominantly propertyless, and those most saddled with the burdens of living with waste, the Geejndar experienced this new waste infrastructure as more a means for the Lebou elite to surveil and to denigrate than a form of infrastructure "for" and "by" the community.

The low-tech community-based waste project served not just to buttress ethnic authority over neighborhood affairs, but also to solidify the Lebou elite's autonomy from the municipal state. The district has a long history of fierce independence and autonomy in the face of external threats to its authority. In the words of one resident, "Yoff is the one village in Senegal never ruled by the French." Indeed, the Lebou declared their republic independent of French authority in 1790. The Lebou Republic lasted until 1857, when the Cape Verde Peninsula was annexed into the French colony; however, they still managed to retain their autonomy (Sylla 1992). Legend has it that the French actually paid the Lebou taxes during the colonial period. In the contemporary moment, the Lebou are acutely preoccupied with their decreasing majority in Yoff and Dakar. A UNESCO report described Yoff's unique history and culture as "besieged" by forces of change and the rapidly invading metropolis of Dakar (UNESCO 2000). At the same time, according to the Yoff historian referenced above, they also have a special advantage: people fear the Lebou—they have land, pride, and also, reportedly, renowned mystical powers. They have preserved an intricate, powerful customary-authority structure and are constantly working to defend their political autonomy. This defense of ethnic claims to belonging resonates with wider research on the resurgence of autochthonous identities in the face of new political economies in African cities, but centers those claims onto the space of infrastructure (see Geschiere and Gugler 1998; Geschiere and Jackson 2006; Marshall-Fratani 2006; Nyamnjoh and Rowlands 1998).

The Lebou elite involved in governing the trash project welcomed the visibility it brought but, perhaps even more importantly, they especially embraced the opportunity provided by this new infrastructure to assert their authority over the neighborhood and their autonomy from the local state, especially Dakar-based public services.[13]

Engaging "their" women in neighborhood trash collection offered a productive opportunity for the Lebou to solidify their tenacious hold on their district through the symbolic ordering of the neighborhood by these municipal housekeepers. Positioning Lebou women as the key technology of the new infrastructure entrenched their authority over the neighborhood through the performance of self-management. The door-to-door service by the animatrices introduced another layer of intimacy and surveillance by the impersonal garbage truck and rendered the municipal state even more distant and ineffectual in the eyes of local residents. As they squeezed out the state from urban public services, the Lebou elite asserted their desire to control the destiny of Yoff in the face of urban change. The animatrices were the vehicle, in other words, for a power grab by the Lebou community association. Though the municipality was an official partner in the project—due to ENDA's declared commitment to collaborative, integrative approaches that productively interface with local government, or "micro-solutions [that] can be integrated into the national action plan" (Gaye and Diallo 1997, 10)—that partnership was a key sticking point for the project that led to its eventual demise.

Embodying Technology

Much of Xadi's life had been, in her words, "all about trash." For as long as she could remember, she was responsible for her household's garbage. When Set/Setal exploded onto Yoff's sandy streets, she was one of the first to dive in and get her hands dirty, cleaning up her neighborhood and ridding Yoff's beautiful beach of unsightly piles of accumulating waste. As Set/Setal matured and captured the interest of Mayor Mamadou Diop, Xadi was keen to take her "commitment to Yoff's cleanliness" to the next level through becoming one of Yoff's regular garbage collectors. When the position became paid and her contract formalized, she was proud to be able to support her family and they, in turn, respected her work ethic and dedication to the well-being of the neighborhood.

A few years later, Xadi was instructed not to show up at work the next day.

She was told to wait for a call that she never received. When she demanded to know why she had been let go, she was given no explanation. Finally the answer came from her neighbor and colleague, Aminata, who had also lost her job: evidently, only the "essential" workers had been retained. All of the women working in Yoff had been let go because, supposedly, they could not do the same work as men, were not household breadwinners, and were out of their element working in the municipal sector. "My husband is out of work," Xadi told me. "Who else is going to take care of our children? Is this my reward for these years of serving my community?" Apparently Xadi's reward was to do more service, but this time for free: just a couple of years later she was called down to speak with the village elders and the coordinator of a new project in the neighborhood. She was asked: "Do you want to do your part to support your neighborhood, your country?" When she responded "Yes," she was informed that she had been chosen to participate in an important new neighborhood initiative.

Xadi and Aminata were two of the six women chosen to be the animatrices of the Yoff community-based waste project. Like the restructuring of state welfare services ushered in with neoliberal reform in the municipal garbage sector, the flexibilization of Xadi and Aminata's labor involved reconfiguring the fabric of activities comprising "life's work" through discourses of participatory citizenship. This new formula of participation deepened the deployment of gendered discourses of waste to render women the new technology of this "more" appropriate waste infrastructure.

The Yoff project instrumentalized associations of waste work in the home as intrinsically women's work in order to idealize women as participants and thereby extend their social-reproductive duties into the neighborhood space. In the words of the project coordinator from ENDA, "as it's women who do the separation at the source, that's what motivated us to place women as key links in the chain" of the project. This exclusive focus on women dovetailed with the overall turn in ENDA's priorities—and in the wider development discourse, for that matter—by the mid-1990s toward a focus on women's participation.[14] Mayor Issa Ndiaye, who had observed the rollout of the project in his dual role as mayor of Yoff (from 1996 to 2002) and a member of APECSY's executive board, further explained:

> [The participation of women] was good because women can speak to
> other women. . . . It was a question of organization. . . . And so, the
> women, while the others went to the beach for money-making activ-

ities, they were taking care of the common interest! [They] had the capacity to withstand this work. Even if people spoke badly to them, they took it in stride! They didn't create any problems. What interested them was the cleanliness of the neighborhood. . . . So, whatever [community] reaction they received, they were incredibly diplomatic! Truly, they withstood lots of grief.

The mayor's revealing statement echoes many of my interviews with those coordinating the project. Women's "natural" attributes, including diplomacy, nonconfrontational style, and intimacy with the community, as well as their altruistic choice to work for "the common interest" in lieu of making money, were celebrated as their key skills as animatrices. Women were positioned as natural community managers who played a "determining role in the education of children, the citizens of the future,"[15] and could most effectively influence the behavior of other women. This reconfiguration of the space of household social-reproductive activities into the community space built on the notion that women should be judged according to their skills and capacities as the managers of order and cleanliness in the home. This resonates with Dipesh Chakrabarty's (1991, 20) observation in India of how "housekeeping"—specifically household trash management—"is meant to express the auspicious qualities of the mistress of the household." These participatory trash projects extended the realm of that responsibility to secure the cleanliness of the neighborhood as a reflection of the auspicious qualities of its female residents.

The notion that women in Tonghor are natural waste managers and community educators facilitated the negation of value for neighborhood trash collection as work deserving of remuneration, and placed the onus of neighborhood waste work on women's skills as project participants. This resonates with other research on the instrumentalization of gender in cheap waste management solutions in neoliberal contexts, defended through a rhetoric of voluntarism, responsibility, and skill acquisition. In their research in Cape Town and Johannesburg, respectively, Melanie Samson (2003, 2007, 2008) and Faranak Miraftab (2004a, 2004b) examine how the privatization of municipal waste collection has exploited African women's vulnerable position in the labor market, in effect "creating new divisions between both workers and citizens."[16] Samson (2007, 136) illustrates how in certain sectors women were given preferential recruitment into street cleaning because of the special skills they were assumed to have developed from their domestic duties, and were then offered lower wages, benefits, and employment security than their male counterparts. This underlines both the predatory and the disciplinary aspects of these forms of participation. The animatrices had no choice but to participate, in the interest of preserving their reputations as good wives and housekeepers but also out of a sense of obligation to their communities, as enforced by the power and authority of community leaders. Behavior is tightly conscripted in Tonghor, and the intimacy of community gives the impression of neighborly surveillance at all times. The ENDA project coordinator was quite explicit about how he kept the women "motivated": "We had a number of meetings with the women explaining why we were counting on them. We told them that we could make them work without paying because they live in this neighborhood. . . . They are obliged to go along with all that is in the neighborhood's best interest. We told them: 'We know the 15,000 [CFA per month] that we give you is nothing at all! But as a resident of the neighborhood, the project could bring other projects that could be beneficial for you.' We let them know that this project was their project!" For many of the neighborhood leaders, women's responsibility was tethered to ideas of tradition. One neighborhood leader spoke nostalgically of times past when women took better care of the neighborhood, rising before dawn to tidy their homes and cleaning the whole village before important events. In this light, women's role in community-based development was rendered not only a historical verity but an obligation on which rested their standing in the community.

The village elders explicitly chose the animatrices using "social criteria" from respected but poor Lebou households, because these women were seen as good representatives of the village who "needed" such an "opportunity." Three of the women were divorced or widowed heads of household, and three were over fifty years of age. For their part, the six women seem to have been taken by surprise when they were notified of their new roles. They felt no choice but to participate out of an obligation to their elders, an honest desire to contribute to neighborhood cleanliness, and a desperate hope that one day their participation would bear fruit. For their part, Xadi and Aminata knew that their selection was motivated by their experience working in municipal garbage collection.

Despite a prevalent rhetoric in ENDA's promotional materials claiming that its participatory waste projects were community-designed and -driven, the animatrices, as well as neighborhood residents in general, were in practice completely excluded from project design. In direct contrast to ENDA's emphasis on women's central roles as project leaders as a key metric of success, the animatrices were emphatic that they had not been consulted prior to the project's rollout and that they would have designed it quite differently. The role of the community in designing the project was exclusively channeled through the two implicated community-based organizations—CGT and APECSY—and discussions took place between older male village elders and community leaders and ENDA's project managers. As such, the project reinforced existing community power dynamics.

Beyond feeling obligated to participate, these women participated hoping that the work might translate into more lucrative opportunities. Because they often lack the education and networks needed to land jobs, women in Dakar are at a stark disadvantage for finding wage labor. The animatrices hoped that this project would be their ticket to paid work. In my interviews with all six participants, it was clear that their participation in the project had been quite onerous and that they were, in the end, deeply disappointed with the lack of compensation or other opportunities gained. One animatrice named Mariama described her daily experience as follows:

> I'd wake up early to do my duties around the house then go meet the horse-cart driver to do our circuit with the other animatrice. We left our kids, left our work at the house, to go rid people's homes of garbage. I would follow behind the cart, whistling and letting everyone know we were coming so they would bring out their garbage. . . . The work was really hard. . . . We continued on because we wanted to work . . . we kept working. Then, you find that even before the end of the month, you'd have a sore chest and then, finally, that what you're supposed to receive, no one gives it to you. What we wanted was to work and that's the chance that God gave us, so we said we would grab that chance . . . but it didn't help to fulfill any of our needs. You would work all day, go home, wash, do the cleaning, do our work, then the next day get back up to do it again.

When I asked the project coordinator if the project's duties interfered with women's duties at home, he said, "Yes, it did! Great question. We analyzed all of these angles!" The solution: move the trash collection two hours later so women had a chance to get their work done at home.

Central to this new labor-intensive infrastructure was a repudiation of the labor these women already performed in the home—or the life's work that the animatrices left behind as they went about their neighborhood trash job. In this sense, we can see how the jobs ended up doubling their unpaid activities by extending the realm of social reproduction into the public space. This extension also came as a fundamental rejection of the value of women's labor in the official trash sector. Fired from municipal trash collection because they were not deemed worthy of those jobs, these women were then installed into the community-based project as idealized volunteers. Quite in contrast to the early experience of women municipal trash workers, whose labors were rendered more valuable when they entered public space to collect garbage, the labors of women in the community-based system were devalued. This underscores the way that so-called formal and "participatory" labors are dialectically constituted and how the categorical distinction between the realms of production and reproduction determines the nature and value of work. Although the women toiled day in and day out alongside the horse-cart drivers, the payment of these men was never in question and was never justified through a narrative of community responsibility. In this light, the case of participatory waste management in Dakar resonates with the growing body of research into the way that the crisis of social reproduction has worked by differentially disciplining gendered bodies through the devaluation of certain spheres of work (Bakker and Gill 2003; Fakier and Cock 2009; Meehan and Strauss 2015; Mitchell, Marston, and Katz 2004; M. Samson 2010). The drivers were clearly seen as workers, whereas the women were seen as participants whose neighborhood trash labor was rendered an "empowering" duty undeserving of compensation.

As was the case in the municipal system, the insidious power of these projects drew from the materiality of trash as it intersected with gendered bodies. The arduous physicality of the collection process joined with the symbolic violence of being associated with waste. Provisioned only with minimal equipment, if any at all, the animatrices did this work with their bare hands. By the end of a workday, they were literally filthy, forced to parade through their neighborhood wearing the smelly remains of other people's waste. In a Muslim society where cleanliness of the body is of utmost importance in terms of spiritual and community standing, this was no small burden. Neither was the vulnerability to disease that came of this risky exposure for people with little or no access to health care. As with the formal trash workers, despite their most fastidious attempts at staying clean, the work often led to infection and disease. Even four years after the project had ended, Mariama was still suffering from a series of infections that had originated with her participation in the project, including a recurring eye infection that had caused her eye to permanently swell shut.

The intimate technology of the door-to-door horse-cart system introduced an entirely different relationship between collector and garbage, and new forms of subjection to waste management's symbolic and material discipline. The deployment of gender stereotypes and devolving technology in these projects entrenched women's connection to waste, dirt, and disorder through literally weighing them down and marking them with the mess of waste. In this way, women's bodies became the embodiment of the new technology, and their labor the animation of the vibrant force of waste. Long after the project's demise, their bodies and reputations still carried with them waste's "toxic vitality" (P. Harvey 2016).

Household Finance

In addition to novel material and social technologies, the infrastructure of community-based waste collection also relied on a new financing technology: the user fee. The fee for trash collection reconfigured the financial burden of waste management for neighborhood women and transformed the value and treatment of garbage within the home. The implementation of fees for service—or the devolution of the costs of basic services to the community—is one of the hallmark elements of the neoliberal model of urban public service reform and its associated reconfiguration of geographies of social reproduction.[17] Consistent with wider trends, the Tonghor community-based trash project was rooted in the principle of the poor paying more for development. The project's feasibility study emphasized that the user fee for the door-to-door trash collection was an important part of involving participants in a sustainable community-driven model of public service. Ironically, in this same document, less than half of Tonghor residents said that they would be willing to contribute financially to the project (ENDA 1999). Despite this, the payment scheme was laid out in an appendix section entitled "When the Poor Finance Development" (ENDA 1999, 136). Each household was asked to pay 1,000 CFA per month (roughly two U.S. dollars), to be collected at the end of the month by the animatrices. A flat rate calculated per household, this fee was separate from the municipal household garbage tax (TEOM), calculated based on property values (see chapter 1 for more details on the TEOM).

The animatrices faced intense resistance to paying the user fee. This impinged on the meager "reward" they received and was a key factor in the decline of the project. Before the project was launched, residents had received their trash collection by the municipality for "free," given that the vast majority of the residents either did not pay the TEOM or were unaware that they paid it. For those who actually did pay the tax, the new fee represented a doubling of their payment for garbage services. The fines imposed on those who continued dumping on the beach, moreover, acted to criminalize those who attempted to opt out. The user fee and efforts to educate neighborhood women on sorting methods transformed the value and treatment of the garbage within the home as well. Charging for the amount of garbage discarded in effect brought women deeper into the management of their waste alongside their neighborly animatrices through incentivizing strategies to reduce waste, including storing, burying, and attempting to dump garbage off the radar of local officials. Given the controversial nature of these fees and their widespread rejection by community members, the animatrices' role in soliciting the user fee was a sticking point, to put it mildly. In effect, it placed these women as the taxman, supposedly drawing on their intimacies in the community, but, in truth, locating them on difficult terrain with their neighbors. As some of the most marginalized members of the community, being asked to solicit money from their neighbors was highly problematic.

The user fee was also a key way that the projects reconfigured the gendered landscape of household waste management and household bargaining power. As was to be expected, the gendered division of trash labor informed household members' priorities regarding household expenditures and valuation of the service. Because they are in charge of managing household cleanliness, women were more willing to pay for the door-to-door service as it alleviated their trash burden and obviated their need to risk dumping on the beach. However, because few women in Tonghor are financially independent, they found it difficult to make this contribution. The user fee interfaced with family power dynamics to disproportionately burden women with the costs associated with maintaining the household. Women shouldered this burden, but often with difficulty.

On the other hand, asking husbands to pay for the service was often problematic if they did not prioritize the service as much as their wives did, or if household finances were already strained. The user fee sometimes precipitated intense conflicts between husbands and wives and the animatrices found themselves unwittingly caught in the middle of this tension. One animatrice described an instance when she was inadvertently ensnarled in a marital clash through simply informing a nosy husband of how much his wife had paid in trash collection fees over a few months. Shocked to hear the difference between what he had given his wife and what she had paid into the project, the husband had asked the animatrice to serve as a witness as he confronted his wife, making the animatrice extremely uncomfortable. Sometimes this tension made for a challenging research environment. On more than one occasion, a joint interview with male and female heads of household devolved into an argument over the fees.

In the end, most households refused to pay the user fee. Beyond their inability to pay was a resistance to paying out of principle. Most residents firmly believed that garbage collection should be a free public service and thus took the user fee as just one more symbol of the state's negligence and incapacity to serve the needs of its citizens. The following statement by a female head of household sums up many residents' perspectives on the fee: "It's good and it's not good! Because we're citizens, the state is supposed to help us . . . the government should be able to pay this money! [The project is] a good thing because we get rid of our garbage, but it's not good because it lessens our [buying] power. . . . If you put your trash on the cart, you are going to pay! It's good because it cleans our neighborhood but bad because it hurts us." This sentiment was particularly intense among the Geejndar, who not only were the least able to pay but also distrusted the Lebou authorities. They viewed the project suspiciously as just one more scheme by the Lebou establishment that did not have their best interests at heart. Together with other residents, their refusal to pay constituted a key reason why the project foundered. The user fee was just one more element in the project's lack of success in actually winning over the community to the idea of individual and community responsibility for waste management.

Municipal Dissent

Though it was an official partner, the district government never fully bought into the project, and municipal officials were quite candid in expressing serious concerns with the model it represented.[18] Issa Ndoye, the official at the Yoff mayor's office charged with coordinating household waste collection with the municipality of Dakar, admitted that he had been opposed to the project from the beginning. When he met with ENDA and the local community group while it was being launched, he warned them that the project would "bring Mbeubeuss [the dump] to Dakar." In response, they reproached him, saying: "You only care about the trucks!" After multiple requests to stop the trucks from collecting in the Tonghor neighborhood, he finally relented and told his guys to skirt the neighborhood. Then, "fifteen days later, it was Mbeubeuss." The issue of the transfer station was trickier than the question of not collecting in the neighborhood. Because the collectors were paid by the ton, the new system, which involved separating out the organics for the pilot compost project, further discouraged the city from coordinating the collection at the transfer station. The challenges of loading the accumulating garbage deposited there made their job even more difficult. Within a short time, the municipality stopped transferring garbage from Yoff to Mbeubeuss and the station quickly began to overflow.

By 2003, after less than a year of operation, the Tonghor community-based trash-collection project was in shambles: many if not most residents refused to pay the user fee, the overworked animatrices were exhausted from—and no longer rewarded for—their labors, and even the horse-cart drivers were fed up as their salaries became increasingly irregular. The dispute between the municipality and the neighborhood authorities over the project, furthermore, had precipitated disaster at the point of coordination near the airport. The transfer station had become a towering mountain of garbage, attracting hundreds of circling birds. When the national aviation administration weighed in over the bird problem, the project was definitively cancelled. After the literal weight of the garbage had kept the municipality away, it was the material force of this trash—its unsightly messiness, insalubrious stench, and the nuisance and danger of the pests it attracted—that hastened the project's abandonment. Precarious labor, moreover, was a weak link in the technology chain forming this infrastructure, threatening its very coherence and sustainability. Issa summed it up in these words: "We can use horse carts in the village, but their place is not here in the city. The horse-cart project was not a good idea. Ask the women [animatrices] who were involved! We need to stick to our trucks." Issa is referring here to much more than infrastructure's function; he's also invoking its affective, material, social, and symbolic dimensions. For him, the technologies employed in the horse-cart project and the structures of feeling to which they gave rise were all wrong. Only investment in the material backbone of the municipal system—the trash trucks—would contribute to a more coherent modern urban infrastructure.

Soon after the project disappeared, the municipal trash trucks began collecting along their usual circuit in Tonghor, with some changes made in an attempt to reach the hard-to-access areas. More recently, the service has improved markedly, tracking gains made to the municipal collectors' working conditions since 2009. Residents currently make do with this service, deploy creative strategies to manage their garbage, and periodically defy the ban and use the beach during collection crises. Besides occasional efforts by the neighborhood's youth and women to clean specific areas when they become clogged with refuse, no comprehensive community-based project has been attempted since 2003.

Conclusions

This chapter has further charted the gendering of splintering urbanism (Graham and Marvin 2001) when infrastructure is devolved onto labor through community-based development. The scaling back of material trash infrastructure and its replacement by coerced voluntary labor of marginalized women fractures this urban public service, leaving women to literally pick up the pieces of a degrading infrastructure as the neighborhood's new "housekeepers." Community—in all of its gendered and ethnicized connotations—is a key technology in processes of governing-through-disposability. Autochthonous claims to the city work through gendered labor and its material power.

The Yoff community-based trash project reconfigured the value of trash work and the image of community, in the name of empowerment and efficiency, with key implications for local politics and state power. Extending women's social-reproductive duties into the public space, it displaced the state's role in managing and sustaining the reproduction of labor power and shifted governmental lines of accountability. Just as in Dakar's municipal trash sector, this precipitated competition between governmental authorities— in this case, between the local municipality and local customary leaders. Despite being an official partner on the project, the Yoff local government was excluded from key project decisions as local customary leaders were seen as closer to the population. It retaliated by ceasing to transfer the garbage to the dump. Far from a simple "technical problem" as ENDA contended, the transfer station was the broken joint in this new infrastructural system, disrupting the orderly flow of waste and filth out of the city that ensured the protection of the city's residents. The unsightly garbage pile was the material manifestation of the disorder wreaked by this increasingly incoherent infrastructural system.

Probing the infrastructure built by community-based development projects and the technologies they instrumentalize illuminates the material power of these new relations and raises some key questions for their functionality and sustainability as public services. If the trucks represented the modernist vision of a comprehensive, networked public service, then the enormous garbage pile was the residue of the archaic horse-cart fantasy of infrastructure's past. In fostering the autonomy of the neighborhood from the local state, the neoliberal vision of NGO-driven development contributed to a fragmenting urbanism of disarticulated infrastructures cast as traditional modes of life. Community-based development introduced here the possibility of an urbanism that is increasingly splintered along divisive, elitist community lines and in which infrastructure may gradually be replaced with women's laboring bodies. The precarity that this introduces for women and their social relations in turn produces new precarities in the infrastructural system as a whole.

So-called green, appropriate technologies were the material scaffolding of these projects' infrastructural vision. Far from the orderly aesthetic of the bourgeois environmentalism associated with world-city-aspirational projects, the aesthetic vision conjured was of a messy urbanism romanticizing the historical virtues of the "local" and harkening back to a sustainable rural past. Not only was the low-tech system assumed to be better suited to this particular type of community, but the Lebou were purported to be better suited for this green approach because of their historically situated "green" lifestyles. What does appropriate technology require and what does it cancel out? What possible future does it render appropriate? In the end, the project only succeeded in pushing the garbage from inside the neighborhood to a festering pile on its periphery. This raises the question of when green becomes greenwash in the service of projects that are no more clean, efficient, or sustainable than municipal services.

What, moreover, do projects like these mean for the aspirations they inspire, or in other words, how do we make sense of their claims for "empowerment"? These low-tech material technologies only work in conjunction with the social technology of labor-intensive participation. But participation has been revealed to marshal discourses of identity to devalue certain spheres of work. In contrast to the women municipal trash workers who benefited from the progressive formalization and thus valuation of their jobs, the animatrices saw no significant benefits to their standing and the project eroded their ability to care for their families. Attention to the vital materiality of infrastructural labor and associated discourses of disposability draws into sharp relief the limitations of amaterial conceptions of empowerment that do not look at the content of the work inspired by participatory infrastructures and their implications for social relations. Conceptions of empowerment that erode the material conditions of everyday life and threaten the stability of the social community are clearly disabling.

An analysis of empowerment must take on, furthermore, the expectations and experiences of those participating. The animatrices often articulated their motivation for participating in these projects as a hope for future "opportunities" that might be made available. Instead, the animatrices witnessed a devaluation of their standing in the community because of the negation of their labor value, the nefarious implications of working with waste, and the uncomfortable tasks they were charged with as the new taxman. This experience stands in sharp contrast to the claims of empowerment that live on in the best-practices literature, and highlights the way that the crisis of social reproduction works through material discipline enacted on women's bodies. The end of the project was bittersweet for the animatrices because of all of the sweat, hope, and pride they had poured into their work. If we understand development to be "the management of a promise" then "what if the promise does not deliver?" (J. N. Pieterse 2000, 176). The mismanagement of hope is perhaps the most disempowering element of these reconfigurations of value at Dakar's margins.

At 11 a.m. on Friday, April 27, 2007, in a large, bare-bones meeting room, a crowd of trash workers waited anxiously for their union's general assembly to begin on "Senegalese time." I had arrived with my research assistant when the meeting was officially convened at 10 a.m. and was excited to witness the gears behind the movement's strike campaign. This was just the beginning of my being brought into the fold of the union's inner workings and I was impressed by the energy in the room. Some of the workers had come straight from work and still wore the tattered remains of old uniforms from a company long since disappeared and plastic sandals that offered minimal protection on the job. The union's leaders sat at one end of the room's huge table, mostly dressed in respectable *boubous* (traditional West African sleeved robes) or button-up shirts. The anticipation was palpable and the temperature continued to rise as more and more workers filled the poorly ventilated room.

The crowd hushed as the union's secretary general, Madany Sy, entered the room. An attractive man in his early forties, he wore smart glasses and a commanding presence. Sy's demeanor demanded respect, yet he appeared humble and approachable. A gifted public speaker, he spoke to a rapt audience that occasionally erupted into applause. The following excerpt from his speech is translated from the Wolof:

> All of you are incited to march on May 1 because this is the day for
> workers. Even if [the event] is a celebration, it's a celebration without

joy. It's a chance for us to show our discontent and our disagreement. . . . Despite the fact of our great difficulties, we are muted, we work in the shadows. . . . Comrades: the authorities of this country do not respect the cleaning workers. They do not take us into account. We have really been deceived. . . . We are the left out, the forgotten of the republic. They treat us like garbage. This must stop today! We must take responsibility for ourselves. . . . The most important thing is that we go together to the end. That we are united. . . . We have worked in this sector for years without being hired on because it was a passage we were obliged to make. This is why, I tell you, we keep working. Each one of us does his job. This is all we've got, and it's a way of living our religion. But if our work is oppressing us, of course we have the right to rise up within the rules of the game. We have addressed ourselves to everyone, and none of them have met with us. We thank the religious leaders because they pray for us. . . . The problem we have is with the politicians. A politician never says where he is going. . . . They have been fooling us for years. That should push each and every one of us to take up our responsibilities. . . .

If they arrest me during the week, I call for you to keep fighting! [The crowd erupts into murmurs and noise, then applause.] My father used to say: "When I am in front, follow me; when I move back, kill me; when I die, avenge me." [Rowdy applause.] I want that to be our slogan because we are doing the most dangerous work that there is. [Someone interjects: "We are all dead."] We are no longer living. We are stressed. Before you receive your salary, you have to fight for it. This needs to stop. Now, we have taken all the other paths we could, without a response. The mayor of Dakar asked me to warn him before I spoke on the radio. He didn't want to hear his name, so I accepted. I waited a year, then I called him. He ignored me. I write to him, without response. He says bad things about me. . . . I don't have much, but I have my dignity. He has more money than me but he is not more dignified. We all have the same dignity, my friends. We are the same as the mayor. We are all human beings. A man has the right to rise up when he feels oppressed by another man. We have the right to speak the truth. If people are afraid to tell the truth to his face, we will do it. . . .

In view of this critical situation, today we launch the second plan of action. We have decided to radicalize the movement from Dakar to Yène [the farthest periphery of the Dakar region]. [Applause.] Comrades, please understand that when I speak of radicalization, that does not mean acts of vandalism, destruction, or fights. Don't forget that we are republicans. . . . The people will support us. . . . The state needs to fulfill its responsibilities and solve the problem of the trash sector. . . . It's thanks to you that Dakar is a nice city to visit, that the people don't fall ill. Do you know this? Do you know that, thanks to you, development is possible in this country? You play a major role in the [protection of the] environment. . . . We, my friends, are strong, thanks to God. We believe in our profession. It's a passion. We are dignified and we do this work for God. We have been sacrificing for this work for fifteen years. . . . God willing, we will be victorious in the end.

Sy's speech was perfectly calibrated to the mood of the moment. It gave voice to the suffering of the workers and praised them for the efficacy and spiritual value of their work, while conjuring the sense of injustice that would be required to wage an audacious strike that would paralyze the city's waste infrastructure—and, by extension, the city as a whole. By taking on the "politicians" who had ignored them for so long, he made it clear that they had exhausted all avenues for a negotiated solution to the crisis. After a few more short speeches and then responses from the crowd, the meeting was adjourned with a short blessing from a religious leader. The workers gradually filed out. The crowd was riled up, but serious; they knew what they had to do and were ready. After the May 1 march, Sy called for a general strike and most of Dakar's sixteen hundred trash workers did not collect the city's trash for two weeks. In solidarity, whole neighborhoods coordinated "trash revolts" of their own, dumping their accumulated household waste into public squares and streets to compel the state to respond to the workers' grievances. As the city choked on its own refuse, the union received its first meeting with Dakar's then mayor, Pape Diop. Within a short while, the union had received two months of back pay and a number of significant concessions. After more than seven grueling years of mobilizing and negotiating, they finally signed their collective bargaining agreement in 2014. Winning formal contracts, medical care, and other benefits, the trash sector pioneered the reversal of austerity management trends, heralding the possibility of a new era of urban governance in Dakar.

Previous chapters have examined the devolution of infrastructure onto labor in Dakar's garbage sector through different formulas of participation as a mode of governing through disposability. This chapter examines how the people who constitute these vital infrastructures refuse their conditions of precarity. Since 2006, the trash-workers union has catapulted trash management and the plight of the city's trash workers to the center of the municipal and national political stage, despite an environment strongly prejudiced against those working with garbage and a political climate generally hostile to labor. I trace here the trash-workers union movement as it gained steam in the 2000s, in order to explain the dynamism of the workers' tactics of refusal and illuminate the intimate communities of affect that forge infrastructures. Through examining their identities as workers and strategies as a union, I show how the particular resonance of their cleaning labor and their refusal to clean through striking have validated garbage work, earned them widespread public support, and, in turn, allowed them to stem the tide of labor flexibilization.

The material and symbolic resonance of waste sculpts the meaning of cleaning labor and, in turn, prefigures the power of trash as a political force. Waste's powers to disrupt and the salience of its opposite—cleanliness—as a symbol of faith and piety are key features of the political valence of trash in Dakar. The counterhegemonic force of trash rebellion in Dakar was forged out of the specific subjectivities conditioned by the corporeal practice of cleaning and manifested in the creative animation of the material itself in rebellion. This chapter begins with an examination of the workers' main lever, the general trash strike, as a powerful disruption of the proper function of disposal infrastructure in organizing the orderly flow of waste out of the city. It then considers the communicative channels that enabled the neighborhood trash revolts to scale up workers' critiques and bestowed meaning onto trash work and protest. Finally, it explores the architectures of faith undergirding the workers' movement, built on the conviction that the labor of cleaning the city is an act of piety. Waste and spirituality are powerfully connected and Islam is central to sculpting the moral geographies surrounding waste work in Dakar. Rooted in the value of purity in Islam and the embodied practice of cleaning, associations between cleaning and virtue evoked a shared moral compass which motivated workers to persevere, won over ordinary residents to their cause, and validated this vital infrastructure on an ethical level.

Chapter 1 explored the representational logic of trash infrastructure, or the political address of different infrastructural assemblages in the performance of governing-through-garbage. This chapter unpacks the values and vernacular moralities through which these infrastructures are felt and understood by the people comprising the social systems they are built upon. In doing so, the chapter expands the definition of what is usually taken into account in studying infrastructure to further demonstrate how the social and affective components of infrastructure matter. Infrastructures are complex ecological arrangements that include feelings and modes of understanding, ritual practices, and spiritual systems of order. The structures of feeling that waste infrastructures evoke emerge out of the material practice of cleaning work. The bricolage labors involved in caring for broken-down machines and a degrading city are bound up, in other words, with bricolage modes of meaning making—a sort of art of conservation of the self in a landscape of disrepair.[1] I describe this art as a piety of refusal that operates as a personal resource as well as a strategic platform for union organizing.

Spirituality is not usually seen as the purview of conventional urban studies nor of studies of infrastructure. However, new materialist scholars and ethnographers of infrastructure are increasingly paying attention to the relevance of spirituality for fully grappling with the force of matter and the wide gamut of relationships embodied in infrastructure. Maria Puig de la Bellacasa draws on Susan Leigh Star in her development of an approach to studying infrastructure that "is not only about materials but also about meanings that are neither separable from, nor reducible to, what we usually conceive as materiality."[2] She argues for spirituality to be taken into account as a key but often overlooked element adhering between the socio-natural communities that make up infrastructures. This conception of "material spirituality" is useful for thinking about Dakar's trash infrastructures because it emphasizes that spirituality is intertwined with material practice but is also something that inspires a "spirit" of community.

Within the growing field of ethnographies of infrastructure, there is an emerging literature on ritual practices animated by infrastructures and the spectral modes through which they are understood and valued. Though this work is important for investigating the vernacular valuations of infrastructure, much of the Africanist literature interprets spiritual understandings (particularly occult imaginings) of infrastructure as reactionary critiques of capitalism, globalization, neoliberalism, and other elements of contemporary modernity.[3] However, as Miho Ishii (2016, 4) points out, reducing spiritual understandings of infrastructure to modes of venting anxieties about modernity is inadequate for fully grappling with the rich "ways in which [people] are entangled with, or encompassed by, nature and divinities." Much more than simple moral panic at neoliberalism's violences, the piety of refusal represents a constructive striving to align moral and material economies in the wake of the failures of the secular nationalist project.

The significance of spirituality in Dakar's waste infrastructures is consistent with the well-documented role of spirituality in making urban publics across diverse African contexts. There is a long tradition of scholarship examining the historical relationship between religious identity and the public sphere in Africa, and it is well recognized that the widespread failures of secular development and patterns of millennial capitalism have catalyzed the rising influence of Christian and Islamic networks in urban areas. A growing literature takes up the shifting role of religion in anchoring urban populations and mediating contests of urban citizenship in the contemporary era.[4] The intensification of religious identification, visibility, and associations in urban areas calls into question normative models of the secular public sphere and long-held associations between secularism, modernity, and democracy.[5] Scholars of Islamic modernities emphasize the increasing role of Muslim civil societies in furnishing a forum for the development of the public sphere and sparking reasoned discourse on modern problems such as labor rights, gender, and democracy.[6] This is a far cry from a view of religious movements as mere self-help initiatives that act to buffer or channel the radicalization of the discontented,[7] or of spiritual conceptions of neoliberal infrastructures as simple modes of venting anxieties about modernity, and offers an important critique of the assumed incompatibility between Islam and forms of public life. Most of the research on Islam and politics, however, focuses on reformist or radical Islamic movements or heightening divisions between communities of faith. Less attention has been paid to movements conjuring a more expansive Muslim identity that aim to reform the state, or, moreover, to how Islam may provide the language for constructively contesting neoliberal austerity.

In the Senegalese context, there is an extensive tradition of scholarship examining the interpenetration of Islam and the political sphere. The thrust of Senegalese Islamic studies, however, has been dominated by perspectives focused on the role of the Sufi brotherhoods and the power of the marabouts. The main current of this research has been concerned with explaining Senegalese "exceptionalism" through rooting the Socialist Party state's hegemony from Independence in 1960 to 2000 within its mutualistic links with the Mouride brotherhood. Instead of privileging the historical social contract between the state and the brotherhoods, the economic utility of Islamic organizations, or the direct involvement of religious leaders in political contests, this chapter joins with other recent interventions that move beyond a preoccupation with the functional aspects of Islamic institutions to a concern with quotidian experiences of religious identity.[8] Building on the work of Mamadou Diouf, Mara Leichtman, and others, I am interested in the way that modes of religiosity craft new communities, political cultures, and moral geographies.[9] In this way, I prioritize deeper investigation into Muslim disciples' identities and experiences of religiosity to foreground the importance of the cultural roots of political consciousness and citizenship practices. The piety of refusal is a lived, embodied, and material mode through which spiritual practice becomes civic virtue.

Striking Disorder in Dakar

Madany Sy and his fellow workers founded their union, le Syndicat National des travailleurs du nettoiement (National Cleaning Workers Union; SNTN), in 2000 in anticipation of the changes under way with the election of President Abdoulaye Wade (known as *Alternance*).[10] The head of his local youth group in a central Dakar neighborhood, Sy had been intensely involved in the Set/Setal movement, and then had emerged as a tireless advocate and leader among the trash workers starting in the mid-1990s. The passion and time that Sy put into the trenches of dirty work as a trash collector was a major element of his popularity. After languishing in informality during Mamadou Diop's participatory sector, the unionists' goal was to reverse the flexibilization of trash labor. In the words of Sy's longtime comrade and union cofounder, Noumou Ndiaye: "The workers were treated more or less like slaves! It was necessary to fight to eradicate all of that!"

One of their key goals in forming the union was to avoid the politicization that had soured their experience of working for Mayor Mamadou Diop. Though many of the union's members and founders (including Sy) were originally active in the Socialist Party during the 1990s, in forming their union they made the important choice to affiliate with an *autonome* (independent) union federation in order to retain their independence from political parties.[11] Their choice of la Confédération des syndicats autonomes du Sénégal (Federation of Independent Unions of Senegal; CSA) was a decision taken explicitly to avoid the influence of political parties. It did not, however, immunize the union from government intervention, which continued in different form under President Wade (Ndiaye 2010). Overall, the 2000s was a period exhibiting what labor scholar Alfred Inis Ndiaye (2008, 2010,

2013) described as a blocked negotiation process and the intensification of conflict between labor and the state. As political parties and government officials continued to try to meddle in unionized labor, and unions had no recourse but to use "hot" strategies (strikes) to resist these and make their voices heard, new labor relations were being forged with difficulty.

After an initially hopeful period in the first half of the decade, with the institutional reconfiguration in 2006 the workers found themselves thrown into another intense period of job insecurity and difficult working conditions.[12] In the otherwise grueling period from 2006 to 2009, they waged a series of strike-based campaigns that maneuvered the question of trash labor to the center of the political stage in Dakar. Waging periodic general strikes that held the city captive to its own garbage, tirelessly educating and agitating over the radio waves, and even reaching out to international observers and activists for their cause,[13] the union won the support of the Dakarois they served and gained the attention of the local and national state. By 2009, they had emerged as one of the most visible and dynamic unions active in contemporary Senegal and had won some key concessions. For the Dakarois, this period was experienced as a full-on trash "crisis" characterized by frequent service disruptions, the accumulation of garbage in the public space, and government inaction.

A series of strikes in 2007 just after President Wade was reelected were particularly important toward crystalizing the union's visibility and public support. Wade was reelected that year to little fanfare as his popularity faded in step with a series of controversies and growing disappointment in his vision for running the country. When the contract with the private waste-management company AMA had been revoked months before, the workers had hoped for a new institutional arrangement for garbage that would put an end to their insecurity once and for all. As months passed and their labor conditions continued to deteriorate, however, they called for a series of trash strikes that wreaked havoc on the city to bring attention to their plight and force the government's hand. In many cases, strikes were called at union general assemblies like that described at the beginning of the chapter, but at other times they were announced by the leadership and radiated out to the workers by word of mouth. The usual directive was simply to refrain from collecting the trash the next day. Often, workers still gathered together at their normal workplace hangouts to discuss the events as they transpired. From the most central Dakar district to the farthest reach into the city's periphery, workers stayed home for as many as two weeks in a row. Garbage accumulated everywhere—in homes, yards, roadsides, drainage canals, construction sites, and empty lots. Neighborhood women went to great lengths to carefully manage their accumulating garbage to avoid dangerous insalubrious conditions, but—as we'll see in the next section—many became fed up and were driven to take drastic action.

Star (1999) describes infrastructure as most visible when it breaks down; similarly, Dakar's labor-intensive infrastructure was most visible during a strike. Given the propensity for quick putrefaction, to maintain urban order the proper functioning of a solid-waste system requires unrelenting daily evacuation out of homes, into the waste grid, and finally to the city's dump in the outskirts of the city. The modern city is a clean, sanitized space where waste is carted out of sight, out of mind, allowing production and consumption to continue. The blockage of that disposal process and the accumulation of urban waste in public spaces is the ultimate indicator of crisis and dysfunction. As Sarah A. Moore (2009, 428) reflected on waste strikes in Oaxaca, "because garbage is inherently misplaced, waste represents a risk to modern urban societies," and a politics of "manifestation"—or rendering garbage visible through striking—becomes an effective political tool because of its potential to destabilize institutions of modernity.

Striking, moreover, is not just an ordinary technical breakdown of infrastructure; it is the purposeful sabotaging of the proper functioning of infrastructure. Trash strikes render infrastructure the "*political terrain* for the negotiation of moral-political questions" and garbage itself a vibrant "protagonist" of protests (von Schnitzler 2013, 671, italics in original). Much in the same way that prepaid water meters in Soweto (von Schnitzler 2013, 2016) and water pipes in Mumbai (Anand 2011) became the material tools of rebellion, so did garbage infrastructures take center stage in wider modes of critiquing logics of governing the city. Such disruption was particularly resonant in Dakar because it exposed the laboring bodies onto which the infrastructure had been devolved. Strikes are the flip side of the performative mode of infrastructure; they are the way that the living components of these socio-technical systems invert the representational logic of governing through garbage by withdrawing their labor. Workers' refusal to be the castaways of society was embodied in their refusal to labor. As the primary technology of the infrastructure, in other words, the laboring body itself became the political terrain of refusal. For those few workers who went so far as to wage hunger strikes in protest, the withdrawal of their labor went even further in manifesting the violences of an infrastructure devolved onto labor.

These were not, furthermore, just any strikes. The material and symbolic force of waste made it a particularly potent matter of rebellion. Those who are associated with garbage are keenly situated for disruption, as not only the most impure in society but also the bridge connecting the outside—which can be "rubbished"—to the clean inside (see Chakrabarty 1991; Furniss 2012; Scanlan 2005; Searle-Chatterjee 1979). Following Mary Searle-Chatterjee's (1979) study of the Benares street sweepers in India, this can be seen as the "power of the polluted," or the capacity of abjected waste workers to trouble the divides between order and disorder.[14] In Dakar, trash workers manifested their power through their strategic alliances with natural processes of decomposition. Festering piles of decomposing garbage amplified workers' grievances, producing a kind of lively, unofficial infrastructure that competed with public rights of way, obstructed other public goods, and obliged new ways of living in the city.[15] The stench and filth of rotting garbage, combined with its resonance as impurity, rendered the city dangerous and called for the resolution of associated risks with urgency. The longer the trash was left to fester, the more hazardous it became. As described in the next section, trash strikes in Dakar exerted particular force because they were multiplied and made manifest by the supportive action of neighborhoods across the city.

Manifesting the Public Secret of Waste

On a warm morning in May 2007, the central Dakar neighborhood of HLM Fass was far too quiet. As household women went about their usual morning cleaning activities, they were well aware of the eerie absence of a sound that usually hastened them along: the incessant honking of their neighborhood trash truck as it did the rounds, emptying this dense neighborhood of its most dangerous product. It was day ten of the trash workers strike, and while most of the Fassois were aware of the conflict between the union and government from the frequent radio coverage of the drama, this was no consolation as they tried to keep their homes clean and their children safe. The smelly remains of the week—including fish guts and goat entrails, plastic bags, and vegetable matter—were building up in the piles, rice sacks, and buckets used as trashcans in the working-class Dakar neighborhood. Although HLM Fass was originally planned to accommodate functionaries in Dakar, with the collapse of state employment in the 1970s and 1980s it came to house a diverse set of mostly working-class families. By 2007, the ill-maintained multistory buildings were home to a mix of renters and owners who made do with the cramped three-room apartments (see figure 4.1). Though they

FIGURE 4.1. One of the main high-rise buildings in HLM Fass, before the trash strikes of 2007. Author's photo, 2007.

added ash to the garbage to mitigate the stench and tied it up in multiple plastic grocery bags, the waste overflowed, cluttering courtyards, balconies, soccer fields, and the local sewage canal (Canal IV) and stinking up homes and public meeting areas.

By sundown, a few neighborhood residents were inspired to tell the government that the problem had continued long enough. After the evening prayer, they gathered more residents together and discussed the idea of a revolt. As midnight approached, the idea spread like wildfire. Mothers, daughters, sons, and fathers alike left their homes that balmy night and went about their task quickly and quietly, piling their week's refuse high in the middle of the boulevard on which they knew the politicians would be traveling the next morning on their way downtown. As a targeted message to the local district mayor, they also sculpted a special tower of detritus directly in front of his dilapidated office in the heart of HLM Fass, a short walk away from the capital's Independence obelisk. Across the city, other neighborhoods did the same, ridding their homes of their dirt and decay and depositing it into the public space. In Tonghor, Yoff, where the pilot participatory garbage collection project had long since disappeared, women and girls' only recourse was to defy a community ordinance and dump their garbage on the beach, where it would inevitably wash into the ocean and tangle their fishermen's nets.

An older female resident, Demba, who was an active participant in the dumping in HLM Fass, explained her motivation for mounting the trash revolt:

> We realized that the trash trucks hadn't come for two weeks. Fass is not very spacious; there was a nauseating smell throughout the neighborhood. People couldn't even breathe normally. What's more, there were children who were playing next to the trash where worms were starting to come out of the ground. They could have gone back home to eat without washing their hands. . . . There was a risk of disease! [Dumping] was the only solution that we had since the mayor refused to resolve the problem. It was our way of letting him know that we were not happy with the situation, of forcing him to react.

Demba's explanation marshaled her authority over household matters and family well-being in order to justify her rebellion through dumping. It was a last resort, she explained, one that any upstanding citizen would take. One of the key organizers, Samba—a young law student born and raised in HLM Fass—described his experience as follows:

One day my older sister said "Don't you smell that odor?" I decided to do something about it. . . . Around 11 p.m., I couldn't wait any longer. . . . I grabbed brooms and sacks [of garbage]. At the beginning, we were two or three people, but then other people passed and saw us and then, all of a sudden, everyone came out. We did it right here [by the mayor's office] and there was also an enormous pile there on the road. [The dumping] was hard work and we finished at the earliest around 3 a.m. . . . But, it worked!

As Samba notes, the trash revolts that day did work: the mayor of Dakar intervened immediately to clean up the trash blocking the streets by noon (see figures 4.2 and 4.3).

Only after the trash workers continued their strike with a second plan of action, however, did the mayor finally meet with the union to resolve the dispute. A few days later, the workers were finally paid two months' back pay and went directly back to work, until the next round of strikes held a couple of months later for other grievances. The media coverage of the neighborhood revolts was extensive (e.g., M. Fall 2007; Nettali 2007; *Sud Quotidien* 2007). The following passage from an article entitled "Insalubrité: Dakar (ré)envahie!" (Insalubrity: Dakar [Re]invaded!) characterizes much of the reporting:

Insalubrity has again taken over the neighborhoods. The Senegalese capital is invaded by heaps of rubbish dumped by angry populations. . . . Colobane, Fass, Gueule Tapée, Médina, HLM Fass are under the yoke of the garbage. Outraged by the inaction of the authorities, the residents have reacted. The week-long strike [by workers,] who claim two months of back pay for a total of 24 million [CFA], seems to be at the source of this situation. . . . We are attacked by the nauseating odors of Dirtiness, queen of the capital. The residents, discontented to see the waste continue to pile up in front of their homes, before our eyes, dump their trash onto the road.[16]

The trash crisis was a lens through which many residents registered their disenchantment with the state of Alternance, the new political era ushered in with the election of President Abdoulaye Wade in 2000. April 2007 was just one month after the recent presidential elections, in which Wade won again with an overwhelming majority but this time little jubilation from the Dakarois. It was generally accepted that these elections signaled not a vote

FIGURES 4.2 AND 4.3. The remains of a 2007 trash revolt in HLM Fass, a few hours after the mayor sent in a special collection force to remove the garbage directly blocking the roads. Author's photos, 2007.

of support for Wade, but rather a vote of no confidence in his rivals, and were a consequence of having many candidates in the final rounds.[17] Support for Wade was dwindling, as Alternance had brought little opportunity to most Dakarois while the cost of living skyrocketed.

The only signs that Wade was "working" were the massive infrastructure projects that had transformed Dakar into a messy construction site. The extensive road-network project in the capital was a central part of Wade's preparations to show off for the international community at the 11th OIC summit to be held in Dakar in spring 2008. "We cannot eat overpasses!" was a common response of residents asked to comment on these investments. Offering up a litany of critiques of Alternance, many jokingly referred to it as "Alternoos"—a play on words disparaging government officials' reputation for partying (noos), instead of working. Wade's acceleration of neoliberal reforms in many sectors was further dismantling welfare services, enabling unprecedented wealth accumulation, and exacerbating social inequalities. Urban infrastructure was the material manifestation of these disparities and the object and symbol of urban protest.

Two of the organizers of the neighborhood trash revolts in HLM Fass—Babacar and Ibrahima—were especially outspoken about their disillusionment with Alternance. Having worked for part of the year in Spain, they were back for a few months to spend time with their families. Becoming embroiled in the trash crisis was far from how they had planned to spend their vacations. Both had been active organizers for Wade's party in 2000, but they admitted that the last seven years had been overwhelmingly disappointing. Interviewed together, they gave an uncensored critique of Alternance: "This problem [the garbage crisis] is the result of a lack of political will. During all of this, they are bypassing the media, buying the presidential airplane, placing government officials in the most optimal working conditions. Really, those people [government officials] are Europeans over there—in an underdeveloped country!" Similarly, the head of the HLM Fass neighborhood association described Alternance in these terms: "What is going on? While [the politicians'] lifestyles improve, the people are dying of hunger! We are talking about [people making] billions! The Senegalese people are still hungry! And what do we have to show for it? A few roads?" These perspectives highlight the injustices of neoliberal accumulation through describing the excesses that came to characterize the ruling regime. President Wade's performative investments in infrastructure had become the signals of uneven development, and garbage in the public space the symbol of political dysfunction.

Though the HLM Fass neighborhood is far from the most disadvantaged district in greater Dakar, accumulating garbage represented for residents their marginalization with regard to urban public services and, more broadly, the landscape of political patronage in the city. For many, it fueled their disenchantment with politics in general. As one HLM Fass resident summed it up, "La politique est poubelle [politics are trash]." Samba (the young law student), for his part, reflected on the garbage crisis by saying he would never, ever, get involved in politics. "All I do in this neighborhood is for God. It's to have grace, never profit."

Like the trash strikes, public dumping by residents deploys the power of waste to contest ordering paradigms. Through a politics of manifestation, residents reveal the public secret of waste, relocate the blame for polluted living conditions, and repudiate their abjection. In the words of one neighborhood revolt organizer who had piled his garbage in the street, "They think we're dirty because we live here. But, we are not dirty! This is the mayor's trash, so we gave it back to him." The act of externalizing the garbage that they had struggled to manage in the home was a refusal to be sullied by the state's negligence. If the proper flow of waste is out of sight, out of mind, then the dumping worked to disrupt the privilege that comes with forgetting and thus the division between those who can discard and forget and those who cannot. Trash strikes and dumping gain their creative power through rendering trash—as dirt—"matter out of place" (Douglas 1966).

Beyond their power as a creative lever of contestation, the trash revolts also reveal the social infrastructure binding the workers and the residents they served. Participants in the HLM Fass revolts were strikingly unified in their support of the trash workers. In aiming their action precisely at "the politicians" (the local district mayor, the mayor of Dakar, and the other political figures who drive along the boulevard to get to their offices downtown), their goals were twofold: to convey their larger discontent with being neglected and to force the government to resolve the dispute with the garbage workers. The following statement by the two main trash-revolt organizers, Babacar and Ibrahima, is illustrative:

> What we did was a total revolt. Because we are revolted by the attitude of the state! It's the state that should fix this problem. We noticed that this was a recurring problem that had returned again. These workers are not well paid. They are the heads of households who live a pitiable existence facing three months without pay. We think that is terrible. . . .

It's revolting [*revoltant*]. Revolting. Revolting. This is a fundamental public service. . . . It's the state's responsibility. It's the state that pays the workers, that pushed them to go on strike. Here in Africa, a father can't go three months without receiving his salary. That's totally impossible! We think that the state is responsible. When we did the "dumping" of the trash on the main road, we knew that was exactly where the [government] authorities passed. The next morning, they went and got people to collect that trash. That goes to show that the only language those people understand is, in the end, violence. When the people don't revolt, [the politicians] don't even think about the people. Before we dumped the garbage on those roads, they had stayed more than two weeks without doing anything. . . . We are not savages, we are citizens. We are educated.

Viewing poor garbage services as a demeaning personal affront, these residents summoned their civility and education to emphasize the irresponsibility of the ruling elite. Invoking their citizenship, moreover, as a right to fair public services and, for the workers, fair wages, rendered Wade's approach to government illiberal and undemocratic.

These statements also illuminate how the union's campaigns to validate their labor had worked to gain the support of many Dakarois. One trash worker's perspective on the revolts echoes many of his colleagues' views toward the neighborhood action:

The people were with us. God made it so that we live in the same zones as we work. They knew us; they were our neighbors. They asked us why the truck no longer came to do the collection. We informed them that we had gone two months without being paid. They felt that wasn't just and that if it had been them, they also wouldn't have accepted it. They pay their garbage tax and are not going to accept to live with garbage in their homes. So, they threw it all in the main arteries where the authorities drive. Therefore, we can say that the people supported us 100 percent.

Beyond striking, the trash workers union had set out from its inception to transform the stigma entailed in working with garbage and to inform ordinary Dakarois of their poor working conditions through a savvy public relations campaign. In an effort to valorize the profession, the union launched a campaign to promote a new language within the sector, insisting that the

FIGURE 4.4. An SNTN press conference in March 2008. The union's secretary general, Madany Sy (*middle*), is shown here reciting the union's grievances and threatening a general strike. Author's photo, 2008.

regular collectors and sweepers who make up the bulk of the sector's workers be called *techniciens de surface* (surface technicians) in lieu of the negatively associated terms *éboueur* (rubbish collector) and *balayeur* (street sweeper) or even the extremely derogatory term *buujumaan* (see chapter 2). Through tireless radio shows, press conferences, and newspaper interviews, the union and its leader, Madany Sy, became household names (see figure 4.4).

Because the activists from the Set/Setal movement were employed as the trash collectors in their own neighborhoods and these relations still persisted in many areas, workers were intimately connected to the neighborhoods they served. Many still collected the garbage of their own families, neighbors, and friends. Even for those who did not serve people they actually knew, the interactive system, which involves direct contact between the workers and residents at the moment of collection in the street, forged communicative channels and spaces of intimacy between workers and the communities they served. As a result, though many respondents admitted to having been prejudiced against the workers before they became familiar with their plight, by 2007 many residents frequently described the workers' labor as "noble" and "dignified" and regularly prayed for them. Although some examples of disrespect persisted, workers equally recounted stories of special consideration they received from their communities. One worker from Yoff recounted this story: "I was collecting the trash with my bare hands. An old man who was teaching the Qur'an nearby to some children stopped what he was doing and came to help me. Afterward, he said, 'My son, you underestimate the importance of the work you are doing.' He knew we knew it, but this was his way of encouraging us to persevere." Many residents were also remarkably informed about the details of the union's grievances and negotiations with the state, and explicitly intended their trash revolts to be an expression of solidarity.

The communicative channels mobilized by participatory waste management provided the basis for the effective mobilization of popular protest and refusal of neoliberal logics. Like roads, bridges, or telephone lines, the practices of sociality encompassing quotidian trash disposal thus served as a social infrastructure that functioned as an affective and symbolic commons that could be "formatted as a public good" (Elyachar 2010, 452). The trash strikes and revolts were the creative product of the flows of "reputation, information, and emotion" (Elyachar 2010, 459) that such infrastructures enabled and, in turn, would serve as the catalyst for new agendas in the garbage sector. The next section will explore the architectures of faith that underpinned these intimate infrastructural relations.

The Piety of Refusal

I sat down with the young, charismatic leader of the trash workers union, Madany Sy, during the heart of the garbage crisis in 2007. Beneath the roar of the only fan in the tiny windowless office at the back of the union headquarters, Sy explained with emotion why he—an articulate, educated Dakarois—was so committed to cleaning the city. He said:

> If I'm here [in the trash sector] to this day, it's because of my beliefs. Because they say that to be a true believer, a true Muslim, one must be clean. One must not be sullied; cleanliness is essential. Thus those who collect the trash of the markets, hospitals, the households, they have a surplus with regard to God. They are like a priesthood. . . . I sacrifice myself today so that people don't have to be contaminated

FIGURE 4.5. Two trash workers in Niari Tali, taking a break from collection on a hot day in July 2007. Author's photo, 2007.

by illnesses. . . . So, it's a very strong gauge of beliefs. If it weren't for the faith, if it weren't this religion, well, we would have quit long ago. But . . . sooner or later, God will pay us for our efforts. . . . It's God that wanted this.

This statement captures Sy's usual passion but it also illuminates a key shared value that has deeply shaped the trash workers' movement. Despite the lamentable circumstances under which they have labored since the early 1990s, the trash workers of Dakar have maintained an intense unity and camaraderie (see figure 4.5). In addition to the shared history and bonds from Set/Setal, the trash workers' solidarity is buttressed by their common faith and conviction that the labor of cleaning the city is a pious act. This architecture of faith undergirds their shared infrastructures of bricolage, serves as an important personal and collective resource, and gives the trash workers' movement its moral authority. Sy and his workers frequently articulated this credo of trash work as God's work and used the idea as a platform from which to demand better conditions. If cleanliness is godliness, they argued, then those who work day in and day out to purge Dakar of its impurities should be rewarded in the here and now. The reward due is simple: respect, job stability, and fair pay. In this way, the workers articulated a refusal to be refuse which inverts the stigma of trash work.

Purity in body and spirit is an indispensable element of Islamic faith. The ablutions performed before praying, including the washing of one's face, hands, and feet, are just one of the myriad ways that cleanliness is essential to Islamic faith and ritual practice. Because a state of purity is a precondition for worship, Muslims cannot offer their prayers with an unclean body, with unclean clothes, or on premises that are seen as polluted. The emphasis on physical cleanliness as a signifier of spiritual cleanliness thus does not stop at the body but is also implicated in the domestic and public space. One's home should be kept clean as a symbol of one's purity and there is an emphasis in specific passages of the Qur'an on the cleanliness of the streets and public spaces.[18] Beyond the cleanliness of the body and environment, moreover, notions of purity in Islam ascribe particular importance to the act of cleaning. The cleansing of holy Muslim sites, for instance, can be understood as an act of deep worship, as demonstrated in the biannual ritual washing ceremony of the Kaaba (inner navel) of the Grand Mosque in Mecca by Saudi dignitaries and similar washing rituals in mosques throughout Senegal. And yet, the act of purging everyday public spaces of their dirt and garbage often comes with immensely negative associations in Islamic settings, as in other contexts.

Perhaps the most well known example of the social stigma of waste work as degraded labor is the connection between sanitation and caste in India. *Dalits* (lower-caste groups) in traditional Hindu society have historically been assigned sanitary work deemed polluting by other castes, "enabl[ing] the higher castes to be free of bodily impurities" (Douglas 1966, 152–53; see also Prashad 2000). In Mary Douglas's formulation, caste was a key example of ritual pollution through which discourses of dirt and danger maintained social categories. In Muslim societies, waste workers can be particularly stigmatized because of the religious associations between waste work and impurity. As a result, in certain places, Christians dominate the waste sector. In her research in Pakistan, for instance, Jo Beall (2006) shows how minority Christians retain a monopoly over sanitation work because of its undesirability to Muslims. Similarly, as marginalized Coptic Christians in a majority Muslim culture, Zabaleen trash collectors have retained an almost exclusive monopoly over Cairo's garbage collection for decades.[19] The cull of all of the Zabaleen's pigs during the H1N1 virus outbreak in 2009 dramatically illuminated the "purity and danger" (Douglas 1966) implications of their waste work.[20]

In Dakar, trash workers are almost exclusively Muslim, mirroring the population at large. Before Set/Setal, however, the majority were workers who came from outside of the city and were considered low-status by Dakarois (see chapter 2). These workers migrated to take positions that, in better times, Dakarois would not deign to consider. When the vast majority of workers were replaced by Set/Setal activists in the early 1990s, the demographics of the sector changed dramatically. With this development, Dakar's garbage sector came to comprise a fairly representative cross section of Dakar society. Women entered into official trash work for the first time and represent a significant minority of trash workers to this day.[21] As mentioned earlier, it took some time for many of these urban—and, in some cases, educated and otherwise privileged—workers to come to terms with the stigmatization of their new professions, particularly for men. However, facing the evisceration of the public sector accompanying structural adjustment and, with it, the prospects for regular work in Dakar, they had little recourse but to persevere in these low-paid but increasingly rare jobs. Many of these workers turned the stigma of trash work on its head through describing their job in terms of its value as religious service.

Trash workers in Dakar have made connections between their work and its spiritual value since they began cleaning in the Set/Setal movement in the late 1980s. Reflecting back, some of the trash workers cite the importance of cleanliness in Islam as a key personal reason why they originally became involved in Set/Setal. As they continued on as workers in the new municipal trash system, the work's religious value served as an inspirational resource in the face of difficult working conditions. For example, Babacar from Médina proudly explained that he had stopped wearing protective *gris-gris* when he started in the profession in the early 1990s because he knew that he was already blessed for his work. Gris-gris are talismans often worn on the body to ward off evil spirits and bring good luck. Although originally derived from African religious practice, gris-gris are commonly incorporated into Senegalese Muslims' spiritual practice. His words sum up the sentiments of many trash workers:

I often say that it's no longer necessary for me to wear gris-gris to protect me. . . . God preaches cleanliness and thus we who make places clean are blessed by God. . . . This is one of my principal motivations in this work and I'm not the only one to think that this is a manner of practicing his religion. In the same way that people pray, we are also endeavoring along the Islamic pathway that preaches cleanliness, one of the precepts of the Islamic religion. Places of worship are ubiquitous in the street, so cleaning the street is a way of reinforcing one's faith. And even if we miss some prayers, we know that God blesses us for the work that we're doing because nothing is more noble and commendable than to clean.

Babacar's practice of piety through cleaning broadens the definition and geography of worship beyond conventional worship practices (e.g., praying, fasting). More provisional and subversive than conventional conceptions of piety, piety through cleaning is the everyday work of bricolage. As a mode of piety, cleaning labor becomes a way of living one's religion, developing personal capacities to endure suffering, and persevering in the face of difficult conditions. Brought to life in the vibrant spaces of the everyday, it involves a moral geography that is centered on the body and deeply rooted in the corporeal practice of laboring. Framed as a collective resource, it becomes a performative practice to lobby for fair labor and better state protections.

Though the spiritual value of cleaning was frequently emphasized in my interviews with trash workers across Dakar as well as in compelling statements made by the union in its work to nurture public support, these responses clearly divided along gendered lines. None of my women respondents volunteered an articulation of the value of their labor in religious terms. When asked directly about the religious value of cleaning, most female respondents did insist that cleanliness was a key element of their spiritual practice and that this was part of why their work was so valuable. However, the key difference was in the force with which men versus women insisted on this value in a public forum. This raises some important questions regarding the gendered space of spirituality and expressions of faith, as well as the gendering of stigma associated with the profession. Because the labor of cleaning in the home is exclusively considered women's work in Senegal, trash work out of the home was not only considered dirty (and thus polluting) but feminized (see chapter 2). Male workers wore masks and tried to hide from their families and girlfriends out of embarrassment. For women, who had always been cleaning in the home, on the other hand, entering the profession was not stigmatizing in the same way. Public articulations by male workers of the value of their labor in religious terms served to at least partly offset some of the stigma of becoming garbage men.

Since the mid-2000s, the trash-workers union has begun publicly articulating religious service through cleaning as a key part of its platform for improved conditions. It centers this positioning on a generic, unifying idea of a common "Muslim" identity that is explicitly not framed in terms of Sufi brotherhoods, specific marabouts, or any other divisions. In fact, when I tried to inquire as to individual workers' affiliations with particular brotherhoods, they went to great lengths to avoid answering the question, insisting instead that they were "all just Muslims" and that which mosque they frequented didn't matter. Conjuring a generic Muslim identity worked to cement solidarity between workers and their communities through downplaying their differences and emphasizing common values. In this way, it inspired a cosmopolitan ethics calling for just treatment to be accorded to all workers, regardless of other divisions. It also conferred moral authority on an otherwise abject population in order to justify claims made on the state. Sy often asked government officials to allow their moral commitments of fraternity with their Muslim brothers to guide their management of the sector.

Forging an understanding of trash work as a service of purification validates trash workers' labor and creates a platform for voicing their grievances. In an era when politicians are strongly distrusted and party values rendered almost meaningless, but where faith and communal religious identity remains an enormous personal and collective resource, they appeal instead to commonly held Senegalese moral values. This renders their grievances difficult to refute and apparently apolitical. Appealing to Islamic morality thus casts a sharp ethical critique of the state's role in the flexibilization of labor and provides a new language through which to understand the value of infrastructure.

Conclusions

Through disrupting the orderly flow of waste out of the city and intentionally externalizing private trash into public spaces, workers and residents manifest disorder to contest the governing prerogatives of government planners and officials and all of the associated dimensions of stigma and abjection implied by living and working in filth. The effectiveness of the trash workers' campaign is evident in the public support the workers have garnered since their campaign ramped up in the mid-2000s and the attention they have finally received from the government over the last few years. Framing their work in religious terms not only acts to validate otherwise stigmatized labor and laborers, but also serves as a platform for making claims on the state. Since that time, the workers have won some important battles, and, as detailed in chapter 1, the sector has figured into important political contests between the mayor of Dakar and the president. During this time, the union was received many times by the mayor and representatives of the national government. From 2006 to 2009, they received a number of concessions, including back pay and indemnities, and then in 2009 their conditions improved markedly when the mayor officially hired on the workers, conferring on them formal contracts, medical coverage, and access to banking services. After more years of hard lobbying, they finally earned the objective of much of their campaigning in 2014 with the signature of their collective bargaining agreement. Although the sector continues to be politicized and workers continue to battle to further improve their working conditions, their grievances have been significantly attenuated over the last few years. The sector represents a pioneer in reversing austerity logics. In the context of continued liberalization of the economy and flexibilization of labor in diverse sectors, this is no small feat.

This chapter has traced the moral geographies of citizenship that emerge from the piety of refusal and that have enabled these transformations. If infrastructure is composed of people, then central to grappling with infrastructural politics is contending with the meanings and values that people place on those infrastructural systems. For systems devolved onto labor, the value of infrastructure derives from the value placed in that labor. The analysis has focused on modes of self-valuation through the embodied cultivation of piety-through-cleaning and the deployment of those values in a public forum. At the same time, it has explored the power of striking, or the withdrawal of infrastructural labors in intentional acts of dirtying. Because waste can be dangerous, trash work has a specific power. The intimate vitality of Dakar's participatory trash collection system and the vibrancy of the material relations of garbage gives the critique its force through rendering politically salient not just the discard process, but also, importantly, its interruption. The natural forces of decomposition take on new meaning as they intersect with the vibrant actions of persons. The spiritual value of trash work is grounded in both the meaning of cleanliness in Islam and the embodied practice of cleaning. As a practice of purification, the labor of cleaning provides a powerful ground on which to contest relations of disposability and lay bare the ethics of infrastructure. In this way, the labor union movement levels a powerful critique of the erosion of the rights and rewards of the city and lays claim to dignity through insisting on the value of labor as an essential infrastructural ingredient.

The piety of refusal raises important questions for the horizon of politics in urban Africa. This study moves away from an exclusive emphasis on religious institutions to emphasize the ways that religious identity shapes individual consciousness and collective organizing. The story of trash workers' religious convictions is not one of marabouts, brotherhoods, Islamism, or instructions from on high about how to wage politics. Instead, the research raises some questions for the critical understandings that may be mobilized through religious identity or the "dialectics of political and spiritual agency" (Diouf and Leichtman 2009, 12). The role of faith and communal religious identity in providing the political consciousness that undergirds oppositional movements is of course not new. Workers' faith has been shown to be crucial in building a strong oppositional culture, both in helping workers to critically reflect on their situations and in legitimizing popular struggles in diverse settings (e.g., Billings 1990; Lubeck 1986). But the piety of refusal offers a novel and significant language for contesting neoliberal austerity and reframing the value of infrastructure.

Given the rising importance of religious movements in African settings, particularly in urban spaces, it has become even more important to ask about the possibilities for critical understandings to emerge through spiritual practices in that context. In Dakar, religious convictions have incited trash workers and their communities to stand up for fair treatment and better jobs. Insisting on the spiritual import of cleaning allowed these workers to find some salvation in a "trashy" job as well as to fight for a measure of respect from the state and populations they serve. The piety of refusal constitutes a mode of bricolage of the self that buttresses the practices of salvage bricolage through which workers forge, maintain, and, sometimes, break down the city's infrastructure. The associations between cleaning and virtue shape the value of the infrastructure and allow citizenship claims to be persuasively staked on a moral-ethical level. Architectures of faith, then, become the scaffolding through which politics and piety are enmeshed and through which new, more ethical infrastructures can be crafted.

Digging beneath Dakar's garbage piles reveals a very different story from the dysfunction and disorder often associated with African cities. Behind the ebb and flow of decay in Dakar's public space lies a rich, dynamic history of political contestation that offers important insights about citizenship and the urban condition in Senegal and beyond. This history make clear the key role of infrastructural politics in shaping access to the rights and rewards of the city while pushing beyond conventional understandings of infrastructure. Dakar's bricolage garbage collection system demands a broader definition of infrastructure that includes labor, materiality, and affective modes of valuation. Urban infrastructures are thus revealed to be ecologies vitally alive with bodies, communities, materials, and ritual practices. Though this liveliness may be more easily discerned in an ordinary Southern city like Dakar, these are potentially essential infrastructural elements anywhere. African cities like Dakar are key sources of theory for urban and infrastructure studies of ordinary cities around the world.

The garbage lining Dakar's city streets, canals, and empty lots is both the stain left by a difficult history of disinvestment in the era of austerity, and the key ingredient in a series of dynamic eruptions by poor and disenfranchised citizens rejecting conditions of precarity. On the one hand, garbage in Dakar bears witness to the vicissitudes of neoliberal development. African cities have been key experimental testing grounds for harsh structural adjustment and urban reform measures that have wreaked havoc on urban livelihoods, labor and environmental conditions, welfare services, and public infrastructures. The tumultuous politics of garbage over the last twenty-five years are the outcome of the starving of the urban public sector with structural adjustment and the wily political maneuvering required to reform within a vibrant democratic context. Urban austerity precipitated intense jockeying for control of this important public sector, especially manifested in a turbulent history of institutional politicking and battles between the mayor of Dakar and the president of the republic. Most generally, these forces accelerated a mode of governing-through-disposability premised upon performative, fragmented infrastructure investments and strategies to flexibilize urban labor. For laborers caught up in these processes, especially women and youth, work was degraded in highly differential ways through discourses of participation. The severe neoliberal experiments that African cities have undergone at the hands of international development loans operate through wasting spaces and bodies in the pursuit of economic growth that rarely materializes.

At the same time, the history of Dakar's garbage reveals that modes of rendering people disposable are met with strategies of refusal that validate labor that has been stigmatized and degraded. Neoliberal experiments spark a host of creative, experimental citizenship practices rooted in the grimy everyday spaces of the city that act to reorder patterns of disposability and insist on different logics for governing the city. Over the last decade in particular, trash workers and the neighborhoods they serve have fostered a critique of the neoliberal logics that have dominated Senegal's political economy. Through their strikes and trash revolts, they have forced a collective reckoning with labor insecurity and uneven urban services. This is just part of a wave of battles that different citizen groups have been waging against the infrastructural elitism, erosion of public services, and degradation of life's work that has taken hold over this period in Dakar. The garbage workers join a chorus of strikers in other municipal sectors, as well as diverse citizens' groups including youth rappers and street vendors, who are reclaiming a more inclusive citizenship and city through often below-the-radar, everyday negotiations and transgressions (Fredericks 2014; Ndiaye 2013; Tandian 2013). Whether dissatisfaction at the current state of affairs will result in long-term political economic change in Senegal remains to be seen. But these events speak to a wider trend across the continent of reckoning with structural adjustment and struggling to chart alternative modes of urban governance. They are consistent, moreover, with the way that urban public infrastructures are the stage for citizenship battles all over the world. Substantive citizenship in Dakar is enacted and contested in the gritty spaces of the city and through the materiality of everyday life.

This book has examined questions of urban citizenship in the neoliberal era through bringing together a materialist understanding of infrastructure and an emphasis on the cultural politics of labor. This has allowed for an innovative approach to both infrastructure and labor that bridges old and new materialist debates. New materialist insights help us to see the ways that the trash itself—its hard-to-manage elements, stench, and processes of decomposition—and the material technologies used to collect it (bodies, trucks, horse carts) shape the trash politics that have seized the capital city. Attention to the cultural politics animating these labor struggles—especially the roles of gender and youth identities as well as the spiritual imaginaries shaping the value of cleaning work—fleshes out these infrastructures as vital systems activated by the differentiated materiality of bodies and the systems of meaning that connect them. Through expert labors of salvage bricolage, Dakar's trash workers piece together complex socio-technical infrastructural systems embedded in communities of affect and vernacular values.

A focus on infrastructural labors thus offers an important corrective to infrastructure studies that elide the bodies, social systems, and affective registers that infrastructures are built upon. Emphasizing materiality reveals the material burdens that exacerbate conditions of precarity and the ways that systems of meaning making may stem from the object of management (here, waste) and its particular properties. An ethnographic perspective allows for an investigation into the strategic alliances that may form between human and nonhuman actants, and into the actual political work that nonhuman actants do in specific settings in order to move beyond the abstract theorizing associated with much new materialist thinking (see, for example, Bennett 2010). This pushes us to ask some questions about how objects have a force, are consequential, and play a role in politics, while retaining a central focus on urban lives, subjectivities, and questions of citizenship.

Considering Dakar's garbage system as political infrastructure illuminates the values that get coded in infrastructural arrangements. A quote from one of my respondents makes this clear. At the end of my last interview with Issa Ndoye, the official in the Yoff mayor's office charged with coordinating household waste collection, he admonished me to be responsible with my analysis of Dakar's trash infrastructure by telling me: "You have to make sure that you are careful in writing up your research on our garbage system. Ideas get quickly taken up and replicated, especially by NGOs. Infrastructure is power. Yes, infrastructure is power, and what matters most is choosing the *right* infrastructure." Issa had been highly critical of the horse-drawn-cart system implemented in Yoff and felt strongly that the municipal garbage infrastructure just needed to be reinforced. Others dismissed him as "obsessed" with garbage trucks because he firmly believed that more advanced technologies like garbage trucks were essential for a more functional, coherent, and just municipal garbage system. I have strived to take Issa's advice to heart in this book. Like Langdon Winner, in his foundational piece "Do Artifacts Have Politics?," Issa was keenly aware that infrastructural choices matter because they codify social-power relations in the city and "establish a framework for public order. . . . The issues that divide or unite people in society are settled not only in the institutions and practices of politics proper, but also, and less obviously, in tangible arrangements of steel and concrete, wires and transistors, nuts and bolts" (Winner 1980, 128). Unjust social relations become entrenched in the material structures of the city through regressive technologies like horse-drawn carts and labor-intensive collection systems. In this light, garbage infrastructures of postadjustment Senegal manifest the moral economies of that political economic conjuncture and highlight questions of distributive justice.

Infrastructures matter in their intersection with human bodies. Though Issa was committed to garbage trucks, he was most concerned with the social technologies employed alongside physical technologies through disingenuous discourses of appropriate technology and empowerment. By placing at the center of this analysis the laboring bodies that serve as the connective tissue tying together steel technologies and waste flows, I hope to crystalize the power relations embedded in different socio-technical systems. Examining the way that human labor and community dynamics serve as technologies in specific infrastructural arrangements reveals who gets access to public welfare benefits, which spaces are slated for decay and pollution, and the corporeal burdens of the crisis of social reproduction.

Human labor is a key, underrecognized ingredient of infrastructures everywhere, but grappling with the burdens of people's infrastructural labors is especially pertinent in bricolage systems that dominate in the Global South. Labor is key to the conditions of the working poor and, as such, forms an important foundation of urban citizenship. Innovative bodily technologies of salvage bricolage may be ingenious tools for navigating austerity but they may also entail violent bodily burdens. Moreover, labor is a key infrastructural technology but it is not equivalent to other technologies. This analysis has endeavored to trace the ways that labor and infrastructure intersect but also the ways that they are in tension and often incommensurate.[1] Suturing labor and infrastructure together produces intersecting precarities that can threaten not just laboring bodies but the integrity of the infrastructure as a whole. Precarious, decaying machines make infrastructural labors riskier while precarious, bricolage labor may, in turn, threaten the integrity of the infrastructural system and the livelihoods it supports. The implications of the relationship between devolving infrastructure and labor are thus unpredictable and potentially perilous.

It is no accident that garbage infrastructure, in particular, became a key battleground for urban citizenship in this dynamic conjuncture in Dakar. As former mayor Mamadou Diop realized, trash is the essence of quotidian life—it is the present, past, and future of the city. As the unavoidable byproduct of consumption and production, garbage represents both an ultimate challenge to and a foundational requirement of development and modernization. Following Mary Douglas, the practice of managing wastes, moreover, is centrally implicated in ordering processes, structuring societies through fears of contagion and risks of impurity. As matter out of place, trash renders places and people impure through threats of contagion (Douglas 1966). It is through the risk of impurity that garbage has been a key mode of governing and rendering abject. At the same time, garbage is universally available and thus a potentially powerful ingredient of creative practices of citizenship by degraded members of society. The symbolic register of trash as waste helps to explain both the power of governing through garbage and the creative possibilities for people to trouble the divides coded by dirt and disorder.

Moreover, the materiality of waste—its messy *thingyness* and "toxic vitality" (P. Harvey 2016)—is inextricable from its symbolic register and is at the root of its power in both governing and claiming citizenship. Though Douglas's foundational insights on the role of dirt in structuring social-power hierarchies are useful to explain the dynamism of trash in Dakar, I have shown here how the force of trash goes far beyond the symbolic. Garbage must be reckoned with not as an abstract concept structuring symbolic oppositions, but as matter oozing with physical, spatial, and affective properties that intersect with bodies in profoundly political ways. Governing and rebelling through garbage are material practices of power. A close materialist reading of discard labor draws our attention to all of the ways that social-power dynamics can be disrupted through reconfiguring the power of waste in a material politics of refusal. Degraded subjects have critiqued the expert knowledge complicit in rendering them disposable through vibrant, messy struggles around garbage. Through strikes and trash revolts, Dakarois engineer "crises" that make plain the inner workings of infrastructure and the inequities it contains. Through the social and communicative investment in their communities, grounded in architectures of faith, moreover, the trash workers resist the negative associations of waste and forge wider communities of affect united around the injustices of uneven urban public services. As they render waste infrastructures "problems of collective existence" (Lakoff and Collier 2010, 244), they politicize the materiality of urban life itself. Given waste's ubiquitous presence in all urban societies and the wide array of contexts that have recently seen trash strikes and crises—from Paris to Beirut to Buenos Aires—it is clear that trash is not just a feature of Senegal's contemporary political landscape. Garbage is a powerful matter of urban citizenship anywhere.

Trash in Dakar makes clear how, as James Ferguson (2012, 562) notes, "the insistence on materiality . . . is at the same time an insistence on morality." Perhaps the most important lesson to learn from Dakar's trash workers comes from their battle to revalorize their labor through sculpting material moralities. At the core of the trash workers' movement is an effort to align their material labors with vernacular moralities. Their citizenship practices refuse moral economies of austerity and their associated infrastructures and call for arrangements of people, objects, and technologies that are more just. Through their conviction that trash work is God's work, and their practical efforts to order the city, the workers demand a remoralization of work and stake claims for a more ethical infrastructure. Trash collection as religious purity, and fair wages and equal public services as Muslim fraternity, enable a very different approach to building this emergent African city. These are the vernacular understandings that mobilize everyday life in Dakar and that could form the basis of a more "ordinary" (see Robinson 2006), more ethical infrastructure. Garbage citizenship, then, draws attention to the injustices of uneven urban infrastructures while charting a new vision for the city that is grounded in the mundane matter, values, and practices of the everyday.

INTRODUCTION. **Trash Matters**

1. See Sharad Chari's (2013, 133) similar notion of "refusal to be detritus."

2. I'm drawing on and reconfiguring AbdouMaliq Simone's (2004b) notion of *people as infrastructure.*

3. For some notable exceptions, see Blundo and Meur (2009) and Chalfin (2010) as well as the political infrastructures literatures discussed later in the chapter.

4. The city is a major financial center, home to a dozen national and regional banks (including la Banque Centrale des états de l'Afrique de l'ouest [Central Bank of the West African States] which manages the unified West African franc [CFA] currency) and numerous international organizations, NGOs, and international research centers, and it is the center of the country's tourist economy.

5. Among other interventions, these literatures have contributed pathbreaking insight toward understanding gendered and generational access to resources, migration and rural-urban connection, and the persistence of "custom" (e.g., Berry 1993; Carney and Watts 1990; Ferguson 1994; Isaacman 1996).

6. Africanist research has been foundational in political ecology (e.g., Bassett and Crummey 1993; Fairhead and Leach 1996; Ribot 1998; Schroeder 1999; Tiffen, Mortimore, and Gichuki 1994; Watts 1983). Though most of the early political ecology scholarship was focused on the rural sphere, there is a growing literature refracting urban political-ecological questions through the lens of African cities (e.g., Lawhon, Ernstson, and Silver 2014; Loftus 2012; McFarlane and Silver 2017; Myers 2005; Njeru 2006).

7. See footnote 12 for a brief discussion of Africanist urban political ecology (UPE).

8. There is a long, important tradition of Africanist urban historiography and ethnography that shifted the rural focus of labor studies to grapple with the transformation of work and labor organizing in the city. For instance, Luise White's ground-

breaking *Comforts of Home* explored the role of prostitution as a means of capital accumulation in colonial Nairobi (1990). Research on urbanism in the Copperbelt, a copper-mining region in Central Africa mostly centered in Zambia's Copperbelt Province, moreover, was central to a new paradigm in urban studies emerging in the middle of the century (see early research coming out of the Rhodes-Livingston Institute [e.g., Gluckman 1961; J. C. Mitchell 1961] and the discussion by J. Robinson [2006]). More recent scholarship on the urban labor question has recalibrated understandings of urban informality (K. Hart 1973), the challenges of economic decline (Ferguson 1999), new patterns of migration (Buggenhagen 2001; Cooper 1983; M. Diouf 2000), the gendered politics of work (Clark 1994; G. Hart 2002), and questions of labor mobilization and unionization (Cooper 1996; Lubeck 1986; Parpart 1983)—to name a few central contributions.

9. For instance, Gillian Hart's (2002) important monograph examines the cultural politics of labor fomented by industrial globalization in black townships in KwaZulu-Natal faced with ongoing legacies of racial dispossession.

10. For instance, my edited volumes with Mamadou Diouf (2013, 2014) brought together a range of established and emerging scholars wrestling ethnographically with the forms of experimentation, adaptation, and negotiation through which African urban dwellers stake claims to the rights and rewards of the city. Other relevant overview pieces include: De Boeck and Plissart (2005), Mbembe and Nuttall (2004b), Murray (2011), Murray and Myers (2011), Myers (2005, 2011), E. Pieterse (2008), J. Robinson (2006), Simone (2004a, 2010), and the debate between Watts (2005a) and Nuttall and Mbembe (2005).

11. For instance, Brenda Chalfin, Daniel Mains, and Antina von Schnitzler have been at the forefront of ethnographic discussions of infrastructural change in the neoliberal era for their work in Ghana, Ethiopia, and South Africa, respectively (Chalfin 2016; Mains 2012; von Schnitzler 2016).

12. These concerns have animated broad swathes of urban geographical debate for some time. Some key foundational texts include Castells (1979), D. Harvey (1996), and Smith (1984). Urban political ecology (UPE) research has made especially important contributions toward emphasizing the socio-power geometries surrounding human-environment relations, the materiality of urban nature, and the key role of urban infrastructures in uneven environment-development relations (e.g., the collection by Heynen et al. [2007]). However, I join with Lawhon, Ernston, and Silver (2014) in arguing for a provincialization of UPE. African urbanisms offer new insights for UPE, which, to date, has been narrow in theoretical scope and dominated by Global North perspectives. This book shares in Lawhon et al.'s call for a more situated UPE that draws on more heterogeneous theoretical influences (especially feminist and postcolonial), particularly through exploring how notions of people as infrastructure, embodied experiences, and situated knowledges are central to urban political ecologies. For some examples of urban political-ecological scholarship that may fall outside the purview of conventional UPE, see Loftus (2012), Myers (2011, 2014), Rademacher and Sivaramakrishnan (2013), and Truelove (2011).

13. The research on political infrastructures has exploded over the last few years. For

some key overview pieces and special issues, see Appel, Anand, and Gupta (2015), Calhoun, Sennett, and Shapira (2013), Collier, Mizes, and von Schnitzler (2016), S. Graham and C. McFarlane (2015), Jensen and Morita (2016), Larkin (2013), Lugo and Lockrem (2012), McFarlane and Rutherford (2008), T. Mitchell (2014), O'Neill and Rodgers (2012), and Star (1999). Water infrastructure has been an especially fertile area of research. See Anand (2017), Björkman (2014), Gandy (2014), Kooy and Bakker (2008), Ranganathan (2014, 2015), and Truelove (2011).

14. There is a wide and established body of urban scholarship, much of which is focused on Global South cities, that emphasizes the rising importance of the city as the key locus of citizenship accompanying the decline of nation-state–based citizenship. The shift to the urban scale is associated with the fading relevance of classic notions of citizenship focused on formal membership and participation in the national polity, and the rising importance of rights-based approaches which focus on access to substantive urban public goods like housing, sanitation, and employment. See the concise summary by Miraftab and Kudva (2015) as well as foundational texts including Holston and Appadurai (1999), J. Robinson (2006), and Roy (2009).

15. Von Schnitzler (2013, 689). See also Appel (2014), Brownell (2014), Chalfin (2014, 2016), Chari (2013), De Boeck (2014), De Boeck and Plissart (2005), De Boeck and Baloji (2016), Doherty (2018), Gandy (2006), Larkin (2008), Loftus and Lumsden (2008), Mains (2012), Masquelier (2002), Mavhunga (2013a), McFarlane and Silver (2017), Mizes (2017), Omezi (2014), Simone (2004b, 2012), and von Schnitzler (2016).

16. Geography has long made its mark on the academy through grappling with the relationship between human activity and material environments (Braun 2007). There has been a resurgence of interest in the last few years, influenced by wider new materialist debates and the rising influence of science studies and the "ontological turn" in anthropology, to bring materiality more fully back into the fold of cultural and political geographical inquiry.

17. See Stephen Graham and Simon Marvin's influential *Splintering Urbanism* (2001). The implied progression in Graham and Marvin's book from networked to individualized and privatized systems is less relevant in African cities. As Matthew Gandy (2006, 389) points out about Lagos, episodic aspirations by colonial and then postcolonial governments to modernize urban space have in reality been "little more than a chimera that characterized sketches, plans and isolated developments, but never constituted the majority experience."

18. See Michael Watts's (2005a) critique of Simone's notion of *people as infrastructure* in the special issue of *Public Culture* on Johannesburg.

19. For some key texts in discard studies examining the culture and materiality of waste, see Alexander and Reno (2012), Gregson and Crang (2010), Hawkins and Muecke (2003), Moore (2012), O'Brien (1999), Reno (2015), and Scanlan (2005).

20. This study joins with a wider body of work in discard studies that pushes beyond Douglas's structural-symbolic approach to foreground waste's materiality (see Reno 2015).

21. Though the examples elaborated here are mostly in the postcolonial world, waste management has also been deeply implicated in city-planning policy and practice in

the West. For example, discourses of cleanliness and indiscipline resonate with a number of other long-running debates including the historic question of pollution and class that can be seen in the progressive era in the United States (Riis 1890).

22. Anand (2012), drawing on Kristeva (1982). Similarly, Michelle Kooy and Karen Bakker (2008) explore how the constitution of modern citizenship is entangled with the provision of water infrastructure in Jakarta through its role in disciplining corporeal subjects.

23. Chakrabarty (1991, 18). D. Asher Ghertner (2010a) argues that such techniques undergird the function of what he terms *aesthetic governmentality* in the service of elite "world-city" aspirations in Delhi. As Ghertner and other scholars of India have observed, bourgeois environmental discourses are frequently invoked in elite projects for urban development, often through mobilizing discourses of order, nuisance, or contamination (Doshi 2013; Ghertner 2010b; McFarlane 2008). It is in this sense that Vinay Gidwani and Rajyashree N. Reddy (2011, 1425) describe contemporary metropolitan governance in India through zones of exclusion, enclosure, and neglect as an "eviscerating urbanism" which operates as a regime of disengagement "for managing bodies and spaces designated as 'wasteful.'"

24. Mbembe (2001). For his part, Esty (1999) argues that the excremental is a governing trope in African and other postcolonial literature, but draws on African satires to emphasize the way that satirists' scatological language fosters an incisive critique of the failures of colonial development and the corruptions of neocolonial politics. See also Lincoln (2008) on excremental allegory in postcolonial African literature.

25. I'm drawing here on Chakrabarty (1991, 19–20).

26. This builds on a focus within critical development studies and urban geography as to how "life's work" is restructured through the instrumentalization of participation in the interest of cheaper urban-development strategies, which roll back the provision of public goods (e.g., Katz 2001; Roberts 2008).

27. For other research looking at the particular burdens of waste work, see Crang (2010), Gidwani (2013), Gidwani and Reddy (2011), Gregson and Crang (2010), Miraftab (2004b), Parizeau (2015), M. Samson (2007, 2009, 2015), Nagle (2013), Reno (2016), and Whitson (2011). For broader explorations of disposability and labor, see Bauman (2003), Butler and Athanasiou (2013), Gilmore (2007), Hecht (2012), Meehan and Strauss (2015), Voyles (2015), Wright (2006), and M. Yates (2011).

28. The discard process is only the beginning of the second life of garbage. A village of people lives at the city's dump, Mbeubeuss, carving lives and value out of the remains left by their better-off neighbors. Although this research did not consider the politics of picking, my new research examines the social life of the dump.

29. Kaplan's article, "The Coming Anarchy," became one of the best-selling issues in *The Atlantic Monthly*'s history, was cited far and wide, and is considered an influential intervention on the current state of world affairs. In his dramatic account of his ride to the airport in Conakry, he described the city as "a nightmarish Dickensian spectacle . . . The streets were one long puddle of floating garbage" (1994, 54).

30. See also Diouf and Fredericks (2013, 2014), Myers (2011), and Roy and Ong (2011) for extended discussion and ethnographic research that resist these two tendencies.

1. Comprising fifty-seven nations, the OIC was formed in 1969 and aims at protecting Muslim interests worldwide.

2. The monument and many of the road projects were not completed for the event but a few key thoroughfares and exchanges were finished in the nick of time.

3. On infrastructure and modernist development, see Gandy (2003), Mrázek (2002), and Scott (1998). On breakdowns, see S. Graham (2010), Lakoff and Collier (2010), Mains (2012), and Star (1999). On abjection, disconnection, and disrepair, see Anand (2012), Appel (2014), Björkman (2014), Chu (2014), Ferguson (1999), Gidwani and Reddy (2011), and Rodgers (2012).

4. Larkin (2013). See also Bazenguissa-Ganga (2014), Ferguson (1999), Harvey and Knox (2012), Ishii (2016), Larkin (2008), Mains (2012), Masquelier (2002), and Trovalla and Trovalla (2015).

5. On international events, see Cavalcanti (2015) and Omezi (2014). On world-class city making and bourgeois environmentalisms, see Ghertner (2010b) and Roy and Ong (2011). Also relevant is research on how infrastructural crisis can be produced for political ends (Giglioli and Swyngedouw 2008), the production of anticipatory security events (Lakoff and Collier 2010), and infrastructural performances for an international-development gaze (Appadurai 2002).

6. Performative practices around infrastructure have not been limited to the state. As we'll see in chapter 4, garbage infrastructure is also the space through which rebellion has been performed by striking workers and ordinary residents through staging breakdowns and exteriorizing waste.

7. Dakar was originally founded by the French as a military base in 1857 at the Lebou village of Ndakarou on the tip of the Cape Verde Peninsula. The Cape Verde Peninsula was originally settled by Lebou—one of Senegal's nine ethnic groups—fishermen no later than the fifteenth century (Sylla 1992). The Portuguese first landed on Gorée (a small island off the peninsula) in 1444, where they founded a settlement that was to become part of the slave trade network. The island, just off the mainland, changed hands between the Portuguese, Dutch, English, and French many times before the French finally took control of it near the end of the seventeenth century. First settling on the African coast in Saint-Louis in 1659, the French took definitive control of the colony of Senegal in 1817 after losing it to English occupation during the French Revolution and Napoleonic Wars.

8. Assimilation was the ideological basis for French colonial policy in the nineteenth and twentieth centuries, premised on the idea that colonial subjects could become French by adopting French language and culture.

9. Although sometimes used to include people of mixed African European descent, the term *originaire* generally referenced Africans living in the Quatre Communes. Demonstrating the required proof of at least five years' residency in one of the communes was often quite complicated.

10. Substantial legal and social barriers prevented the full exercise of "citizens'" rights. These struggles lend significant insight into the contradictions intrinsic to

the ideals and practices of the French *mission civilisatrice* (civilizing mission), at once rooted in republican egalitarianism and premised on authoritarian violence and racism (Conklin 1997).

11. The concentration of investment and power in the coastal administrative cities and the hierarchies of citizenship established in the colonial period have had lasting impacts for the postcolony. A core legacy of colonial administration is the bifurcation between urban "citizens" and rural "subjects" (Mamdani 1996). Compared with rural areas and secondary cities, Dakar has long dominated planning and infrastructure development.

12. Swanson (1977) coined the term in describing how colonial policy surrounding the bubonic plague acted as an instrument of racial segregation in some South African cities. Some other notable examples of the interlocking politics of difference and sanitation in the colonial era include Warwick Anderson's (1995) study of "excremental colonialism" in the Philippines, Sidney Chalhoub's (1993) inquiry into yellow fever in Rio de Janeiro, Vijay Prashad's (1994) study of "native dirt/imperial ordure" in India, Brenda S. A. Yeoh's (2003) research in Singapore, and, of particular relevance to my study setting, Myron Echenberg's (2002) analysis of the bubonic plague in Senegal.

13. The Socialist Party was originally named the Union Progressiste Sénégalaise (Senegalese Progressive Union) until 1976.

14. After considerable growth in the 1960s, the public sector exploded in the 1970s, with thirty-three new public and state-owned enterprises created from 1973 to 1975 (Bellitto 2001, 79). The water sector was nationalized in 1971, followed by electricity two years later (Bellitto 2001, 94). The trash sector did not follow until 1985 with the creation of the parastatal corporation, la Société Industrielle d'aménagement urbain du Sénégal (Industrial Urban Planning Company of Senegal; SIAS). By the 1980s the government was the sole or majority entity of eighty-six public and parastatal companies, representing 20 percent of GDP and employing thirty-five thousand workers (Somerville 1991, 153). Dakar's graduates were particularly well placed for government jobs during this period (Zeilig and Ansell 2008).

15. Collignon (1984) discusses the *déguerpissements* (displacement) of urban residents seen as "overpopulating" the area, as well as specific marginalized members of the urban landscape, including *talibé* children (young boys, who in an extremely controversial practice, beg for money for their *marabouts*), handicapped people, and the mentally ill.

16. Cohen (2007, 148). The World Bank's first urban development loan was US$8 million to Senegal for the Sites and Services Project, approved in 1972, to construct the Parcelles Assainies district in Dakar. Despite the fanfare, the project was inadequate and failed to make much of a dent in Dakar's housing crisis.

17. The management of household garbage was specified by the Code de l'administration communale (Municipal Administration Code, Law 66–64 of June 30, 1966, modified in 1969, 1970, and 1972). The financing of household waste management is covered by the Taxe d'enlèvement des ordures ménagères (Tax on the Removal of Household Waste; TEOM), which dates back to the law of August 13, 1926, and an amendment from February 3, 1958, which required that all properties be subjected to

the TEOM, calculated based on the built property values. Household waste is collected by the Treasury Service of the Ministry of Finance. The recovery rates are infamously low and inadequate for covering service costs. For instance, in 1995, 18 percent of the total trash budget was covered by the TEOM, and in 2001, only 15 percent was covered (Chagnon 1996, 109; Direction des collectivités locales, personal communication, 2007).

18. In Diouf's (1997, 308) words, the protection of the economy by the state had contributed to the "development of an attitude of total irresponsibility on the parts of those associated with power. In fact, political protection that guaranteed impunity generalized bad management, clientelism, corruption, and the total absence of sanctions, positive or negative."

19. Whether continued economic decline in Africa was the result of the reforms themselves or the poor implementation of them is an extremely complicated question that has been the subject of vast debate over the last few decades (e.g., Mkandawire and Soludo 1999).

20. The CUD was created in 1983 as a governing structure over the greater *Région de Dakar* (region of Dakar) (joining the three *départements* [departments] of Dakar, Rufisque, and Pikine). As stipulated in Decree 83–1131 (October 1983), the CUD was responsible for household waste management in the region of Dakar.

21. At the onset of structural adjustment, the wage bill had reached 60 percent of government spending (B. Fall 2002, 52). Reform of the civil service was centered on several major strategies aimed at controlling recruitment practices and minimizing new hires (B. Fall 2002). The formal jobs that did remain became more flexible with the passage of more liberal labor regulations and policies that made it easier for employers to fire workers and use contract labor (Somerville 1991). Reform of the public sector was slow and sectoral at first, and some public and parastatal ("mixed economy") companies continued to be created up until 1988.

22. It is beyond the scope of this analysis to explore in detail the origins of the industrial crisis in Senegal. For one particularly illuminating case, see Catherine Boone's (1992) thorough and persuasive examination of the rise and fall of the Dakar textile industry.

23. Political reforms had begun in 1976 when President Senghor adopted a new constitution that transformed the one-party state into a tripartite political system. Although some scholars emphasize that the democratic gains in the 1980s only made Senegal a "quasi-democracy" that was really more about political consensus (Vengroff and Creevey 1997), real gains were made in opening up the political playing field. Robert Fatton (1986) argues that through deftly ushering in unlimited pluralism, Diouf was able to neutralize threats from the left opposition in order to retain popularity in the early 1980s. This popularity was, however, to be short lived. While political liberalization was to ensure the survival of the Socialist government into the late 1980s, this was to prove temporary in the face of the diminishing capacity of the state to shape and benefit from the economy.

24. Though first associated with Donal B. Cruise O'Brien, the Senegalese social contract theory has gained the attention of, and been revised by, a significant scholarly

field (see, for instance, Creevey 1985; Cruise O'Brien and Coulon 1988; Diop and Diouf 1990; Fatton 1987; D. Robinson 2000; Villalon 1995). For important recent interventions and revisions, see M. Diouf (2013), especially the chapter by Babou (2013).

25. See Cruise O'Brien (2003) on these factors, including the challenges to brotherhood authority stemming from generational differences, quarrels over succession, and competition between marabouts over shrinking resources.

26. Ironically, the evidence that this compulsion was fading first showed up in the 1983 elections even though the Socialist Party fared quite well. In those presidential elections, despite the Mouride leader's preelection ndigal to vote for the Socialist Party, a significant number of Mouride voters appear to have defied these instructions and voted for the opposition party, even in the Mouride heartland (Cruise O'Brien 2003).

27. Diplomatic ties between the neighboring countries were severed, and several hundred people (estimates vary between a hundred and a thousand) were killed in April and May 1989 in a spate of looting, rioting, and reprisals in both Dakar and the Mauritanian capital Nouakchott, as well as in other towns on both sides of the border. The ethnic violence was allegedly sparked by a dispute over grazing rights along the Senegal River (Parker 1991).

28. Diop and Diouf (1992) describe mayors as "prisoners" dependent upon "mercenary support" from the central state. Despite new policies and agendas for decentralization stretching back to 1972, in practice these reforms were maneuvered to reinforce power in the central state and keep the municipalities hemmed in. A key restriction on the mayor of Dakar's power is his lack of control over financial resources sufficient to the responsibilities of the post. Even local taxes (including the TEOM) are not automatically at the mayor's disposal, but must, rather, be collected by the central treasury and sent back to the municipality, which is rarely assured. Poor recovery rates on local taxes and the politicization of their dispersal are just two of the financial challenges facing the mayor of Dakar.

29. Diop had served multiple posts as minister under Senghor. He served as mayor of Dakar from 1984 to 2002.

30. The devaluation precipitated widespread social dislocation, protests, and further economic inequality in the country (Creevey, Vengroff, and Gaye 1995).

31. Senegal received a comprehensive debt-reduction package from the World Bank and IMF under the enhanced Heavily Indebted Poor Countries (HIPC) Initiative from 2000 to 2006 (World Bank 2000).

32. At first named the Haute Autorité pour la propreté de Dakar (High Authority for the Cleanliness of Dakar; HAPD), transformed shortly after to Propreté de Dakar (Cleanliness of Dakar; PRODAK), the agency then became Agence pour la propreté de Dakar (Agency for the Cleanliness of Dakar; APRODAK) in 2001.

33. The Swiss company Alcyon was selected for the exclusive market of Dakar's garbage collection in 2001 and the twenty-five-year contract was eventually ceded on November 11, 2003, to Alcyon's main subcontractor, AMA. The company AMA-Senegal was created as a private subsidiary of the Italian AMA-Rome (République du Sénégal 2002). The story behind the choice of these contracting companies was the subject of enormous controversy, stemming from allegations of direct personal links discovered with

the president or his family. The conditions under which AMA, which had no previous experience in the developing world, was selected are extremely muddy.

34. Oumar Cissé and Salimata Seck Wone (2013) detail some of the troubling aspects of AMA's shady equipment and managerial practices.

35. The government first broke the contract with AMA in October 2005, citing widespread corruption, mismanagement, and devastating public health consequences. Under pressure from the World Bank, the state quickly reinstated its contract with AMA, building in some new checks and balances. The World Bank pressured for the contract to be reinstated because AMA's investments were insured by the Multilateral Investment Guarantee Agency (MIGA) (Project no. 5498). Although most trash workers were retained, the administrative and mechanical staff were fired with the rupture of the contract.

36. Officially titled the Entente CADAK-CAR, the acronym stands for Communauté d'agglomérations de Dakar–Communauté d'agglomérations de Rufisque (the agreement of the urban agglomerations of Dakar and Rufisque).

37. Remarkably, the expertise of the CUD did not form the basis for the creation of CADAK-CAR, as most of the staff, reports, etc., had been expunged in the shake-up after 2000. Symbolizing this erasure, only vestiges of CUD publications were found scattered across administrative offices and homes of former employees. In terms of leadership and charge, the mayor of Dakar served as the president of the CADAK-CAR, and its official mission revolved around the management of household garbage, the roadway network, and public street lighting.

38. The Code des collectivités locales (Decentralization Law) is Law 96–06 (March 22, 1996) and the addendum is Law 2002–16 (April 15, 2002).

39. See Cissé and Wone (2013) for critiques of Veolia's contract.

40. They were hired and managed through a temping agency, did not receive benefits or formal contracts, and were paid the same salaries as those in the rest of the sector.

41. For media coverage of the trash strikes, see Dieng (2009) and Le Quotidien (2009).

42. The newly created Mutuelle de santé des travailleurs du nettoiement (Health Insurance for Cleaning Workers; MSTN) counted close to three thousand members in 2016 (trash workers and their families).

43. Monthly salaries for the average trash worker had stagnated between 65,000 and 80,000 CFA per month for some time. From 2009 to 2012, the base salary was gradually raised to between 90,000 and 95,000 CFA per month. In 2012, the union leader, Madany Sy, indicated that the union still did not consider this a liveable wage, and that they advocated for a minimum base salary of 150,000 CFA per month.

44. Banque Internationale pour le commerce et l'industrie du Sénégal (International Bank for Trade and Industry of Senegal).

45. The new agency, la Société pour la propreté du Sénégal (Company for the Cleanliness of Senegal; SOPROSEN), was voted on by the National Assembly on August 16, 2011.

46. In removing this foundational element of the urban economy, he made it clear

that access to work was about one's ability to conform to specific aesthetic regimes. The forced removal of the vendors precipitated a major riot in November 2007 and proved a vexing and highly politicized issue for years to come (Tandian 2013).

47. The monument was despised because the family it portrays is viewed as culturally inappropriate, the cost of its production was exorbitant and did not rely on local labor, and all visitation proceeds went directly into the president's pocket (see Roberts 2013).

48. On December 17, 2012, the National Assembly unanimously voted to dissolve SOPROSEN and officially return the management of garbage to the Ministry of Local Governments.

49. The unit was created in 2011 under President Wade but was charged only with garbage management outside of Dakar.

50. Like its preceding organizations, the UCG has organized cleanup events with *voluntaires* (day laborers), instead of recruiting more permanent workers into the sector. The union insists that new recruitment and increased salaries are necessary to keep up with increasing workloads and the rising cost of living in Dakar.

TWO. **Vital Infrastructures of Labor**

1. Associations sportives et culturelles (Sporting and Cultural Associations), Groupements d'intérêt economique (Economic Interest Groups), and Groupements promotion féminine (Women's Interest Groups).

2. This phenomenon varied by neighborhood and by flavor of the association. In more affluent neighborhoods, the youth tended to be more educated, for example, but because of the level of unemployment, often even these educated youth were very active in their youth groups. The implications of this phenomenon—and the strong presence of young intellectuals in Set/Setal—for the trash union battle are considered in chapter 4. In terms of ethnicity and other divisions, youth associations are quite representative of local demographics, so in some neighborhoods specific ethnic groups dominated (e.g., the Lebou in Yoff).

3. This quotation, and all other uncited quotations throughout this book, are from my own interviews with trash workers, residents, government officials, and waste experts in Dakar, conducted between 2006 and 2016. The majority of the more than two hundred fifty interviews I conducted took place in the course of my dissertation fieldwork, in 2007–8. The interviews were originally conducted in French and Wolof, some with the assistance of my Senegalese research assistant. She and two other assistants transcribed the interviews into French and, unless otherwise noted, I translated them into English. With the exception of government officials or those who explicitly asked that I use their real names, I have withheld the names of my respondents in the interest of confidentiality. The ethnographic research was centered in the department of Dakar although research into the institutional history of the sector covered the greater Dakar region. Trash workers at multiple sites across Dakar were interviewed, mainly on their collection routes or, most commonly, at the workers' hangout spots where

they took their breaks. Two neighborhood ethnographies were conducted in HLM Fass and Tonghor, Yoff. These interviews were conducted in fifty households in each neighborhood, with a mixture of household members. The large majority took place within these respondents' homes.

4. Women's connection to ritual impurity through Islamic custom may reinforce their association with cleaning duties, but I did not explore this connection directly in the present research. For a discussion of the South Asian context, see Beall (1997).

5. Single women are of lower status than married women, and older wives are considered higher in social rank than younger wives.

6. Better-off families in Senegal have *bonnes* (household maids) who help with the domestic duties of cleaning, cooking, and child care.

7. Based in Dakar and intervening in areas related to urban livelihoods across the Global South, ENDA is one of the best-known NGOs in West Africa. The book's full title is *Set Setal, Des Murs Qui Parlent: Nouvelle Culture Urbaine à Dakar* (ENDA 1991).

8. N'Dour and Le Super Étoile (1990). N'Dour is the father of the popular music genre *mbalax*, and is Senegal's most famous musician. The original lyrics are in Wolof and the translation is provided by the author with the assistance of Sophie Coly.

9. The integration of the SIAS workers into the new system was not an easy one and those involved remember deep disagreement at the time between the older "professionals" from SIAS and the Set/Setal youth.

10. This project was actually the second of two major attempts in Senegal at quelling the social discontent unleashed by structural adjustment in the late 1980s. The first, Délégation à l'insertion à la réinsertion et à l'emploi (Delegation for Inclusion, Reintegration, and Employment; DIRE), though established in 1987, received more attention after the events of 1988. Funded by the state and international donors, DIRE was aimed at the people who were least happy with the economic reforms: parastatal workers who were laid off, civil servants who voluntarily retired, and university graduates. Designed primarily as an expensive "sweetener" for buying off these groups, DIRE was, for a variety of reasons, considered a failure (C. L. Graham 1994).

11. For the first phase of the AGETIP project (1989–92), the World Bank dispersed a US$20 million loan, and there was additional cofinancing from the African Development ment Bank, other funders, and the Senegalese national and municipal governments. In the second phase (1993–97), the World Bank distributed $38 billion, and there was additional cofunding from other sources (World Bank 1997).

12. SIAS was officially dissolved on September 27, 1995, and the Nouveau Système de nettoiement (New Cleaning System; NSN) was codified in October (République du Sénégal, n.d.). It consisted of 109 GIES and their 1,542 members (Doucouré 2002). The CAMCUD was created to federate these associations as a new arm of Mayor Diop's municipal organization, the CUD. The principal objectives of the new system were stated as follows: "1) the rationalization of the collection and transport system for solid municipal wastes; 2) the involvement of the population in the improvement and management of their quality of life; 3) the mastery of the collection and evacuation systems; 4) the reduction of the costs of collection and disposal" (République du Sénégal 1998, 27).

13. For a general document on the forum, see Whittaker (1995).

14. The term was originally used to describe the young oyster collectors of Mbour (*buuj* means "oyster" in Wolof) (Diop and Faye 2002, 698), but in present-day parlance is used to derogatorily describe informal recyclers and trash pickers and, at times, formal trash workers.

15. Sweeping (*balayer* in French and *balé* in Wolof) is a term used in Senegal to describe general cleaning activities.

16. Women represented over 25 percent of national candidates for most political parties, with the number of women elected to political office increasing at all levels of government (Beck 2003, 158). Amy S. Patterson (2002), however, demonstrates that despite the growing mobilization of women and some of the possibilities opened up by decentralization reforms, there were many blockages to women being equal participants in the political system in Senegal during this time.

17. This resonates with research in South Africa that found gendered discourses of waste to be instrumentalized in the service of cheap, exploitative labor (Miraftab 2004a; M. Samson 2008). See also chapter 3.

18. The social category *youth* (*les jeunes*) in Senegal is often coded male and separated from the category *women* (*les femmes*), in both official and popular discourse, as well as scholarly writing.

19. The French verb *bricoler* means to tinker, "do it yourself" (DIY), or cobble together. Bricolage, or the act of piecing something together from diverse elements, is usually seen as an informal activity associated with DIY or hacking systems and related to the art form of collage.

20. These are two common homemade juices in Senegal. Bissap is made as a tea from hibiscus leaves and bouye is made from the fruit of the baobab tree.

21. For instance, a cholera outbreak in 2005 was directly connected to a crisis in garbage collection. See N. Diouf (2005).

22. This is not an unusual predicament for African youth in the postcolonial period. Best understood as a relational, social category of persons, not a biological one, African youth's passage into adulthood can be complicated and frustrated by their social, political, and/or economic situations. For a useful discussion of youth as a category of analysis, see Durham (2000). For a collection of essays on contemporary youth politics in Africa, see Honwana and De Boeck (2005).

23. A key element of the problem is that the trucks were (and still are) provided by a number of unregulated private contractors and employed at all levels of disrepair. Even the large international companies with whom the state has contracted at various moments to provide the collection materials have often failed to provide quality hardware.

24. See Chu (2014) and Mains (2007) for two other ethnographic perspectives on the lived effects of disrepair in very different settings.

1. As the city sprawls outward into its banlieue, Yoff represents a sort of inner periphery that is increasingly incorporated into central Dakar. Other similar projects were implemented in Pikine and Rufisque, outer departments within the region of Dakar.

2. Most of the community-based sanitation projects (including Tonghor) were coordinated by ENDA's program Relais pour le développement urbain participé (Relay for Participatory Urban Development; RUP).

3. For instance: in the *Best Practices for Human Settlements* report by the United Nations Educational, Scientific and Cultural Organization (UNESCO), as a case study for the Institute for Development Studies at the University of Sussex (UNESCO, n.d.); and in the widely circulated article written by ENDA in *Environment and Urbanization* (Gaye and Diallo 1997).

4. Because of their claim to land on the peninsula, the Lebou constituted a large percentage of the originaires of the first four urban areas of Senegal, the Quatres Communes (M. Diouf 1998). Land has been a key element of their political influence and independence in the postcolonial era.

5. I use *tradition* not to denote a static, unchanging nature, but, rather, to engage the discourse of tradition employed by the Lebou and the historical roots of their contemporary neighborhood governance structures.

6. The Tonghor project was patterned after a model developed by the same RUP program at ENDA in the district of Rufisque on the far outskirts of Dakar (Gaye and Diallo 1997).

7. *Waa Geejndar* or *Geejndar* translates directly from the Wolof as "people from the Saint-Louis sea." The Geejndar are the largest ethnic minority in Tonghor, and a rough estimate would put them at 10 percent of the population at least.

8. The pilot in Tonghor also had a liquid-sanitation element that was aimed at treating wastewater with small-scale (off-grid) "eco-sanitation stations." Though this was not the subject of this research, it should be noted that the liquid-waste project also experienced enormous problems and did not come to fruition. The mural in figure 3.3 is painted on the wall of one of the stations.

9. A study conducted in 1997 as a baseline for the community-based trash project estimated that 60 percent of Tonghor households disposed of their garbage on the ground or by burying it; over half of these discarded their garbage on the beach or in the ocean (Zeitlin and Diouf 1998, 4).

10. Horse-cart owners come in from the countryside to offer their services in the city on a seasonal basis. This rate was a regular rate for such a service. The drivers combined this work with other odd collection jobs in the city.

11. August 2003.

12. The conference was held from January 8 to 12, 1996. Over a hundred foreign participants attended from thirty countries, and local attendance topped two thousand at the opening ceremony. See Register and Peeks (1997) for a detailed report from the conference.

13. In practice, there is some overlap between customary authority and the Yoff district mayor's office, which was founded in 1996 with the decentralization law. Many of the district's municipal leaders are also members of Yoff's powerful community association, APECSY. Tension still arises between the district government and the Yoff community associations. Disagreements and competition for authority are even more pronounced between the community authorities and Dakar-based local government and public services.

14. For a concise overview of the history of "mainstreaming" gender in development discourse, see R. Pearson (2005).

15. This quote is taken from the "Forum on Household Waste Collection Using Carts: Resolutions and Action Plans" for Rufisque, dated December 22, 1994, as reprinted in Gaye (1996, 122).

16. M. Samson (2007, 121). Other research by Ali, Olley, and Cotton (1998) and Beall, Crankshaw, and Parnell (2000) shows how cheap waste-management solutions disproportionately subject marginalized populations to dirty-labor burdens.

17. User fees, especially in health care and education, have been extremely controversial in low- and middle-income countries and communities for their lackluster revenue generation and disproportionate impact on the poor. By the mid-2000s, a number of development agencies and countries had begun to move away from user fees, especially in the health sector. See Nyanator and Kutzin (1999), M. Pearson (2004), WHO (2005), and R. Yates (2009).

18. The district mayor quoted earlier, Issa Ndiaye, had been involved in the rollout of the project in his capacity with APECSY and agreed with the idea of enlisting neighborhood women in neighborhood cleaning activities, but he too saw problems with this model of public service provision.

FOUR. **The Piety of Refusal**

1. I am indebted to an anonymous reviewer for some thoughts on this idea.

2. Puig de la Bellacasa (2016), drawing on Star's (1995) introduction to *Ecologies of Knowledge* and also Barad (2007).

3. See for example Masquelier (2002). This is part of a broader Africanist literature (much of which is not reactionary in the same way) exploring the "modernity of witchcraft" (Geschiere 1997). See also Comaroff and Comaroff (1999).

4. For just a few selections from a growing literature: on Christianity, see Bornstein (2003), Comaroff and Comaroff (2000), Gifford (2004), Marshall (2009, 2013), Meyer (1995), and Osinulu (2013); and on Islam, see Brenner (1993), Gueye (2002), Lubeck (1986), Lubeck and Britts (2002), Simone (1994), Soares and Otayek (2007), and Watts (1996).

5. See Hirschkind (2001) and Hoexter, Eisenstadt, and Levtzion (2002) for a challenge to notions, most famously associated with Habermas ([1962] 1991), that Islamic societies are bereft of a public sphere.

6. See, for instance, Watts (1996), Hirschkind (2001), Lubeck and Britts (2002), Kane (2003), and Soares and Otayek (2007).

7. For instance, Mike Davis (2004, 33–34), in his widely read "Planet of Slums," suggests that religious movements in the "slums" of Africa represent the apocalyptic visions of what has been rendered "a surplus humanity" and not the possible building blocks for an alternative future.

8. For instance, see the important collection of essays edited by Diouf and Leichtman (2009). See also Babou (2007) and M. Diouf (2013).

9. Diouf and Leichtman (2009). For work in geography, see McGuire (2008) on "lived religion" and Tse (2014) on "grounded theologies." For geographical scholarship on new moral geographies, see Kong's very useful literature surveys (1990, 2001, 2010).

10. Although a few smaller unions did form over the next few years, my research focuses on SNTN, as it represented the majority of workers (around thirteen hundred in 2008) and was to lead the other unions in a number of mobilizations.

11. The Socialist Party state had long tried to rein in organized labor through its doctrine of state-affiliated unionism or "responsible participation," but as this lost steam, two major poles of autonomous unions emerged in 1989. During the 1990s, although a certain level of unity and compromise was reached between the unions through federations as they rallied against the common cause of structural adjustment and its devastating impacts, labor was weakened by the state's attempt to infiltrate autonomous unions (Ndiaye 2002, 2010). In the face of de-unionization and the weakening of unions in the 1990s due to their internal fragmentation, politicization, and the informalization of labor, the unions attempted to regroup into federations after 1990 as a survival strategy (Diallo 2002). Two major trends were under way: (1) the formation of *intersyndicales* (union federations or umbrella organizations grouping together existing unions); and (2) the growing number and power of *syndicats autonomes* (independent or "autonomous" unions). This period ushered in more conflictual mobilization: two general strikes were held in the 1990s (1993 and 1999), whereas there had not been any in the 1970s or 1980s. With the election of opposition candidate Abdoulaye Wade in 2000, "responsible participation" was officially rendered meaningless, and the main union—la Confédération Nationale des travailleurs du Sénégal (National Confederation of Trade Unions of Senegal; CNTS)—finally officially disaffiliated itself from the Socialist Party. In spite of this, political tendencies and party connections persisted within the major union federations (including the officially "independent" unions) during the Wade era. The 2000s were an even more conflictual period with frequent strikes taking place, especially in the health and education sectors (Ndiaye 2013).

12. For more details on the institutional reconfigurations, see chapter 1. For more details on the workers' labor conditions in the mid-2000s, see chapter 2.

13. Their relationship with labor activists in Italy, for instance, led to widespread Italian press coverage in 2007 and even protests in Rome—the home base of the company AMA, which had left Dakar trash workers in limbo when it lost its contract with the state of Senegal in 2006. These connections eventually led to the trash-workers union

going on a diplomatic mission to Rome in the summer of 2007, where the leaders were warmly received by Italian unionists and government officials.

14. See also Prashad (2000) on the Balmiki sanitation workers of Delhi.

15. I am grateful to an anonymous reviewer for development of this point.

16. Excerpt from an article in the newspaper *Sud Quotidien* (2007); my translation.

17. There were thirteen candidates for president in the final round, which greatly diminished any chance for the opposition to get enough support to rival Wade.

18. Kuscular (2007). A growing body of scholarship and philosophy explores Islamic views on nature and the roots of environmental ethics and justice in Islamic thought. Scholars of ecology and Islam point to a number of injunctions against pollution, wasteful consumption, and the general abuse of nature to highlight foundational guidelines within Islam for the faithful stewardship of the environment. For a collection of essays aimed at both a scholarly and lay audience, see *Islam and Ecology: A Bestowed Trust* (Foltz, Frederick, and Baharuddin 2003). Some other resources include Haleem (1998), Khalid and O'Brien (1992), and Nasr (1996).

19. See Fahmi and Sutton (2010) and Kuppinger (2014) for a description of the Zabaleen's waste-management system and some of the challenges it faces with neoliberal privatization.

20. The Zabaleen traditionally fed organic material that they collected to pigs, which were then later sold for meat. However, in the fear surrounding the so-called swine flu or H1N1 virus, the pigs were all killed in a massive cull in 2009. Bound up with associations of impurity and contagion, the slaughter appears to have represented more discrimination against the Copts than a rational policy (see Leach and Tadros 2014).

21. In 2016 it was estimated that about one-fifth of garbage workers were women. The numbers have been slowly declining since Set/Setal.

CONCLUSION. **Garbage Citizenship**

1. I am indebted to an anonymous reviewer for clarifying this point.

Abdoul, Mohamadou. 2002. "The Production of the City and Urban Informalities: The Borough of Thiaroye-sur-Mer in the City of Pikine, Senegal." In *Under Siege: Four African Cities—Freetown, Johannesburg, Kinshasa, Lagos: Documenta 11_Platform 4*, edited by Okwui Enwezor, Carlos Basualdo, Ute Meta Bauer, Susanne Ghez, Sarat Majaraj, Mark Nash, and Octavio Zaya, 337–58. Ostfildern-Ruit, Germany: Hatje Cantz.

Abrahamsson, Sebastian, Filippo Bertoni, and Annemarie Mol. 2015. "Living with Omega-3: New Materialism and Enduring Concerns." *Environment and Planning D: Society and Space* 33:4–19.

Alexander, Catherine, and Joshua Reno, eds. 2012. *Economies of Recycling: The Global Transformation of Materials, Values and Social Relations*. London: Zed Books.

Ali, Mansoor, Jane Olley, and Andrew Cotton. 1998. "Agents of Change: The Case of Karachi City's Waste Management." *Third World Planning Review* 20, no. 33: 255–66.

Anand, Nikhil. 2011. "Pressure: The PoliTechnics of Water Supply in Mumbai." *Cultural Anthropology* 26, no. 4: 542–64.

Anand, Nikhil. 2012. "Municipal Disconnect: On Abject Water and Its Urban Infrastructures." *Ethnography* 13, no. 4: 487–509.

Anand, Nikhil. 2017. *Hydraulic City: Water and the Infrastructures of Citizenship in Mumbai*. Durham, NC: Duke University Press.

Anderson, Warwick. 1995. "Excremental Colonialism: Public Health and the Poetics of Pollution." *Critical Inquiry* (spring): 640–69.

Appadurai, Arjun. 2002. "Deep Democracy: Urban Governmentality and the Horizon of Politics." *Public Culture* 14, no. 1: 21–47.

Appel, Hannah. 2014. "Walls and White Elephants: Oil, Infrastructure, and the Materiality of Citizenship in Urban Equatorial Guinea." In *The Arts of Citizenship in African Cities: Infrastructures and Spaces of Belonging*, edited by Mamadou Diouf and Rosalind Fredericks, 253–76. New York: Palgrave Macmillan.

Appel, Hannah, Nikhil Anand, and Akhil Gupta. 2015. "Introduction: The Infrastructure Toolbox." *Cultural Anthropology.* http://www.culanth.org/fieldsights /714-introduction-the-infrastructure-toolbox.

Audrain, Xavier. 2004. "Du "'*ndigël*" avorté' au parti de la vérité: Évolution du rapport religion/politique à travers le parcours de Cheikh Modou Kara (1999–2004)." *Politique Africaine* 96:96–118.

Babou, Cheikh Anta. 2007. "Urbanizing Mystical Islam: Making Murid Space in the Cities of Senegal." *International Journal of African Historical Studies* 40, no. 2: 197–223.

Babou, Cheikh Anta. 2013. "The Senegalese 'Social Contract' Revisited: The Muridiyya Muslim Order and State Politics in Postcolonial Senegal." In *Tolerance, Democracy, and Sufis in Senegal*, edited by Mamadou Diouf, 125–46. New York: Columbia University Press.

Bakker, Isabella, and Stephen Gill, eds. 2003. *Power, Production and Social Reproduction: Human In/security in the Global Political Economy.* New York: Palgrave Macmillan.

Bakker, Karen, and Gavin Bridge. 2006. "Material Worlds? Resource Geographies and the 'Matter of Nature'." *Progress in Human Geography* 30, no. 1: 5–27.

Barad, Karen. 2007. *Meeting the Universe Halfway: Quantum Physics and the Entanglement of Matter and Meaning.* Durham, NC: Duke University Press.

Bassett, Thomas J., and Donald Crummey. 1993. *Land in African Agrarian Systems.* Madison: University of Wisconsin Press.

Bauman, Zygmunt. 2003. *Wasted Lives: Modernity and Its Outcasts.* Cambridge: Polity.

Bayart, Jean-François. 1989. *L'état en Afrique: La politique du ventre.* Paris: Editions Fayard.

Bayart, Jean-François. 1999."Africa in the World: A History of Extraversion." *African Affairs* 99, no. 395: 217–67.

Bazenguissa-Ganga, Rémy. 2014. "Beautifying Brazzaville: Arts of Citizenship in the Congo." In *The Arts of Citizenship in African Cities: Infrastructures and Spaces of Belonging*, edited by Mamadou Diouf and Rosalind Fredericks, 163–86. New York: Palgrave Macmillan.

BCEOM (Bureau central d'études pour les équipements d'outre-mer). 1986. *Etude des systèmes de gestion des déchets et de récupération des ressources dans la zone métropolitaine de Dakar.* Dakar: Communauté Urbaine de Dakar.

Beall, Jo. 1997. "Thoughts on Poverty from a South Asian Rubbish Dump: Gender, Inequality, and Household Waste." *IDS Bulletin* 28, no. 3: 73–90.

Beall, Jo. 2006. "Dealing with Dirt and the Disorder of Development: Managing Rubbish in Urban Pakistan." *Oxford Development Studies* 34, no. 1: 81–97.

Beall, Jo, Owen Crankshaw, and Susan Parnell. 2000. "Victims, Villains and Fixers: The Urban Environment and Johannesburg's Poor." *Journal of Southern African Studies* 26, no. 4: 833–55.

Beck, Linda. 2003. "Democratization and the Hidden Public: The Impact of Patronage Networks on Senegalese Women." *Comparative Politics* 35, no. 2: 147–69.

Bellitto, Marc. 2001. *Une histoire du Sénégal et de ses entreprises publiques Paris.* Paris: Harmattan.

Bennett, Jane. 2010. *Vibrant Matter: A Political Ecology of Things*. Durham, NC: Duke University Press.

Benrabia, Nora. 2002. "Choix organisationnels et institutions: La reform du secteur des dechets menagers en Afrique subsaharienne." PhD diss., Université de Versailles Saint-Quentin-en-Yvelines.

Berg, Elliot. 1981. *Accelerated Development in Sub-Saharan Africa: An Agenda for Action*. Washington, DC: World Bank.

Berg, Elliot. 1990. *Adjustment Postponed: Economic Policy Reform in Senegal in the 1980s*. Dakar: USAID.

Berry, Sara. 1993. *No Condition Is Permanent: The Social Dynamics of Agrarian Change in Sub-Saharan Africa*. Madison: University of Wisconsin Press.

Betts, Raymond F. 1971. "The Establishment of the Medina in Dakar, Senegal, 1914." *Africa* 41, no. 2: 143–52.

Bigon, Liora. 2009. *A History of Urban Planning in Two West African Colonial Capitals: Residential Segregation in British Lagos and French Dakar (1850–1930)*. Lewiston, NY: Edwin Mellen.

Billings, Dwight B. 1990. "Religion as Opposition: A Gramscian Analysis." *American Journal of Sociology* 96, no. 1: 1–31.

Björkman, Lisa. 2014. "Un/known Waters: Navigating Everyday Risks of Infrastructural Breakdown in Mumbai." *Comparative Studies of South Asia, Africa and the Middle East* 34, no. 3: 497–517.

Blundo, Giorgio, and Pierre-Yves Le Meur, eds. 2009. *The Governance of Daily Life in Africa: Ethnographic Explorations of Public and Collective Services*. Leiden, Netherlands: Brill.

Bond, Patrick. 2005. "Gramsci, Polanyi and Impressions from Africa on the Social Forum Phenomenon." *International Journal of Urban and Regional Research* 29, no. 2: 433–40.

Boone, Catherine. 1990. "State Power and Economic Crisis in Senegal." *Comparative Politics* 22, no. 3: 341–57.

Boone, Catherine. 1992. *Merchant Capital and the Roots of State Power in Senegal 1930–1985*. Cambridge: Cambridge University Press.

Bornstein, Erica. 2003. *The Spirit of Development: Protestant NGOs, Morality, and Economics in Zimbabwe*. New York: Routledge.

Braun, Bruce. 2007. "Theorizing the Nature-Society Divide." In *The SAGE Handbook of Political Geography*, edited by Kevin Cox, Murray Low, and Jenny Robinson, 189–204. London: SAGE.

Braun, Bruce, Ben Anderson, Steve Hinchliffe, Christian Abrahamsson, Nicky Gregson, and Jane Bennett. 2011. "Book Review Forum: Vibrant Matter: A Political Ecology of Things." *Dialogues in Human Geography* 1, no. 3: 390–406.

Braun, Bruce, and Sarah J. Whatmore, eds. 2010. *Political Matter: Technoscience, Democracy, and Public Life*. Minneapolis: University of Minnesota Press.

Brenner, Louis, ed. 1993. *Muslim Identity and Social Change in Africa*. London: Hurst and Company.

Brownell, Emily. 2014. "Seeing Dirt in Dar es Salaam: Sanitation, Waste and Citizenship in the Post-Colonial City." In *The Art of Citizenship in African Cities: Infrastructures and Spaces of Belonging*, edited by Mamadou Diouf and Rosalind Fredericks, 209–29. New York: Palgrave Macmillan.

Buggenhagen, Beth A. 2001. "Prophets and Profits: Gendered and Generational Visions of Wealth and Value in Senegalese Murid Households." *Journal of Religion in Africa* 31, no. 4: 373–401.

Butler, Judith, and Athena Athanasiou. 2013. *Dispossession: The Performative in the Political*. Cambridge: Polity.

Calhoun, Craig, Richard Sennett, and Harel Shapira. 2013. "Introduction: *Poesis* Means Making." *Public Culture* 25, no. 2: 195–200.

Callaway, Barbara, and Lucy Creevey. 1994. *The Heritage of Islam: Women, Religion, and Politics in West Africa*. Boulder, CO: Lynne Rienner.

Carney, Judith, and Michael Watts. 1990. "Manufacturing Dissent: Work, Gender and the Politics of Meaning in a Peasant Society." *Africa* 60, no. 2: 205–41.

Castells, Manuel. 1979. *The Urban Question: A Marxist Approach*. Cambridge, MA: MIT Press.

Cavalcanti, Mariana. 2015. "Waiting in the Ruins: The Aesthetics and Politics of Favela Urbanization in 'PACification' Rio de Janeiro." In *Infrastructural Lives: Urban Infrastructure in Context*, edited by Stephen Graham and Colin McFarlane, 86–113. New York: Routledge.

Chakrabarty, Dipesh. 1991. "Open Space/Public Place: Garbage, Modernity, and India." *South Asia* 14, no. 1: 15–31.

Chalfin, Brenda. 2010. *Neoliberal Frontiers: An Ethnography of Sovereignty in West Africa*. Chicago: University of Chicago Press.

Chalfin, Brenda. 2014. "Public Things, Excremental Politics, and the Infrastructure of Bare Life in Ghana's City of Tema." *American Ethnologist* 41, no. 1: 92–109.

Chalfin, Brenda. 2016. "'Wastelandia': Infrastructure and the Commonwealth of Waste in Urban Ghana." *Ethnos* 82, no. 4: 648–71.

Chalhoub, Sidney. 1993. "The Politics of Disease Control: Yellow Fever and Race in Nineteenth Century Rio de Janeiro." *Journal of Latin American Studies* 25:441–63.

Chari, Sharad. 2013. "Detritus in Durban: Polluted Environs and the Biopolitics of Refusal." In *Imperial Debris: On Ruins and Ruination*, edited by Ann Laura Stoler, 131–61. Durham, NC: Duke University Press.

Chu, Julie Y. 2014. "When Infrastructures Attack: The Workings of Disrepair in China." *American Ethnologist* 41, no. 2: 351–67.

CIA (Central Intelligence Agency). 2016. "The World Factbook: Senegal." Central Intelligence Agency. https://www.cia.gov/library/publications/the-world-factbook/geos/sg.html.

Cissé, Oumar, and Salimata Seck Wone. 2013. "La gestion des déchets de Dakar (2000–2012): L'imbroglio institutionnel." In *Sénégal (2000–2012): Les institutions et politiques publiques à l'épreuve d'une gouvernance libérale*, edited by Momar-Coumba Diop, 729–58. Paris: Karthala.

Cissokho, Aboubacar Demba. 2011. "Wade soutient une prise en charge de l'électricité et des ordures des mairies." *APS*, April 28.

Clark, Gracia. 1994. *Onions Are My Husband: Survival and Accumulation by West African Market Women*. Chicago: University of Chicago Press.

Cohen, Michael. 2007. "Aid, Density, and Urban Form: Anticipating Dakar." *Built Environment* 33, no. 2: 145–56.

Collier, Stephen J., James Christopher Mizes, and Antina von Schnitzler. 2016. "Preface: Public Infrastructures/Infrastructural Publics." *Limn* 7. http://limn.it/issue/07/.

Collignon, René. 1984. "La lutte des pouvoirs publics contre les 'encombrements humains' à Dakar." *Canadian Journal of African Studies/Revue Canadienne des études africaines* 18, no. 3: 573–82.

Comaroff, Jean, and John L. Comaroff. 1999. "Occult Economies and the Violence of Abstraction: Notes from the South African Postcolony." *American Ethnologist* 26, no. 2: 279–303.

Comaroff, Jean, and John L. Comaroff. 2000. "Privatizing the Millennium: New Protestant Ethics and Spirits of Capitalism in Africa, and Elsewhere." *Afrika Spectrum* 35, no. 3: 293–312.

Comaroff, Jean, and John L. Comaroff. 2012. "Theory from the South: Or, How Euro-America Is Evolving Toward Africa." *Anthropological Forum: A Journal of Social Anthropology and Comparative Sociology* 22, no. 2: 113–31.

Conklin, Alice L. 1997. *A Mission to Civilize: The Republican Idea of Empire in France and West Africa (1895–1930)*. Stanford, CA: Stanford University Press.

Connolly, William E. 2010. "Materiality, Experience, and Surveillance." In *Political Matter: Technoscience, Democracy, and Public Life*, edited by Bruce Braun and Sarah J. Whatmore, 63–88. Minneapolis: University of Minnesota Press.

Cooper, Frederick, ed. 1983. *Struggle for the City: Migrant Labor, Capital, and the State in Urban Africa*. Beverly Hills, CA: SAGE.

Cooper, Frederick. 1996. *Decolonization and African Society: The Labor Question in French and British Africa*. Cambridge: Cambridge University Press.

Copans, Jean. 1980. *Les marabouts de l'arachide*. Paris: Harmattan.

Coulon, Christian, and Donal B. Cruise O'Brien. 1990. "Senegal." In *Contemporary West African States*, edited by Donal B. Cruise O'Brien, John Dunn, and Richard Rathbone, 145–64. Cambridge: Cambridge University Press.

Crang, Michael. 2010. "The Death of Great Ships: Photography, Politics, and Waste in the Global Imaginary." *Environment and Planning A* 42, no. 5: 1084–102.

Creevey, Lucy. 1985. "Muslim Brotherhood and Politics in Senegal." *Journal of Modern African Studies* 22:715–21.

Creevey, Lucy. 1996. "Islam, Women and the Role of the State in Senegal." *Journal of Religion in Africa* 26, no. 3: 268–307.

Creevey, Lucy, Richard Vengroff, and Ibrahima Gaye. 1995. "Devaluation of the CFA Franc in Senegal: The Reaction of Small Businesses." *Journal of Modern African Studies* 33, no. 44: 669–83.

Cruise O'Brien, Donal B. 1971. *The Mourides of Senegal: The Political and Economic Organization of an Islamic Brotherhood*. Oxford: Clarendon.

Cruise O'Brien, Donal B. 1975. *Saints and Politicians: Essays on the Organisation of a Senegalese Peasant Society*. New York: Cambridge University Press.

Cruise O'Brien, Donal B. 1996. "A Lost Generation? Youth Identity and State Decay in West Africa." In *Postcolonial Identities in Africa*, edited by Richard Werbner and Terrance Ranger, 55–74. London: Zed Books.

Cruise O'Brien, Donal B. 2003. *Symbolic Confrontations: Muslims Imagining the State in Africa*. New York: Palgrave Macmillan.

Cruise O'Brien, Donal B. 2007. "Show and State in Senegal: Play-Acting on the Threshold of Power." In *Staging Politics: Power and Performance in Asia and Africa*, edited by Julia C. Strauss and Donal B. Cruise O'Brien, 15–30. New York: I. B. Tauris.

Cruise O'Brien, Donal B., and Christian Coulon. 1988. *Charisma and Brotherhood in African Islam*. Oxford: Clarendon.

Dahou, Tarik, and Vincent Foucher. 2004. "Le Sénégal, entre changement politique et révolution passé: Sopi or not sopi?" *Politique Africaine* 96:5–21.

Davis, Mike. 2004. "Planet of Slums: Urban Involution and the Informal Proletariat." *New Left Review* 26 (March–April): 5–34.

De Boeck, Filip. 2014. "Challenges of Urban Growth: Toward an Anthropology of Urban Infrastructure in Africa." In *Afritecture: Building Social Change*, edited by A. Lepik, 92–102. Ostfildern-Ruit, Germany: Hatje Cantz.

De Boeck, Filip, and Sammy Baloji. 2016. *Suturing the City: Living Together in Congo's Urban Worlds*. London: Autograph.

De Boeck, Filip, and Marie-Françoise Plissart. 2005. *Kinshasa: Tales of the Invisible City*. Antwerp, Belgium: Ludion.

Diallo, Kalidou. 2002. "Le mouvement syndical: Crises et recompositions." In *La société sénégalaise entre le local et le global*, edited by Momar-Coumba Diop, 441–64. Paris: Karthala.

Diaw, Aminata, and Mamadou Diouf. 1998. "The Senegalese Opposition and Its Quest for Power." In *The Politics of Opposition in Contemporary Africa*, edited by Adebayo O. Olukoshi, 113–43. Uppsala, Sweden: Nordiska Afrikainstitutet.

Dieng, Moctar. 2009. "Greve des agents du nettoiement: Dakar sous la menace des ordures." APS, February 18.

Diop, Mamadou. n.d. "Propos d'un maire: Mon combat pour Dakar." Unpublished manuscript.

Diop, Momar-Coumba. 2013a. "Introduction: Essai sur un mode de gouvernance des institutions et des politiques publiques." In *Sénégal (2000–2012): Les institutions et politiques publiques à l'épreuve d'une gouvernance libérale*, edited by Momar-Coumba Diop, 33–84. Paris: Karthala.

Diop, Momar-Coumba, ed. 2013b. *Le Sénégal sous Abdoulaye Wade: Le sopi à l'épreuve du pouvoir*. Paris: Karthala.

Diop, Momar-Coumba, ed. 2013c. *Sénégal (2000–2012): Les institutions et politiques publiques à l'épreuve d'une gouvernance libérale*. Paris: Karthala.

Diop, Momar-Coumba, and Mamadou Diouf. 1990. *Le Sénégal sous Abdou Diouf*. Paris: Karthala.

Diop, Momar-Coumba, and Mamadou Diouf. 1992. "Enjeux et contraintes politiques de la gestion municipale au Sénégal." *Canadian Journal of African Studies/Revue Canadienne des études africaines* 26, no. 1: 1–23.

Diop, Momar-Coumba, Mamadou Diouf, and Aminata Diaw. 2000. "Le baobab a eté déraciné: L'alternance au Sénégal." *Politique Africaine* 78:157–79.

Diop, Momar-Coumba, and Faye Ousseynou. 2002. "Les jeunes et la gouvernance de la ville." In *La société sénégalaise entre le local et le global*, edited by Momar-Coumba Diop, 687–720. Paris: Karthala.

Diouf, Mamadou. 1992. "Fresques murales et écriture de l'histoire: Le Set/Setal a Dakar." *Politique Africaine* 46:41–54.

Diouf, Mamadou. 1996. "Urban Youth and Senegalese Politics: Dakar 1988–1994." *Public Culture* 8:225–49.

Diouf, Mamadou. 1997. "Senegalese Development: From Mass Mobilization to Technocratic Elitism." In *International Development and the Social Sciences: Essays on the History and Politics of Knowledge*, edited by F. Cooper and R. Packard, 291–319. Berkeley: University of California Press.

Diouf, Mamadou. 1998. "The French Colonial Policy and the Civility of the Originaires of the Four Communes (Senegal): A Nineteenth Century Globalization Project." *Development and Change* 29:671–96.

Diouf, Mamadou. 2000. "The Senegalese Murid Trade Diaspora and the Making of a Vernacular Cosmopolitanism." *Public Culture* 12, no. 3: 679–702.

Diouf, Mamadou. 2002. "Des cultures urbaines entre traditions et mondialisations." In *Le Sénégal contemporain*, edited by Momar-Coumba Diop, 261–88. Paris: Karthala.

Diouf, Mamadou. 2003. "Engaging Postcolonial Cultures: African Youth and Public Space." *African Studies Review* 46, no. 2: 1–12.

Diouf, Mamadou, ed. 2013. *Tolerance, Democracy, and Sufis in Senegal*. New York: Columbia University Press.

Diouf, Mamadou. n.d. Synthèse du rapport sur le contentieux soadip-ex commune de Dakar. Direction des collectivités locales. Ministère de l'interieur. République du Sénégal.

Diouf, Mamadou, and Rosalind Fredericks, eds. 2013. *Les arts de la citoyenneté au Sénégal: Espaces contestés et civilités urbaines*. Paris: Karthala.

Diouf, Mamadou, and Rosalind Fredericks, eds. 2014. *The Arts of Citizenship in African Cities: Infrastructures and Spaces of Belonging*. New York: Palgrave Macmillan.

Diouf, Mamadou, and Mara Leichtman, eds. 2009. *New Perspectives on Islam in Senegal*. New York: Palgrave Macmillan.

Diouf, Nafi. 2005. "Cholera Epidemic Spreads in Senegal, Infecting Dozens." *Associated Press Worldstream*, April 5.

Doherty, Jacob. 2018. "Maintenance Space: The Political Authority of Garbage in Kampala." *Current Anthropology*, forthcoming.

Doshi, Sapana. 2013. "Resettlement Ecologies: Environmental Subjectivity and Graduated Citizenship in Mumbai." In *Ecologies of Urbanism in India: Metropolitan Civility and Sustainability*, edited by Anne Rademacher and Kalyanakrishnan Sivaramakrishnan, 225–48. Hong Kong: Hong Kong University Press.

Doucouré, Djibril. 2002. "La gestion des dechets à Dakar: Evolutions institutionnelles récentes et impact sur le financement." *Atelier regional thématique: "Pour une gestion partagée des dechets solides en Afrique."* Cotonou: IAGU-Waste Net Sénégal.

Douglas, Mary. 1966. *Purity and Danger: An Analysis of the Concepts of Pollution and Taboo*. London: Routledge.

Durham, Deborah. 2000. "Youth and the Social Imagination in Africa: Introduction to Parts 1 and 2." *Anthropological Quarterly* 73, no. 3: 113–20.

Echenberg, Myron. 2002. *Black Death, White Medicine: Bubonic Plague and the Politics of Public Health in Colonial Senegal, 1914–1945*. Oxford: James Currey.

Elyachar, Julia. 2010. "Phatic Labor, Infrastructure, and the Question of Empowerment in Cairo." *American Ethnologist* 37, no. 3: 452–64.

ENDA (Environnement et développement du tiers monde). 1991. *Set Setal, des murs qui parlent: Nouvelle culture urbaine à Dakar*. Dakar: ENDA Tiers Monde.

ENDA (Environnement et développement du tiers monde). 1999. *Volet collecte des déchets et assainissement du quartier traditionnel de Yoff-Tonghor: Etude de faisabilité*. Dakar: ENDA Tiers Monde.

Esty, Joshua D. 1999. "Excremental Postcolonialism." *Contemporary Literature* 40, no. 1: 22–59.

Fahmi, Wael, and Keith Sutton. 2010. "Cairo's Contested Garbage: Sustainable Solid Waste Management and the Zabaleen's Right to the City." *Sustainability* 2:1765–83.

Fairhead, James, and Melissa Leach. 1996. *Misreading the African Landscape: Society and Ecology in a Forest-Savanna Mosaic*. Cambridge: Cambridge University Press.

Fakier, Khayaat, and Jacklyn Cock. 2009. "A Gendered Analysis of the Crisis of Social Reproduction in Contemporary South Africa." *International Feminist Journal of Politics* 11, no. 3: 353–71.

Fall, Babacar. 2002. *Social History in French West Africa: Forced Labour, Labour Market, Women and Politics*. Amsterdam/India: South-South Exchange Programme for Research on the History of Development (SEPHIS) and the Centre for Studies in Social Sciences, Calcutta (CSSSC).

Fall, Madior. 2007. "Sénégal: l'insalubrité "recolonise" Dakar." *Sud Quotidien*, May 3.

Fatton, Robert. 1986. "Gramsci and the Legitimization of the State: The Case of the Senegalese Passive Revolution." *Canadian Journal of Political Science* 19, no. 4: 729–50.

Fatton, Robert. 1987. *The Making of a Liberal Democracy: Senegal's Passive Revolution, 1975–1985*. Boulder, CO: Lynne Rienner.

Fennell, Catherine. 2016. "Are We All Flint?" *Limn* 7. http://limn.it/issue/07/.

Ferguson, James. 1994. *The Anti-politics Machine: Development, Depoliticization, and Bureaucratic Power in Lesotho*. Minneapolis: University of Minnesota Press.

Ferguson, James. 1999. *Expectations of Modernity: Myths and Meanings of Urban Life on the Zambian Copperbelt*. Berkeley: University of California Press.

Ferguson, James. 2006. *Global Shadows: Africa in the Neoliberal World Order*. Durham, NC: Duke University Press.

Ferguson, James. 2012. "Afterward: Structures of Responsibility." *Ethnography* 13, no. 4: 558–62.

Foley, Ellen E. 2010. *Your Pocket Is What Cures You: The Politics of Health in Senegal*. New Brunswick, NJ: Rutgers University Press.

Foley, Ellen E., and Fatou Maria Drame. 2013. "Mbaraan and the Shifting Political Economy of Sex in Urban Senegal." *Culture, Health and Sexuality* 15, no. 2: 121–34.

Foltz, Richard C., Denny M. Frederick, and Azizan Baharuddin, eds. 2003. *Islam and Ecology: A Bestowed Trust*. Cambridge, MA: Harvard University Press.

Foucher, Vincent. 2007. "'Blue Marches': Public Performance and Political Turnover in Senegal." In *Staging Politics: Power and Performance in Asia and Africa*, edited by Julia C. Strauss and Donal B. Cruise O'Brien, 111–32. New York: I. B. Tauris.

Fouquet, Thomas. 2013. "Esquisses d'un art de la citadinité subalterne: Les aventurières de la nuit dakaroise." In *Les arts de la citoyenneté au Sénégal: Espaces contestés et civilités urbaines*, edited by Mamadou Diouf and Rosalind Fredericks, 131–58. Paris: Karthala.

Fredericks, Rosalind. 2014. "'The Old Man Is Dead': Youth, Hip Hop, and the Elections of 2012 in Senegal." *Antipode* 46, no. 1: 130–48.

Furniss, Philip Jamie. 2012. "Metaphors of Waste: Several Ways of Seeing 'Development' and Cairo's Garbage Collectors." DPhil diss., Oxford University.

Gandy, Matthew. 2003. *Concrete and Clay: Reworking Nature in New York City*. Cambridge, MA: MIT Press.

Gandy, Matthew. 2006. "Planning, Anti-planning and the Infrastructure Crisis Facing Metropolitan Lagos." *Urban Studies* 43, no. 2: 371–96.

Gandy, Matthew. 2014. *The Fabric of Space: Water, Modernity, and the Urban Imagination*. Cambridge, MA: MIT Press.

Gaye, Malick. 1996. *Entrepreneurial Cities*. Dakar: ENDA.

Gaye, Malick, and Fodé Diallo. 1997. "Community Participation in the Management of the Urban Environment in Rufisque (Senegal)." *Environment and Urbanization* 9, no. 1: 9–29.

Gellar, Sheldon. 2005. *Democracy in Senegal: Tocquevillian Analytics in Africa*. New York: Palgrave Macmillan.

Geschiere, Peter. 1997. *The Modernity of Witchcraft: Politics and the Occult in Postcolonial Africa*. Charlottesville: University of Virginia Press.

Geschiere, Peter, and Josef Gugler. 1998. "The Urban-Rural Connection: Changing Issues of Belonging and Identification." *Africa: Journal of the International African Institute* 68, no. 3: 309–19.

Geschiere, Peter, and Stephen Jackson. 2006. "Autochthony and the Crisis of Citizenship: Democratization, Decentralization, and the Politics of Belonging." *African Studies Review* 49, no. 2: 1–7.

Ghertner, D. Asher. 2010a. "Calculating without Numbers: Aesthetic Governmentality in Delhi's Slums." *Economy and Society* 39, no. 2: 185–217.

Ghertner, D. Asher. 2010b. "Green Evictions: Clearing Slums, Saving Nature in Delhi." In *Global Political Ecology*, edited by Paul Robbins, Richard Peet, and Michael Watts, 145–66. London: Routledge.

Gidwani, Vinay. 2013. "Value Struggles: Waste Work and Urban Ecology in Delhi." In *Ecologies of Urbanism in India: Metropolitan Civility and Sustainability*, edited by Anne Rademacher and Kalyanakrishnan Sivaramakrishnan, 169–200. Hong Kong: Hong Kong University Press.

Gidwani, Vinay, and Rajyashree N. Reddy. 2011. "The Afterlives of 'Waste': Notes from India for a Minor History of Capitalist Surplus." *Antipode* 43, no. 5: 1625–58.

Gifford, Paul. 2004. *Ghana's New Christianity: Pentecostalism in a Globalizing African Economy*. Bloomington: Indiana University Press.

Giglioli, Ilaria, and Eric Swyngedouw. 2008. "Let's Drink to the Great Thirst!: Water and the Politics of Fractured Techno-natures in Sicily." *International Journal of Urban and Regional Research* 32, no. 2: 392–414.

Gilmore, Ruth Wilson. 2007. *Golden Gulag: Prisons, Surplus, Crisis, and Opposition in Globalizing California*. Berkeley: University of California Press.

Gluckman, Max. 1961. "Anthropological Problems Arising from the African Industrial Revolution." In *Social Change in Modern Africa*, edited by Aidan Southall, 67–83. London: Oxford University Press.

Graham, Carol L. 1994. *Safety Nets, Politics, and the Poor: Transitions to Market Economies*. Washington, DC: Brookings Institution.

Graham, Stephen, ed. 2010. *Disrupted Cities: When Infrastructure Fails*. New York: Routledge.

Graham, Stephen, and Simon Marvin. 2001. *Splintering Urbanism: Networked Infrastructures, Technological Mobilities and the Urban Condition*. New York: Routledge.

Graham, Stephen, and Colin McFarlane, eds. 2015. *Infrastructural Lives: Urban Infrastructure in Context*. New York: Routledge.

Graham, Stephen, and Nigel Thrift. 2007. "Out of Order: Understanding Repair and Maintenance." *Theory, Culture and Society* 24, no. 3: 1–25.

Gregson, Nicky, and Michael Crang. 2010. "Materiality and Waste: Inorganic Vitality in a Networked World." *Environment and Planning A* 42, no. 5: 1026–32.

Gregson, Nicky, Helen Watkins, and Melania Calestani. 2010. "Inextinguishable Fibres: Demolition and the Vital Materialisms of Asbestos." *Environment and Planning A* 42, no. 5: 1065–83.

Groupe Chagnon Ltée. 1996. *Nouveau systeme de nettoiement de la communauté urbaine de Dakar*. Montreal: Groupe Chagnon.

Gueye, Cheikh. 2002. *Touba: La capitale des Mourides*. Paris: Karthala.

Habermas, Jürgen. [1962] 1991. *The Structural Transformation of the Public Sphere*. Cambridge, MA: MIT Press.

Haleem, Harfiyah Abdel, ed. 1998. *Islam and the Environment*. London: Ta-Ha.

Hansen, Thomas Blom, and Finn Stepputat, eds. 2001. *States of Imagination: Ethnographic Explorations of the Postcolonial State*. Durham, NC: Duke University Press.

Hart, Gillian. 2001. "Development Critiques in the 1990s: Culs de Sac and Promising Paths." *Progress in Human Geography* 25, no. 4: 649–58.

Hart, Gillian. 2002. *Disabling Globalization: Places of Power in Post-apartheid South Africa*. Berkeley: University of California Press.

Hart, Keith. 1973. "Informal Income Opportunities and Urban Employment in Ghana." *Journal of Modern African Studies* 11, no. 1: 61–89.

Harvey, David. 1996. *Justice, Nature, and the Geography of Difference*. Oxford: Blackwell.

Harvey, Penelope. 2016. "Waste Futures: Infrastructures and Political Experimentation in Southern Peru." *Ethnos* 82, no. 4: 672–89.

Harvey, Penelope, and Hannah Knox. 2012. "The Enchantments of Infrastructure." *Mobilities* 7, no. 4: 521–36.

Hawkins, Gay. 2003. "Down the Drain: Shit and the Politics of Disturbance." In *Culture and Waste: The Creation and Destruction of Value*, edited by Gay Hawkins and Stephen Muecke, 39–52. Lanham, MD: Rowman and Littlefield.

Hawkins, Gay, and Stephen Muecke, eds. 2003. *Culture and Waste: The Creation and Destruction of Value*. Lanham, MD: Rowman and Littlefield.

Hecht, Gabrielle. 2012. *Being Nuclear: Africans and the Global Uranium Trade*. Cambridge MA: MIT Press.

Heynen, Nik, James McCarthy, Scott Prudham, and Paul Robbins, eds. 2007. *Neoliberal Environments: False Promises and Unnatural Consequences*. London: Routledge.

Hirschkind, Charles. 2001. "Civic Virtue and Religious Reason: An Islamic Counter-public." *Cultural Anthropology* 16, no. 1: 3–34.

Hoexter, Miriam, Shmuel N. Eisenstadt, and Nehemia Levtzion, eds. 2002. *The Public Sphere in Muslim Societies*. Albany: State University of New York Press.

Holston, James. 2010. "Right to the City, Right to Rights, and Urban Citizenship." Paper presented at the Globalization, Institutions, and Economic Security Workshop at the Mershon Center for International Security Studies, Columbus, OH, March 3.

Holston, James, and Arjun Appadurai. 1999. "Introduction: Cities and Citizenship." In *Cities and Citizenship*, edited by James Holston, 1–20. Durham, NC: Duke University Press.

Honwana, Alcinda. 2012. *The Time of Youth: Work, Social Change, and Politics in Africa*. Sterling, VA: Kumarian.

Honwana, Alcinda, and Filip De Boeck, eds. 2005. *Makers and Breakers: Children and Youth in Postcolonial Africa*. Trenton, NJ: Africa World Press.

ICLEI (International Council for Local Environmental Initiatives). 1997. *Case Study 45—Participatory Solid Waste Management (Dakar, Senegal)*. Toronto: ICLEI-Canada.

Isaacman, Allen. 1996. *Cotton Is the Mother of Poverty: Peasants, Work, and Rural Struggle in Colonial Mozambique, 1938–1961*. London: Heinemann.

Ishii, Miho. 2016. "Caring for Divine Infrastructures: Nature and Spirits in a Special Economic Zone in India." *Ethnos* 82, no. 4: 690–710.

Jackson, Peter. 2000. "Rematerializing Social and Cultural Geography." *Social and Cultural Geography* 1:9–14.

Jensen, Casper Bruun, and Atsuro Morita. 2016. "Infrastructures as Ontological Experiments." *Ethnos* 82, no. 4: 615–26.

Johnson, G. Wesley. 1971. *The Emergence of Black Politics in Senegal: The Struggle for Power in the Four Communes 1900–1920*. Stanford, CA: Stanford University Press.

Kane, Ousmane. 2003. *Muslim Modernity in Postcolonial Nigeria: A Study of the Society for the Removal of Innovation and Reinstatement of Tradition*. Boston: Brill.

Kaplan, Robert. D. 1994. "The Coming Anarchy." *Atlantic Monthly* (February): 44–76.

Katz, Cindi. 2001. "Vagabond Capitalism and the Necessity of Social Reproduction." *Antipode* 33, no. 4: 709–14.

Khalid, Fazlun, and Joanne O'Brien, eds. 1992. *Islam and Ecology*. New York: Cassell.

Kirsch, Scott. 2013. "Cultural Geography I: Materialist Turns." *Progress in Human Geography* 37, no. 3: 433–41.

Kong, Lily. 1990. "Geography and Religion: Trends and Prospects." *Progress in Human Geography* 14:355–71.

Kong, Lily. 2001. "Mapping 'New' Geographies of Religion: Politics and Poetics in Modernity." *Progress in Human Geography* 25, no. 2: 211–33.

Kong, Lily. 2010. "Global Shifts, Theoretical Shifts: Changing Geographies of Religion." *Progress in Human Geography* 34, no. 6: 755–76.

Kooy, Michelle, and Karen Bakker. 2008. "Technologies of Government: Constituting Subjectivities, Spaces, and Infrastructures in Colonial and Contemporary Jakarta." *International Journal of Urban and Regional Research* 32, no. 2: 375–91.

Kristeva, Julia. 1982. *Powers of Horror: An Essay on Abjection.* New York: Columbia University Press.

Kuppinger, Petra. 2014. "Crushed?: Cairo's Garbage Collectors and Neoliberal Urban Politics." *Journal of Urban Affairs* 36:621–33.

Kuscular, Remzi. 2007. *Cleanliness in Islam.* Somerset, NJ: The Light.

Lakoff, Andrew, and Stephen J. Collier. 2010. "Infrastructure and Event: The Political Technology of Preparedness." In *Political Matter: Technoscience, Democracy, and Public Life*, edited by Bruce Braun and Sarah J. Whatmore, 243–66. Minneapolis: University of Minnesota Press.

Larkin, Brian. 2008. *Signal and Noise: Media, Infrastructure, and Urban Culture in Nigeria.* Durham, NC: Duke University Press.

Larkin, Brian. 2013. "The Politics and Poetics of Infrastructure." *Annual Review of Anthropology* 42:327–43.

Larner, Wendy. 2003. "Guest Editorial: Neoliberalism?" *Environment and Planning D: Society and Space* 21:509–12.

Lawhon, Mary, Henrik Ernstson, and Jonathan Silver. 2014. "Provincializing Urban Political Ecology: Towards a Situated UPE through African Urbanism." *Antipode* 46, no. 2: 497–516.

Leach, Melissa, and Mariz Tadros. 2014. "Epidemics and the Politics of Knowledge: Contested Narratives in Egypt's H1N1 Response." *Medical Anthropology* 33, no. 3: 240–54.

Le Quotidien. 2009. "Ses camarades éboueurs inondent Dakar d'ordures: Madani Sy en garde à vue au Commissariat." *Le Quotidien*, February 20.

Li, Tania Murray. 1996. "Images of Community: Discourse and Strategy in Property Relations." *Development and Change* 27: 501–27.

Lincoln, Sarah L. 2008. "Expensive Shit: Aesthetic Economies of Waste in Postcolonial Africa." PhD Diss., Duke University.

Loftus, Alex. 2012. *Everyday Environmentalism: Creating an Urban Political Ecology.* Minneapolis: University of Minnesota Press.

Loftus, Alex, and Fiona Lumsden. 2008. "Reworking Hegemony in the Urban Waterscape." *Transactions of the Institute of British Geographers* 33, no. 1: 109–26.

Lubeck, Paul. 1986. *Islam and Urban Labor in Northern Nigeria: The Making of a Muslim Working Class.* Cambridge: Cambridge University Press.

Lubeck, Paul, and Bryana Britts. 2002. "Muslim Civil Society in Urban Public Spaces:

Globalization, Discursive Shifts, and Social Movements." In *Understanding the City: Contemporary and Future Perspectives*, edited by John Eade and Christopher Mele, 305–36. Oxford: Blackwell.

Lugo, Adonia, and Jessica Lockrem, eds. 2012. Curated collection on "Infrastructure," *Cultural Anthropology*, November 26. https://culanth.org/curated_collections /11-infrastructure.

Mains, Daniel. 2007. "Neoliberal Times: Progress, Boredom, and Shame among Young Men in Urban Ethiopia." *American Ethnologist* 34, no. 4: 659–73.

Mains, Daniel. 2012. "Blackouts and Progress: Privatization, Infrastructure, and a Developmentalist State in Jimma, Ethiopia." *Cultural Anthropology* 27, no. 1: 3–27.

Mamdani, Mahmood. 1996. *Citizen and Subject: Contemporary Africa and the Legacy of Late Colonialism*. Princeton, NJ: Princeton University Press.

Mamdani, Mahmood, and Ernest Wamba-dia-Wamba, eds. 1995. *African Studies in Social Movements and Democracy*. Dakar: CODESRIA.

Mann, Michael. 1984. "The Autonomous Power of the State: Its Origins, Mechanisms and Results." *European Journal of Sociology* 25:185–213.

Marshall, Ruth. 2009. *Political Spiritualities: The Pentecostal Revolution in Nigeria*. Chicago: University of Chicago Press.

Marshall, Ruth. 2013. "'Dealing with the Prince over Lagos': Pentecostal Arts of Citizenship." In *The Arts of Citizenship in African Cities: Infrastructures and Spaces of Belonging*, edited by Mamadou Diouf and Rosalind Fredericks, 91–114. New York: Palgrave Macmillan.

Marshall-Fratani, Ruth. 2006. "The War of 'Who Is Who': Autochthony, Nationalism and Citizenship in the Ivorian Crisis." *African Studies Review* 49, no. 2: 9–43.

Masquelier, Adeline. 2002. "Road Mythographies: Space, Mobility, and the Historical Imagination in Postcolonial Niger." *American Ethnologist* 29, no. 4: 829–56.

Mavhunga, Clapperton Chakanetsa. 2013a. "*Cidades Esfumaçadas*: Energy and the Rural-Urban Connection in Mozambique." *Public Culture* 25, no. 2: 261–71.

Mavhunga, Clapperton Chakanetsa. 2013b. "What Is Africa in Technology? What Is Technology in Africa?" Keynote presented at the MIT-Africa Interest Group, Cambridge, MA, October 1.

Mbembe, Achille. 2001. *On the Postcolony*. Berkeley: University of California Press.

Mbembe, Achille, and Sarah Nuttall. 2004a. "Writing the World from an African Metropolis." *Public Culture* 16, no. 3: 347–72.

Mbembe, Achille, and Sarah Nuttall, eds. 2004b. *Johannesburg: The Elusive Metropolis*. Durham, NC: Duke University Press.

Mbengue, Cheikh Tidiane. 1997. "An Introduction to the Traditional Villages of Yoff, Ngor, and Ouakam." In *Village Wisdom, Future Cities: Proceedings from the Third International Ecocity and Ecovillage Conference Held in Yoff, January 8–12, 1996*, edited by Richard Register and Brady Peeks. Oakland, CA: Ecocity Builders.

Mbow, Penda. 2003. "Civisme, Laïcité, République." Unpublished manuscript.

Mbow, Penda. 2008. "Senegal: The Return of Personalism." *Journal of Democracy* 19, no. 1: 156–69.

McFarlane, Colin. 2008. "Governing the Contaminated City: Infrastructure and Sanitation in Colonial and Post-colonial Bombay." *International Journal of Urban and Regional Research* 32, no. 2: 415–35.

McFarlane, Colin, and Jonathan Rutherford. 2008. "Political Infrastructures: Governing and Experiencing the Fabric of the City." *International Journal of Urban and Regional Research* 32, no. 2: 363–74.

McFarlane, Colin, and Jonathan Silver. 2017. "The Poolitical City: 'Seeing Sanitation' and Making the Urban Political in Cape Town." *Antipode* 49:125–48.

McGuire, Meredith. 2008. *Lived Religion: Faith and Practice in Everyday Life.* Oxford: Oxford University Press.

Meehan, Katie, and Strauss, Kendra, eds. 2015. *Precarious Worlds: New Geographies of Social Reproduction.* Athens: University of Georgia Press.

Melly, Caroline. 2013. "Ethnography on the Road: Infrastructural Vision and the Unruly Present in Contemporary Dakar." *Africa* 83, no. 3: 385–402.

Meyer, Birgit. 1995. "Delivered from the Powers of Darkness: Confession of Satanic Riches in Christian Ghana." *Africa: Journal of the International African Institute* 65, no. 2: 236–55.

Millar, Kathleen M. 2012. "Trash Ties: Urban Politics, Economic Crisis, and Rio de Janeiro's Garbage Dump." In *Economies of Recycling: The Global Transformation of Materials, Values, and Social Relations*, edited by Catherine Alexander and Joshua Reno, 164–84. London: Zed Books.

Miraftab, Faranak. 2004a. "Making Neo-liberal Governance: The Disempowering Work of Empowerment." *International Planning Studies* 9, no. 4: 239–59.

Miraftab, Faranak. 2004b. "Neoliberalism and Casualization of Public Sector Services: The Case of Waste Collection Services in Cape Town, South Africa." *International Journal of Urban and Regional Research* 28, no. 4: 874–92.

Miraftab, Faranak, and Neema Kudva. 2015. "Urban Citizenship." In *Cities of the Global South Reader*, edited by Faranak Miraftab and Neema Kudva, 270–76. New York: Routledge.

Mitchell, J. Clyde. 1961. *An Outline of the Sociological Background to African Labour.* Salisbury, Southern Rhodesia: Ensign Publishers.

Mitchell, Katharyne, Sally A. Marston, and Cindi Katz, eds. 2004. *Life's Work: Geographies of Social Reproduction.* Malden, MA: Blackwell.

Mitchell, Timothy. 2014. "Introduction: Life of Infrastructure." *Comparative Studies of South Asia, Africa and the Middle East* 34, no. 3: 401–12.

Mizes, James Christopher. 2016. "Who Owns Africa's Infrastructure?" *Limn* 7. http://limn.it/issue/07/.

Mkandawire, Thandika, and Charles C. Soludo. 1999. *Our Continent Our Future: African Perspectives on Structural Adjustment.* Trenton, NJ: Africa World Press.

Mohan, Giles, and Kristian Stokke. 2000. "Participatory Development and Empowerment: The Dangers of Localism." *Third World Quarterly* 20:247–68.

Moore, Sarah A. 2009. "The Excess of Modernity: Garbage Politics in Oaxaca, Mexico." *The Professional Geographer* 61, no. 4: 426–37.

Moore, Sarah A. 2012. "Garbage Matters: Concepts in New Geographies of Waste." *Progress in Human Geography* 36, no. 6: 780–99.

Mrázek, Rudolph. 2002. *Engineers of Happy Land: Technology and Nationalism in a Colony.* Princeton, NJ: Princeton University Press.

Mudimbe, V. Y. 1994. *The Idea of Africa.* Bloomington: Indiana University Press.

Murphy, Michelle. 2013. "Chemical Infrastructures of the St. Clair River." In *Toxicants, Health, and Regulation since 1945*, edited by Soraya Boudia and Nathalie Jas, 103–15. London: Pickering and Chatto.

Murray, Martin J. 2011. *City of Extremes: The Spatial Politics of Johannesburg.* Durham, NC: Duke University Press.

Murray, Martin J., and Garth Myers, eds. 2011. *Cities in Contemporary Africa.* New York: Palgrave Macmillan.

Myers, Garth Andrew. 2005. *Disposable Cities: Garbage, Governance, and Sustainable Development in Urban Africa.* Aldershot, UK: Ashgate.

Myers, Garth Andrew. 2011. *African Cities: Alternative Visions of Urban Theory and Practice.* London: Zed Books.

Myers, Garth Andrew. 2014. "From Expected to Unexpected Comparisons: Changing the Flows of Ideas about Cities in a Postcolonial Urban World." *Singapore Journal of Tropical Geography* 35:104–18.

Nagle, Robin. 2013. *Picking Up: On the Streets and Behind the Trucks with the Sanitation Workers of New York City.* New York: Farrar, Straus and Giroux.

Nasr, Seyyed Hossein. 1996. *Religion and the Order of Nature.* New York: Oxford University Press.

Ndiaye, Alfred Inis. 2002. "Le partenariat social en question?: Vers de nouvelles relations de travail." In *La société sénégalaise entre le local et le global*, edited by Momar-Coumba Diop, 397–440. Paris: Karthala.

Ndiaye, Alfred Inis. 2008. "Genre et flexibilité du travail: Le temps de travail en devenir?" Working paper, CODESRIA Institut sur le genre, Dakar.

Ndiaye, Alfred Inis. 2010. "Autonomy or Political Affiliation?: Senegalese Trade Unions in the Face of Economics and Political Reform." In *Trade Unions and Party Politics: Labour Movements in Africa*, edited by Björn Beckman, Sakhela Buhlungu, and Lloyd Sachikonye, 23–38. Cape Town: HSRC.

Ndiaye, Alfred Inis. 2013. "Le partenariat social dans les années 2000: Une décennie perdue?" In *Sénégal (2000–2012): Les institutions et politiques publiques à l'épreuve d'une gouvernance libérale*, edited by Momar-Coumba Diop, 313–46. Paris: Karthala.

N'Dour, Youssou. 1990. *Set.* Youssou N'Dour and Le Super Étoile. CD.

Ndoye, Ndeye Bineta Laye. 2005. "Problématique de l'assainissement dans la Commune d'Arrondissement de Yoff: L'état de lieux d'une espace fragile." Masters diss., Université Gaston Berger de Saint-Louis, Senegal.

Ndoye, Ousmane. 2013. "Le gouvernement à l'épreuve de la gestion du système de planification." In *Sénégal (2000–2012): Les institutions et politiques publiques à l'épreuve d'une gouvernance libérale*, edited by Momar-Coumba Diop, 115–48. Paris: Karthala.

Nettali. 2007. "Insalubrité: Plusieurs quartiers de Dakar envahis par les ordures." *Nettali*, April 25.

Njeru, Jeremia. 2006. "The Urban Political Ecology of Plastic Bag Waste Problem in Nairobi, Kenya." *Geoforum* 37, no. 6: 1046–58.

Nuttall, Sarah, and Achille Mbembe. 2005. "A Blasé Attitude: A Response to Michael Watts." *Public Culture* 17, no. 1: 193–201.

Nyamnjoh, Francis B. 2005. "Fishing in Troubled Waters: *Disquettes* and *Thiofs* in Dakar." *Africa* 73, no. 3: 295–324.

Nyamnjoh, Francis B., and Michael Rowlands. 1998. "Elite Associations and the Politics of Belonging in Cameroon." *Africa: Journal of the International African Institute* 68, no. 3: 320–37.

Nyanator, Frank K., and Joseph Kutzin. 1999. "Health for Some?: The Effects of User Fees in the Volta Region of Ghana." *Health Policy and Planning* 14:329–41.

O'Brien, Martin. 1999. "Rubbish-Power: Towards a Sociology of the Rubbish Society." In *Consuming Cultures: Power and Resistance*, edited by Jeff Hearn and Sasha Roseneil, 262–77. New York: St. Martin's.

Omezi, Giles. 2014. "Nigerian Modernity and the City: Lagos 1960–1980." In *The Arts of Citizenship in African Cities: Infrastructures and Spaces of Belonging*, edited by Mamadou Diouf and Rosalind Fredericks, 277–96. New York: Palgrave Macmillan.

O'Neill, Bruce, and Dennis Rodgers. 2012. "Infrastructural Violence: Introduction to the Special Issue." *Ethnography* 13, no. 4: 437–39.

Osinulu, Adedamola. 2013. "The Road to Redemption: Performing Pentecostal Citizenship in Lagos." In *The Arts of Citizenship in African Cities: Infrastructures and Spaces of Belonging*, edited by Mamadou Diouf and Rosalind Fredericks, 115–36. New York: Palgrave Macmillan.

Parizeau, Kate. 2015. "When Assets Are Vulnerabilities: An Assessment of Informal Recyclers' Livelihood Strategies in Buenos Aires, Argentina." *World Development* 67:161–73.

Parker, Ron. 1991. "The Senegal-Mauritania Conflict of 1989: A Fragile Equilibrium." *Journal of Modern African Studies* 29, no. 1: 155–71.

Parnell, Susan, and Jennifer Robinson. 2012. "(Re)Theorizing Cities from the Global South: Looking Beyond Neoliberalism." *Urban Geography* 33, no. 4: 593–617.

Parpart, Jane L. 1983. *Labor and Capital on the African Copperbelt*. Philadelphia: Temple University Press.

Patterson, Amy S. 2002. "The Impact of Senegal's Decentralization on Women in Local Governance." *Canadian Journal of African Studies/Revue Canadienne des Études Africaines* 36, no. 3: 490–529.

Pearson, Mark. 2004. "Issues Paper: The Case for Abolition of User Fees for Primary Health Services." Issues paper, DFID Health Systems Resource Centre, London.

Pearson, Ruth. 2005. "The Rise and Rise of Gender and Development." In *A Radical History of Development Studies: Individuals, Institutiions, and Ideologies*, edited by Uma Kothari, 157–79. London: Zed Books.

Peck, Jamie. 2010. *Constructions of Neoliberal Reason*. Oxford: Oxford University Press.

Petrocelli, Rachel Marie. 2011. *City Dwellers and the State: Making Modern Urbanism in Colonial Dakar, 1914–1944*. Stanford, CA: Stanford University.

Pieterse, Edgar. 2008. *City Futures: Confronting the Crisis of Urban Development.* London: Zed Books.

Pieterse, Jan Nederveen. 2000. "After Post-development." *Third World Quarterly* 21, no. 2: 175–91.

Prashad, Vijay. 1994. "Native Dirt/Imperial Ordure: The Cholera of 1832 and the Morbid Resolutions of Modernity." *Journal of Historical Sociology* 7, no. 3: 243–60.

Prashad, Vijay. 2000. *Untouchable Freedom: A Social History of a Dalit Community.* New York: Oxford University Press.

Puig de la Bellacasa, Maria. 2016. "Ecological Thinking, Material Spirituality, and the Poetics of Infrastructure." In *Boundary Objects and Beyond: Working with Leigh Star,* edited by Geoffrey C. Bowker, Stefan Timmermans, Adele E. Clarke, and Ellen Balka, 47–68. Cambridge, MA: MIT Press.

Rabine, Leslie. 2013. "Pratiques multimédias et constructions d'identité à Dakar." In *Arts de la cittoyenneté et esthétiques du politiques au Sénégal: Espaces contestés et civilités urbaines,* edited by Mamadou Diouf and Rosalind Fredericks, 291–326. Paris: Karthala.

Rabinow, Paul. 1989. "Governing Morocco: Modernity and Difference." *International Journal of Urban and Regional Research* 13:32–46.

Rademacher, Anne, and Kalyanakrishnan Sivaramakrishnan, eds. 2013. *Ecologies of Urbanism in India: Metropolitan Civility and Sustainability.* Hong Kong: Hong Kong University Press.

Ralph, Michael. 2008. "Killing Time." *Social Text* 26, no. 4: 1–29.

Ranganathan, Malini. 2014. "Paying for Pipes, Claiming Citizenship: Political Agency and Water Reforms at the Urban Periphery." *International Journal of Urban and Regional Research* 38, no. 2: 590–608.

Ranganathan, Malini. 2015. "Storm Drains as Assemblages: The Political Ecology of Flood Risk in Post-Colonial Bangalore." *Antipode* 47, no. 5: 1300–1320.

Register, Richard, and Brady Peeks, eds. 1997. *Village Wisdom, Future Cities: Proceedings from the Third International Ecocity and Ecovillage Conference Held in Yoff, January 8–12, 1996.* Oakland, CA: Ecocity Builders.

Reno, Joshua. 2015. "Waste and Waste Management." *Annual Review of Anthropology* 44:557–72.

Reno, Joshua. 2016. *Waste Away: Working and Living with a North American Landfill.* Berkeley: University of California Press.

République du Sénégal. 1998. "Rapport sur le nettoiement." Ministère de l'intérieur. Dakar, December 11.

République du Sénégal. 2002. "Communiqué officiel: Eclairages sur le contrat liant l'Etat du Sénégal à la société ALCYON.SA." La Primature. Dakar, April 24.

République du Sénégal. 2014. "Convention collective du secteur du nettoiement au Sénégal." Le Ministre de la Fonction Publique, et du Dialogue Sociale et des Organisations Professionnelles. Dakar, June 24.

République du Sénégal. n.d. "Collecte, enlevement, et evacuation des ordures menageres sur le territoire de la Communauté Urbaine de Dakar." Contrat de sous-traitance entre Groupement d'intérêt economique (GIE) et la Société Concessionaire. Communauté Urbaine de Dakar (CUD). Dakar.

Ribot, Jesse C. 1998. "Theorizing Access: Forest Profits along Senegal's Charcoal Commodity Chain." *Development and Change* 29, no. 2: 307–41.

Riis, Jacob A. 1890. *How the Other Half Lives: Studies among the Tenements of New York.* New York: Charles Scribner's Sons.

Roberts, Adrienne. 2008. "Privatizing Social Reproduction: The Primitive Accumulation of Water in an Era of Neoliberalism." *Antipode* 40, no. 4: 535–60.

Roberts, Allen F. 2013. "Citoyennetés visuelles en compétition dans le Sénégal contemporain." In *Les arts de la citoyenneté au Sénégal: Espaces contestés et civilités urbaines,* edited by Mamadou Diouf and Rosalind Fredericks, 195–236. Paris: Karthala.

Roberts, Allen F., Mary Nooter Roberts, Gassia Aremenian, and Ousmane Gueye. 2003. *A Saint in the City: Sufi Arts of Urban Senegal.* Los Angeles: UCLA Fowler Museum of Cultural History.

Robinson, David. 2000. *Paths of Accommodation: Muslim Societies and French Colonial Authorities in Senegal and Mauritania, 1880–1920.* Oxford: James Currey.

Robinson, Jennifer. 2002. "Global and World Cities: A View from Off the Map." *International Journal of Urban and Regional Research* 26, no. 3: 531–54.

Robinson, Jennifer. 2006. *Ordinary Cities: Between Modernity and Development.* London: Routledge.

Rodgers, Dennis. 2012. "Haussmannization in the Tropics: Abject Urbanism and Infrastructural Violence in Nicaragua." *Ethnography* 13, no. 4: 413–38.

Roy, Ananya. 2009. "The 21st-Century Metropolis: New Geographies of Theory." *Regional Studies* 43, no. 6: 819–30.

Roy, Ananya, Wendy Larner, and Jamie Peck. 2012. "Book Review Symposium: Jamie Peck (2010) Constructions of Neoliberal Reason." *Progress in Human Geography* 36, no. 2: 273–81.

Roy, Ananya, and Aiwha Ong, eds. 2011. *Worlding Cities: Asian Experiments and the Art of Being Global.* Oxford: Wiley Blackwell.

Samson, Fabienne. 2000. "La place du religieux dans l'élection présidentielle sénégalaise." *Afrique contemporaine* 194:5–11.

Samson, Melanie. 2003. *Dumping on Women: Gender and the Privatization of Waste Management.* Cape Town: Municipal Services Project and South African Municipal Workers Union.

Samson, Melanie. 2007. "Privatizing Collective Public Goods—Re-fracturing the 'Public' and Re-segmenting Labour Markets: A Case Study of Street Cleaning in Johannesburg, South Africa." *Studies in Political Economy* 79 (spring): 119–43.

Samson, Melanie. 2008. "Rescaling the State, Restructuring Social Relations: Local Government Transformation and Waste Management Privatization in Post-apartheid Johannesburg." *International Feminist Journal of Politics* 10, no. 1: 19–39.

Samson, Melanie. 2009. "Wasted Citizenship?: Reclaimers and the Privatised Expansion of the Public Sphere." *Africa Development* 34, nos. 3–4: 1–25.

Samson, Melanie. 2010. "Producing Privatization: Re-articulating Race, Gender, Class and Space." *Antipode* 42, no. 2: 404–32.

Samson, Melanie. 2015. "Accumulation by Dispossession and the Informal Economy:

Struggles over Knowledge, Being and Waste at a Soweto Garbage Dump." *Environment and Planning D: Society and Space* 33, no. 5: 813–30.

Scanlan, John. 2005. *On Garbage*. London: Reaktion Books.

Scheld, Suzanne. 2007. "Youth Cosmopolitanism: Clothing, the City and Globalization in Dakar, Senegal." *City and Society* 19, no. 2: 232–53.

Schroeder, Richard A. 1999. *Shady Practices: Agroforestry and Gender Politics in The Gambia*. Berkeley: University of California Press.

Scott, James C. 1998. *Seeing Like a State: How Certain Schemes to Improve the Human Condition Have Failed*. New Haven, CT: Yale University Press.

Searle-Chatterjee, Mary. 1979. "The Polluted Identity of Work: A Study of Benares Sweepers." In *Social Anthropology of Work*, edited by Sandra Wallman, 269–86. London: Academic Press.

Sennett, Richard. 1970. *The Uses of Disorder: Personal Identity and City Life*. New York: Knopf.

Simone, AbdouMaliq. 1994. *In Whose Image?: Political Islam and Urban Practices in Sudan*. Chicago: University of Chicago Press.

Simone, AbdouMaliq. 2003. "Reaching the Larger World: New Forms of Social Collaboration in Pikine, Senegal." *Africa* 73, no. 2: 226–50.

Simone, AbdouMaliq. 2004a. *For the City Yet to Come: Changing Life in Four African Cities*. Durham, NC: Duke University Press.

Simone, AbdouMaliq. 2004b. "People as Infrastructure: People as Intersecting Fragments in Johannesburg." *Public Culture* 16, no. 3: 407–29.

Simone, AbdouMaliq. 2010. *City Life from Jakarta to Dakar: Movements at the Crossroads*. New York: Routledge.

Simone, AbdouMaliq. 2012. "Infrastructure: Introductory Commentary by AbdouMaliq Simone." Curated collection on "Infrastructure," *Cultural Anthropology*, November 26. https://culanth.org/curated_collections/11-infrastructure /discussions/12-infrastructure-introductory-commentary-by-abdoumaliq-simone.

Smith, Neil. 1984. *Uneven Development: Nature, Capital, and the Production of Space*. Oxford: Blackwell.

Soares, Benjamin F., and René Otayek, eds. 2007. *Islam and Muslim Politics in Africa*. New York: Palgrave Macmillan.

Le Soleil. 2011. "Gestion des dechets à Dakar: Khalifa Sall engage la bataille de l'or dur contre l'état." *Le Soleil*, April 8.

Somerville, Carolyn M. 1991. "The Impact of the Reforms on the Urban Population: How the Dakarois View the Crisis." In *The Political Economy of Senegal under Structural Adjustment*, edited by Christopher L. Delgado and Sidi Jammeh, 151–73. New York: Praeger.

Soumaré, Mohamed. 2002. "Local Initiatives and Poverty Reduction in Urban Areas: The Example of Yeumbeul in Senegal." *International Social Science Journal* 52, no. 172: 261–66.

Star, Susan Leigh. 1995. *Ecologies of Knowledge: Work and Politics in Science and Technology*. Albany: State of New York University Press.

Star, Susan Leigh. 1999. "The Ethnography of Infrastructure." *American Behavioral Scientist* 43, no. 3: 377–91.

Stoler, Ann Laura. 2008. "Imperial Debris: Reflections on Ruins and Ruination." *Cultural Anthropology* 23, no. 2: 191–219.

Sud Quotidien. 2007. "Insalubrité: Dakar (ré)envahie!" *Sud Quotidien*, April 25.

Swanson, Maynard W. 1977. "The Sanitation Syndrome: Bubonic Plague and Urban Native Policy in the Cape Colony, 1900–1909." *Journal of African History* 18, no. 3: 387–410.

Sylla, Assane. 1992. *Le peuple Lebou de la presqu'ile du Cap-Vert.* Dakar: Les Nouvelles Editions Africaines du Sénégal.

Tandian, Aly. 2013. "L'an 2000: Un rendez-vous crucial pour la jeunesse sénégalaise? Entre espoirs et désillusion." In *Le Sénégal sous Abdoulaye Wade: Le sopi a l'épreuve du pouvoir,* edited by Momar-Coumba Diop, 547–67. Paris: Karthala.

Thioub, Ibrahima, Momar-Coumba Diop, and Catherine Boone. 1998. "Economic Liberalization in Senegal: Shifting Politics of Indigenous Business Interests." *African Studies Review* 41, no. 2: 63–89.

Tiffen, Mary, Michael Mortimore, and Francis Gichuki. 1994. *More People, Less Erosion: Environmental Recovery in Kenya.* Chichester, UK: John Wiley and Sons.

Trovalla, Eric, and Ulrika Trovalla. 2015. "Infrastructure as a Divination Tool: Whispers from the Grids in a Nigerian City." *City* 19, nos. 2–3: 332–43.

Truelove, Yaffa. 2011. "(Re-)Conceptualizing Water Inequality in Delhi, India through a Feminist Political Ecology Framework." *Geoforum* 42, no. 2: 143–52.

Tse, Justin K. H. 2014. "Grounded Theologies: 'Religion' and the 'Secular' in Human Geography." *Progress in Human Geography* 38, no. 2: 201–20.

UNCHS (United Nations Centre for Human Settlements). 1996. *An Urbanizing World: Global Report on Human Settlements.* Oxford: Oxford University Press.

UNESCO (United Nations Educational, Scientific and Cultural Organization). 2000. *Yoff, le territoire assiégé: Un village lébou dans la banlieue de Dakar.* Paris: UNESCO.

UNESCO (United Nations Educational, Scientific and Cultural Organization). n.d. "Community Participation in the Management of the Urban Environment in Senegal." *MOST Best Practices for Human Settlements.* http://www.unesco.org/most/africa6.htm.

Van de Walle, Nicolas. 2001. *African Economies and the Politics of Permanent Crisis, 1979–1999.* Cambridge: Cambridge University Press.

Vengroff, Richard, and Lucy Creevey. 1997. "Senegal: The Evolution of a Quasi-Democracy." In *Political Reform in Francophone Africa,* edited by John F. Clark and David E. Gardiner, 204–22. Boulder, CO: Lynne Rienner.

Vernière, Marc. 1977. *Dakar et son double: Dagoudane Pikine.* Paris: Bibliothèque Nationale.

Villalon, Leonardo A. 1995. *Islamic Society and State Power in Senegal: Disciples and Citizens in Fatick.* Cambridge: Cambridge University Press.

Villalon, Leonardo A. 1999. "Generational Changes, Political Stagnation, and the Evolving Dynamics of Religion and Politics in Senegal." *Africa Today* 46, nos. 3–4: 129–47.

Villalon, Leonardo A. 2004. "ASR Focus: Islamism in West Africa: Senegal." *African Studies Review* 47, no. 2: 61–71.

von Schnitzler, Antina. 2013. "Traveling Technologies: Infrastructure, Ethical Regimes, and the Materiality of Politics in South Africa." *Cultural Anthropology* 28, no. 4: 670–93.

von Schnitzler, Antina. 2016. *Democracy's Infrastructure: Techno-Politics and Protest after Apartheid*. Princeton, NJ: Princeton University Press.

Voyles, Traci Brynne. 2015. *Wastelanding: Legacies of Uranium Mining in Navajo Country*. Minneapolis: University of Minnesota.

Watts, Michael. 1983. *Silent Violence: Food, Famine and Peasantry in Northern Nigeria*. Berkeley: University of California Press.

Watts, Michael. 1996. "Islamic Modernities?: Citizenship, Civil Society, and Islamism in a Nigerian City." *Public Culture* 8:251–89.

Watts, Michael. 2005a. "Baudelaire over Berea, Simmel over Sandton?" *Public Culture* 17, no. 1: 181–92.

Watts, Michael. 2005b. "The Sinister Political Life of Community: Economies of Violence and Governable Spaces in the Niger Delta, Nigeria." In *The Romance of Community*, edited by Gerald Creed, 101–42. Santa Fe, NM: SAR.

Watts, Michael. 2009. "The Rule of Oil: Petro-Politics and the Anatomy of an Insurgency." *Journal of African Development* 11, no. 2: 27–56.

White, Luise. 1990. *The Comforts of Home: Prostitution in Colonial Nairobi*. Chicago: University of Chicago Press.

Whitington, Jerome. 2016. "Carbon as a Metric of the Human." *PoLAR: Political and Legal Anthropology Review* 39, no. 1: 46–63.

Whitson, Risa. 2011. "Negotiating Place and Value: Geographies of Waste and Scavenging in Buenos Aires." *Antipode* 43, no. 4: 1404–33.

Whittaker, Stella, ed. 1995. *First Steps—Local Agenda 21 in Practice: Municipal Strategies for Sustainability as Presented at Global Forum 94 in Manchester*. London: HMSO.

WHO (World Health Organization). 2005. "World Health Assembly Resolution WHA 58.31: Working towards Universal Coverage of Maternal, Newborn and Child Health Interventions." Geneva: World Health Organization.

Winner, Langdon. 1980. "Do Artifacts Have Politics?" *Daedalus* 109, no. 1: 121–36.

World Bank. 1989. *Sub-Saharan Africa: From Crisis to Sustainable Growth*. Washington, DC: World Bank.

World Bank. 1992. "Staff Appraisal Report (SAR) for the Second Public Works and Employment Program (Republic of Senegal)." No. 10421-SE. Washington, DC: World Bank, Infrastructure and Operations Division, Sahelian Department, Africa Region.

World Bank. 1997. "Performance Audit Report (PAR) for the First and Second Public Works and Employment projects (AGETIP) (Republic of Senegal)." No. 16516. Washington, DC: World Bank, Operations and Evaluations Department.

World Bank. 2000. "Senegal to Receive US$800 Million in Debt Relief: World Bank and IMF Support Debt Relief under the Enhanced HIPC Initiative." Press release no. 2000/449/S (June 23). Washington, DC: World Bank.

Wright, Gwendolyn. 1987. "Tradition in the Service of Modernity: Architecture and Urbanism in French Colonial Policy, 1900–1930." *Journal of Modern History* 59, no. 2: 291–316.

Wright, Melissa. 2006. *Disposable Women and Other Myths of Global Capitalism*. New York: Routledge.

Yates, Michelle. 2011. "The Human-as-Waste, the Labor Theory of Value and Disposability in Contemporary Capitalism." *Antipode* 43:1679–95.

Yates, Rob. 2009. "Universal Health Care and the Removal of User Fees." *The Lancet* 373:2078–81.

Yeoh, Brenda S. A. 2003. *Contesting Space: Power Relations and the Urban Built Environment in Colonial Singapore*. Singapore: Singapore University Press.

Young, Crawford, and Babacar Kante. 1992. "Governance, Democracy, and the 1988 Senegalese Elections." In *Governance and Politics in Africa*, edited by Goran Hyden and Michael Bratton, 57–74. Boulder, CO: Lynne Rienner.

Zeilig, Leo. 2007. *Revolt and Protest: Student Politics and Activism in Sub-Saharan Africa*. London: I. B. Tauris.

Zeilig, Leo, and Nicola Ansell. 2008. "Spaces and Scales of African Student Activism: Senegalese and Zimbabwean University Students at the Intersection of Campus, Nation and Globe." *Antipode* 40, no. 1: 31–54.

Zeitlin, Marian F., and Loly Diouf. 1998. *Etudes Socio-économiques et d'assainissement du quartier de Tonghor du village traditionnel de Yoff, 16 Commune d'Arrondisement Yoff-Dakar, Sénégal*. Dakar: Programme Eco-Communautaire de Yoff for ENDA-RUP.

Page numbers followed by *f* indicate a figure; those followed by *t* indicate a table.

African cities, 5–8, 23–25, 155nn5–6, 155–56nn8–11, 157n14; making theory from the South in, 24–25; narratives of failure of, 23–24; neoliberal reforms in, 5–8, 149–50; political discourses of waste in, 20–23; public religious practices in, 128; racial regulation and segregation in, 19–20, 24, 158n23, 160n12; socioenvironmental power relations in, 7; urban political ecologies of, 6–7, 155n6, 156n12; waste infrastructures of, 7. *See also* Dakar; infrastructures; labor of urban infrastructures

Afrique Occidentale Française, 35

Agence d'exécution des travaux d'intérêt public contre le sous-emploi (AGETIP), 30–31*t*, 70–74, 165nn10–11

l'Agence Nationale de l'organisation de la conférence islamique (ANOCI), 27, 29

Agence pour la propreté de Dakar (APRODAK), 30–31*t*

Agence pour la propreté du Sénégal (APROSEN), 30–31*t*

Alcyon, 30*t*, 162n33

Les Amazones of Gueule Tapée, 78, 89

Anand, Nikhil, 19–20

Anderson, Warwick, 160n12

architectures of faith. *See* Islam; religious and spiritual practices

Army Corps of Engineers, 30*t*

Association pour la promotion social, economique et culturelle de Yoff (APECSY), 103, 107, 111–12, 114, 168n13, 168n19

austerity programs. *See* Structural Adjustment Programs

Azienda Municipalizzata per l'Ambiente (AMA), 30*t*, 48–49, 53, 82, 130, 162n33, 163n35, 169n13

Bakker, Karen, 158n22

Beall, Jo, 143

Bennett, Jane, 16

BICIS, 51

Boone, Catherine, 161n22

Braun, Bruce, 15–16

Bretton Woods institutions, 39, 48

bricolage. *See* salvage bricolage

bubonic plague, 36, 160n12

Cape Verde Peninsula, 10, 11*f*, 101, 109, 159n7

Castells, Manuel, 156n11

Chakrabarty, Dipesh, 112

Chalfin, Brenda, 14–15, 156n11
Chalhoub, Sidney, 160n12
charrettes (horese-drawn carts), 85, 106, 110, 114–16, 119
cholera, 49, 166n22
citizenship. *See* participatory citizenship; urban citizenship
civil service, 5, 161n21
Code de l'administration communale, 160n17
Collignon, René, 37
colonial legacies, 34–36, 109, 159–60nn7–12
Comaroff, Jean, 24
Comaroff, John, 24
Comforts of Home (White), 155n8
"The Coming Anarchy" (Kaplan), 158n29
Comité de gestion de Tonghor (CGT), 102–5, 114
Communauté d'agglomérations de Dakar–Communauté d'agglomérations de Rufisque (CADAK-CAR), 30–31t, 49–52, 55–56, 163nn36–37
Communauté Urbaine de Dakar (CUD), 30–31t, 40, 48–50, 161n20, 163n37, 165n12
community-based trash collection, 12–13, 26, 97–122; animatrice work in, 110–18, 121–22; community empowerment claims of, 100–101; compensated male drivers of, 105, 115; difficult-to-access neighborhoods of, 98, 101–4; education and participation focus of, 104–6; ENDA's technological vision for, 99, 102, 120–21; failure of, 118–20; fired female trash workers in, 100–101, 110–11, 115; free women's labor of, 100–101, 111, 112, 114–15; gendered discourses of waste in, 111–13; horse-drawn-cart technology of, 12, 89, 97–100, 103–6, 119, 121, 152, 167n10; local politics of garbage in, 106–10; pilot compost project of, 108, 119; project design of, 114; user fees in, 103, 106, 108–9, 116–18, 168n18; waste-related diseases of workers in, 115–16; wastewater treatment project of, 167n8
community participation. *See* participatory citizenship
Confédération des syndicats autonomes du Sénégal (CSA), 129–30
Confédération Nationale des travailleurs du Sénégal (CNTS), 169n11

Constitution of 1976, 161n23
Coordination des associations et mouvements de la communauté urbaine de Dakar (CAMCUD), 70, 165n12
crises. *See* garbage crises
Cruise O'Brien, Donal B., 161n24

Dakar, 6–7, 9–14, 30–31t; colonial legacies in, 34–36, 109, 159–60nn7–12; ENDA's technological vision for, 99, 102, 120–21; founding of, 34–35, 159n7; infrastructure projects in, 27, 28f, 29f; Lebou neighborhoods in, 101–10, 167nn4–5; map of, 11f; OIC summit in, 27–29, 55, 159nn1–2; population of, 11f; racial segregation in, 19–20, 24, 35–36, 158n23, 160n12; regional and international role of, 6, 35, 155n4; segregated infrastructural systems of, 10–12, 19–22, 28–29, 36–37, 50, 53–54, 100–101, 106–10, 160n15; state and local power-sharing in, 50–56, 163n45, 164n48; TEOM in, 116–17, 160n17, 162n28; trash collection process in, 83–87; urban public services in, 10; urban sprawl of, 167n1; vibrant street life of, 64; waste dump in, 11f, 38; waste storage challenges in, 83, 85–86. *See also* garbage crises; names of specific neighborhoods, e.g., Yoff; politics of garbage
Dalits, 143
Davis, Mike, 169n7
decentralization laws of 1996, 50, 52, 163n38, 166n17, 168n13
Diagne, Blaise, 35–36
Diene, Serigne Mbaye, 107
Diop, Mamadou, 39, 42–46, 48, 56, 58, 153, 162n29; garbage crisis of 1988 and, 2–3, 9, 13, 40, 42–43; Journées de Propreté of, 44–45, 70–72, 77; participatory trash sector under, 68–82, 100, 110–11, 129; patronage system of, 45–46; recruitment of women by, 80–81; Set/Setal movement and, 43–46, 48, 68–74, 162n28, 165n9. *See also* Set/Setal movement
Diop, Pape, 48, 50–51, 124–25
Diouf, Abdou, 39–47, 161n18, 161n23
Diouf, Mamadou, 38, 63, 65, 129, 156n10
"Do Artifacts Have Politics?" (Winner), 152

Douglas, Mary, 18–19, 143, 153–54, 157n20
dump work, 158n28. *See also* Mbeubeuss dump

Echenberg, Myron, 160n12
Environnement et développement du tiers
    monde (ENDA), 64–66, 98–120, 165n7;
    "best practices" approach in projects of,
    98, 167n3; on Dakar's traditional neighbor-
    hoods, 107; inclusivity rhetoric of, 109–10;
    on local education and participation, 104–6;
    RUP program of, 167n2, 167n6; sustainable
    development narrative of, 107; technologi-
    cal vision for Dakar of, 99, 102, 120–21;
    on user fees for basic services, 116; on
    women's participation, 111, 113–14. *See also*
    community-based trash collection; murals
Ernstson, Henrik, 156n12
Esty, Joshua D., 158n24
ethnographies of infrastructure, 14–15,
    127–29, 156n11
excremental politics, 20, 158n24, 160n12

Fass. *See* HLM Fass neighborhood
Fatton, Robert, 161n23
Ferguson, James, 154

Gandy, Matthew, 157n17
garbage crises, 1–14, 27–29, 86–87; of 1988,
    2–3, 9, 13, 40, 42–43, 63, 75; of 2005, 49;
    of 2006–9, 49, 130–41, 146; disease risks
    of, 19, 49, 90, 134, 166n22; household
    waste management challenges of, 82–87;
    poor neighborhoods affected by, 10–12,
    19–22; public support of workers in, 1–2,
    13, 86–87, 130, 138–40; trash worker
    strikes of, 1–3, 13, 22–23, 26–27, 51, 82,
    93–94, 123–26, 129–41, 146–47; of Yoff's
    community-based trash collection project,
    97, 118–20. *See also* politics of garbage; Set/
    Setal movement
garbage trucks. *See* trash trucks
Geejndar communities, 102, 105, 107–9, 118,
    167n7
gendered discourses, 8, 21–22, 62; on bread-
    winning, 89; on clothing for trash work,
    77; in community-based trash collection

projects, 12–13, 26, 78, 89, 97–122, 166n16;
    on household cleaning roles, 64, 76, 78–81,
    111–15, 165nn4–6, 166n19; on household
    finances, 117–18; in Islamic custom, 165n4;
    on moral citizenship, 78–80; neoliberal in-
    strumentalization of, 111–13; on participa-
    tion in political life, 80–81, 166n17; in the
    participatory trash sector, 76–81, 88–89,
    100, 110–11, 143, 170n21; in response to
    garbage crises, 82–87; in the Set/Setal
    movement, 64, 68, 77, 80–81; on spiritual
    value of cleaning, 145; women's traditional
    responsibilities in, 113
geographical debates, 7, 14, 16, 156n12, 157n16
Ghertner, D. Asher, 158n23
Gidwani, Vinay, 20, 158n23
governing-through-disposability, 3–5, 7, 22,
    32–34, 58–59, 149–54. *See also* politics of
    garbage
Graham, Stephen, 54, 157n17
Guédiwaye, 36

Hart, Gillian, 156n9
Harvey, David, 156n12
Haute autorité pour la propreté de Dakar
    (HAPD), 30–31t, 162n32
Heavily Indebted Poor Countries (HIPC) Ini-
    tiative, 162n31
HLM Fass neighborhood, 164n3; household
    waste management challenges in, 85; trash
    revolts in, 1–2, 13, 132–38

infrastructures, 4–5, 25, 149–54, 155n2; affec-
    tive components of, 17–18, 32–33, 126–29,
    140–41, 154; codified segregation through,
    10–12, 19–22, 28–29, 36–37, 50, 53–54,
    100–101, 106–10, 160n15; colonial legacies
    in, 34–36, 159–60nn7–12; cultural politics
    of labor in, 4–8; as ecologies of socio-
    technical relationships, 14–16, 98–101,
    120–22, 157nn16–17; ethnographic
    scholarship on, 127–29; expansion under
    Senghor of, 36–38, 160nn14–17; familiar
    technologies in, 99–100; materialization
    of power in, 4–6, 8, 14–18, 20–23, 32–34,
    101, 131–32, 156n12; people as infra-
    structure and, 16–17, 61–62, 157n18;

infrastructures (*continued*)
    precarity in management of, 21–23, 26;
    racial boundary-making by, 19–20, 35–36,
    158n23, 160n12. *See also* labor of urban
    infrastructures; neoliberal reforms; politics
    of garbage
International Ecocity and Ecovillage Confer-
    ence of 1996, 107, 167n12
International Monetary Fund (IMF), 39,
    162n31. *See also* Bretton Woods institutions;
    Structural Adjustment Programs
interview methodology, 164n3
Ishii, Miho, 127–28
Islam, 4, 23, 26, 126–29, 141–48; centrality in
    Senegal of, 28, 143; environmental ethics
    in, 170n18; everyday practices of piety
    in, 129, 144–45, 147–48; expansion into
    the public sphere of, 128, 145–46, 168n5;
    female ritual impurity in, 165n4; gris-gris
    talismans in, 144; OIC summit of, 27–29,
    55, 159nn1–2; political authority of, 41–43,
    47, 161–62nn24–26; radical forms of, 128,
    147; spiritual value of cleanliness in, 13, 16,
    21, 115, 126–27, 141–46, 153–54; stigma of
    waste work in, 143–46; Sufi brotherhoods of,
    41–43, 128, 145, 147, 160n15, 162nn25–26;
    washing ceremonies in, 142–43

Journées de Propreté (Days of Cleanliness),
    44–45, 52, 70–72, 77

Kaplan, Robert D., 24, 158n29
Kooy, Michelle, 158n22
Kristeva, Julia, 19

labor of urban infrastructures, 4–8, 25, 59,
    149–54, 155n2, 155n8; devaluation by
    neoliberal reforms of, 7, 12–13, 87–94,
    114–16, 120, 122; flexibilization of, 40–41,
    48, 54–55, 62–63, 111, 129, 161n21, 164n50;
    grounding of urban citizenship in, 6–8, 151;
    materiality of, 16–17, 61–62; precarities of
    bodies in, 21–23, 61–62, 152–53; as salvage
    bricolage, 5, 17–18, 62–63, 81–94, 127,
    149–54, 166n20. *See also* organized labor;
    participatory citizenship; trash work

Larkin, Brian, 33
Lawhon, Mary, 156n12
Lebou ethnic group, 101–10, 167nn4–5
Lebou Republic, 109
Leichtman, Mara, 129
life's work, 81–87, 95, 100, 111, 114, 158n26.
    See also social reproduction

Mains, Daniel, 156n11
Mann, Michael, 32
map of Dakar, 11f
marabouts, 41–43, 128, 145, 147, 160n15,
    162nn25–26
Marvin, Simon, 54, 157n17
Mauritanian crisis of 1989, 43, 60, 162n27
Mbembe, Achille, 20
Mbeubeuss dump, 38, 40, 106, 158n28
Médina district, 11f, 36, 50
Meehan, Katie, 22
Melly, Caroline, 48
Ministry of Culture, 52
Ministry of Finance, 160n17
Ministry of the Environment, 30t, 50
Miraftab, Faranak, 7, 112–13
Monument de la Renaissance africaine, 27,
    29f, 55, 164n47
Moore, Sarah A., 131
moral citizenship, 74–76, 78–81; religious
    values in, 80, 144–48, 154; of women's in-
    trinsic commitment to cleaning, 78–80
Mouride brotherhood, 41–43, 47, 128, 162n26
Multilateral Investment Guarantee Agency
    (MIGA), 163n35
murals, 3f, 63–68, 69f, 105f
My Combat for Dakar (M. Diop), 74

nationalist era, 36–38, 160nn14–17
N'Dour, Youssou, 45, 66, 165n8
neighborhood ethnographies, 164n3
neoliberal reforms, 3–9, 149–54; in African
    cities, 5–8; basic service fees in, 116–18; co-
    lonial logic of, 24; cultural politics of labor
    in, 4–5, 7–9, 21–23, 158n26; degradation of
    infrastructure under, 46–47, 57–58, 60–61;
    devaluation of labor by, 7, 12–13, 87–94,
    114–16, 120, 122; fragmented infrastruc-
    tures of, 17; governing-through-disposability

in, 3–5, 32–34, 58–59, 125–26; hybrid and "soft" forms of, 5, 9–10, 12, 30–31*t*, 46, 70–74; informalization of economies in, 40–41, 64; instrumentalization of gender in, 111–13; NGO-sponsored community-development projects of, 98–101, 120–22; politics of garbage and, 38–42, 46–47, 56–59; sustainable development discourses of, 101, 107; theory from the South on, 6–7. *See also* infrastructures; politics of garbage; Structural Adjustment Programs

new materialism, 14–19, 95–96, 127, 151–54, 157n16

NGO projects: on community-based trash collection, 12–13, 26, 89, 97–122; community-development focus of, 98–101, 120–22; empowerment discourses of, 121–22. *See also* Environnement et développement du tiers monde

Niari Tali neighborhood, 11*f*, 66, 87–92, 142*f*

Nouveau Système de nettoiement (NSN), 165n12

Operation Augias, 38, 45

Organisation de la conférence islamique (OIC) summit, 27–29, 55, 159nn1–2

organized labor, 69, 82, 123–48; formal contracts negotiated by, 13, 32, 50–51, 55–56, 82, 125, 146, 163n40, 163nn42–43; political autonomy of, 129–30, 169n11; politician responses to, 124–25; public support of, 1–2, 13, 86–87, 130, 138–40, 146; religious motivations of, 13, 141, 145–48; SNTN's mobilizations and, 129–41, 146–47, 169nn10–11; state recognition of, 92–94; strategies of, 126; Sy's leadership of, 123–25, 129; trash strikes of, 1–3, 13, 22–23, 26–27, 51, 82, 93–94, 123–26, 129–41, 146–47

originaires, 35, 159nn9–10

participatory citizenship, 2–4, 21–23, 94–96, 158n26; of community-based trash collection project, 12–13, 26, 89, 97–122; in Diop's participatory trash sector, 68–82, 100, 110–11, 129; gendered discourses of, 62, 64, 76–81, 88–89, 100–101; of Journées de Propreté, 44–45, 52, 70–72, 77; low-cost

flexible labor of, 72–73; in NGO community development projects, 98–101, 120–22; of Set/Setal movement, 2, 9, 12, 25–26, 34, 43–46, 48, 61–80, 162n28. *See also* community-based trash collection; trash work

Patterson, Amy S., 166n17

people as infrastructure, 5, 16–17, 61–74. *See also* Simone, AbdouMaliq

piety. *See* Islam; religious and spiritual practices

Pikine, 36

"Planet of Slums" (Davis), 169n7

Plateau district, 10, 11*f*, 36, 50

politics of garbage, 25, 27–59, 95–96, 149–54; codified segregation of poor neighborhoods in, 10–12, 19–22, 28–29, 36–37, 50, 53–54, 100–101, 106–10, 160n15; colonial legacies in, 34–36, 109, 159–60nn7–12; in community-based trash infrastructures, 101–2, 106–10, 168n13; customary authorities in, 101–2, 168n13; decentralization laws and, 50, 52, 163n38, 166n17, 168n13; under Diouf, 39–47, 161n18, 162n28; HLM Fass neighborhood revolt in, 1–2, 13, 132–38; materialization of state power in, 20–23, 32–34, 101, 159n6; under M. Diop, 42–46, 48, 58, 68–74, 129, 162nn28–29; under M. Sall, 55–56, 58, 164nn49–50; neoliberal governing-through-disposability in, 3–5, 32–34, 58–59, 125–26, 149–54; official regulatory management in, 160n17; OIC summit and, 27–29, 55, 159nn1–2; organizations involved in, 29, 30–31*t*; religious authority in, 42, 47; in Senghor's developmentalist agenda, 36–38, 160nn14–17; state and local power-sharing in, 50–56, 163n45, 164n48; structural adjustment and, 38–42, 46–48, 56–59, 160n16, 161nn21–23; structures of feeling in, 32–33, 126–29, 140–41; Sufi Mouride brotherhood in, 41–43; under Wade, 27–32, 34, 47–58, 75, 81–96, 129–41, 162n33; youth involvement in, 40–44, 60–63, 67, 70. *See also* garbage crises; neoliberal reforms; organized labor; Set/Setal movement

Prashad, Vijay, 160n12

precarity, 21–23, 61–62, 81, 121, 126, 151–53

public services. *See* infrastructures

Puig de la Bellacasa, Maria, 127

Quatre Communes, 34–36

race: in narratives of African alterity, 23; in segregation of urban spaces, 19–20, 24, 35–36, 158n23, 160n12

Reddy, Rajyashree N., 158n23

Relais pour le développement urbain participé (RUP) program, 167n2, 167n6. *See also* Environnement et développement du tiers monde

religious and spiritual practices, 15, 126–29, 141–48, 153–54; everyday practices of piety in, 129, 144–45, 147–48; expansion into the public sphere of, 128, 145–46, 168n5; formal institutions of, 8, 128–29, 147; spaces of affiliation in, 6, 8, 18, 26. *See also* Islam

Robinson, Jennifer, 24

Sall, Khalifa, 51–52, 55–58

Sall, Macky, 29–32, 55–56

salvage bricolage, 5, 17–18, 62–63, 81–94, 127, 149–54, 166n20; degradation of trash work and equipment and, 87–94; household waste management challenges and, 82–87

Samson, Melanie, 112–13

sanitation syndrome, 36, 160n12

Searle-Chatterjee, Mary, 132

Senegalese Democratic Party (Parti Démocratique Sénégalais, PDS), 47, 51, 161n23

Senghor, Léopold Sédar, 35–39, 42, 160nn14–17

"Set" (N'Dour), 66, 165n8

Set Setal, des murs qi parlent (ENDA), 64–66, 67f, 165n7

Set/Setal movement, 2–3, 9, 25–26, 30t, 43–46, 60–74, 143–44, 162n28; AGETIP project of, 70–72, 165nn10–11; community projects of, 66–68; demographics of participants in, 63–64, 75–76, 143, 164n2; international recognition of, 74; low-cost flexible labor of, 72–73; murals of, 3f, 63–68, 69f; origins of, 63–64, 73; participatory citizenship of, 2, 9, 12, 26, 34, 44–46, 48, 61–62, 94; state instrumentalization of,

61; transformation into Diop's participatory trash system of, 68–77, 110–11, 165nn9–10; women's roles in, 64, 68, 77, 80–81, 143, 170n21

Set Wecc event, 39–40

Silver, Jonathan, 156n12

Simone, AbdouMaliq, 17, 62, 155n2, 157n18. *See also* people as infrastructure

slave trade, 35, 159n7

Smith, Neil, 156n12

Socialist Party (Parti Socialiste), 36–51, 58, 69, 129, 160n13; organized labor and, 129–30, 169n11; Set/Setal movement and, 72–73; Sufi Mouride brotherhood and, 41–43, 47, 128, 162n26. *See also* politics of garbage

social reproduction, 21–22, 62, 81, 95, 115–16, 158n26. *See also* life's work

Société africaine de diffusion et de promotion (SOADIP), 30–31t, 38

Société industrielle d'aménagement urbain du Sénégal (SIAS), 30–31t, 40, 63, 68–70, 76, 160n14, 165n9, 165n12

Société pour la propreté du Sénégal (SOPROSEN), 30–31t, 163n45, 164n48

soft neoliberalism, 12

spirituality. *See* Islam; religious and spiritual practices

Splintering Urbanism (Graham and Marvin), 157n17

Star, Susan Leigh, 127, 131

state power: materialization in urban infrastructures of, 4–6, 8, 14–18, 156n12; materialization in waste management of, 20–23, 32–34, 101; performative practices in, 33–34, 159n6. *See also* politics of garbage

Strauss, Kendra, 22

street vendors, 55, 163n45

Structural Adjustment Programs (SAPS), 3–6, 9, 32, 146, 161n19; currency devaluations of, 46, 162n30; debt reduction packages of, 47–48, 162n31; degradation of infrastructure under, 46–47, 57–58, 60–61; flexibilization of labor under, 40–41, 48, 54–55, 62–63, 111, 129, 161n21, 164n50; impact on youth of, 60, 67, 70–74; politics of garbage and, 38–42, 46, 56–59, 149–54, 160n16, 161nn21–23; relaxation of, 47–48; third-sector initiatives in, 98–103. *See also*

International Monetary Fund; neoliberal reforms; World Bank

Sufi brotherhoods, 41–43, 128, 145, 147, 160n15, 162nn25–26

Le Super Étoile, 165n8

Swanson, Maynard W., 36, 160n12

Sy, Madany, 123–25, 129, 139–41, 145

Syndicat National des travailleurs du nettoiement (SNTN), 129–41, 169n10; leadership of, 123–25, 129, 139, 140f; political autonomy of, 129–30, 169n11; public support for, 138–40; strike-based campaigns of, 130–41, 146–47

Taxe d'enlèvement des ordures ménagères (TEOM), 116–17, 160n17, 162n28

Thioub, Ibrahima, et al., 41

Tijani brotherhood, 41

Tonghor (Yoff) neighborhood, 58, 98, 101–6, 134, 164n3. *See also* community-based trash collection; Yoff district

toxic vitality, 18, 85, 116, 153

trash. *See* garbage crises; infrastructures; politics of garbage; waste

trash trucks: collection process of, 83, 84f; community-based trash collection and, 118–19, 152; poor condition of, 49, 54f, 90–92, 166n24; during Set/Setal, 77–79

trash work, 7–8, 25–26, 28–29, 33–34, 60–96, 149–54; of Christians in Muslim societies, 143, 170n20; as employees of AMA, 48–49, 82, 130, 162n33, 163n35, 169n13; as employees of CADAK-CAR, 51, 163n40; flexibilized labor of, 40–41, 48, 54–55, 62–63, 82, 111, 129, 161n21, 164n50; formal contracts for, 13, 32, 50–51, 55–56, 82, 125, 146, 163n40, 163nn42–43; hybrid institutions of, 9–10, 12, 30–31t; as intrinsic to women, 64, 76, 78–81, 111–15, 165nn4–6, 166n18; material precarities of bodies in, 21–23, 61–62, 152–53; at the Mbeubeuss dump, 158n28; as moral citizenship, 74–75, 78–81, 144–48, 154; neglected trucks and equipment in, 24, 49, 54f, 90–92, 166n24; neoliberal reforms and degradation of, 7, 12–13, 87–94, 114–16, 153–54; public support of workers in, 1–2, 13, 86–87, 130, 138–40;

salvage bricolage of, 5, 62–63, 81–94, 127, 149–54, 166n20; Set/Setal movement and, 2–3, 9, 25–26, 30t, 43–46, 60–74, 162n28; social stigma attached to, 75–78, 80, 90, 139, 143–46, 166n15; spiritual value of, 13, 16, 21, 115, 126–29, 141–46, 153; terminology used for, 76, 139; trash strikes of, 1–3, 13, 22–23, 26–27, 51, 82, 93–94, 123–26, 129–41, 146–47; of women in the participatory trash sector, 76–81, 88–89, 100–101, 110–11, 143, 170n21. *See also* labor of urban infrastructures; organized labor; participatory citizenship; politics of garbage

tuberculosis, 90

unions. *See* organized labor

Unité de coordination et de gestion des déchets (UCG), 30–31t, 56, 164nn49–50

urban citizenship, 3, 5–8, 13–14, 151; codified segregation in, 10–12, 19–22, 28–29, 36–37, 50, 53–54, 100–101, 106–10, 160n15; in colonial Dakar, 35, 159–60nn9–12; grounding in urban labor of, 6–8; racial boundaries of, 19–20, 24, 35–36, 158n23, 160n12. *See also* participatory citizenship

urban political ecology (UPE), 6–7, 155n6, 156n12

Veolia Propreté, 50, 51, 53

Vivendi, 50

von Schnitzler, Antina, 14, 156n11

Wade, Abdoulaye, 28f, 61, 82, 87–96, 169n11; Alternance election of 2000 of, 47, 135–36; flexibilized labor under, 54–55, 62–63, 82, 111, 164n50; garbage crisis of 2006–2009 under, 129–41; household waste management challenges under, 82–87; infrastructure development goals of, 47–49, 53–55, 136–37, 163n45; management of public services by, 10, 12, 27, 52–54; Monument de la Renaissance africaine of, 27, 29f, 55, 164n47; politics of garbage of, 27–32, 34, 47–58, 75, 129, 162n33; presidential campaign of 1988 of, 42–43;

Wade, Abdoulaye (*continued*)
reelection of 2007 of, 1, 2*f*, 130, 135–36,
170n18; salvage bricolage under, 62–63,
81–94
Wade, Karim, 27, 29, 50
waste, 18–25; composition in Dakar of, 83; in
discourses of failed African cities, 23–24;
diseases associated with, 19, 49, 90, 115–16,
134, 166n22; as index of value, 18–20, 132,
157–58nn20–22; material power of, 4,
18–23, 32–34, 101, 131–41, 153; material
properties of, 18, 83, 86, 131–32; precarity
in management of, 21–23, 26; social engineering projects and, 36; storage of, 83,
85–86. *See also* garbage crises; infrastructures; politics of garbage; trash work
waste labor. *See* trash work
Watts, Michael, 101
Whatmore, Sarah J., 15–16
White, Luise, 155n8
Winner, Langdon, 152
women. *See* gendered discourses
World Bank, 38–39, 70–74, 160n16, 162n31,
163n35, 165nn10–11. *See also* Bretton

Woods institutions; Structural Adjustment
Programs

Yeoh, Brenda S. A., 160n12
Yoff district, 11*f*, 97–122, 167n1; APECSY community association of, 103, 107, 111–12,
114, 168n13, 168n19; dumping practices
in, 104*f*, 105–6, 108, 120, 134, 167n9; ethnic divisions in, 106–10; firing of female
trash workers in, 89, 100–101, 110–11,
115; garbage crisis of 2003 in, 97, 118–20;
Geejndar communities in, 102, 105, 107–9,
118, 167n7; Lebou ethnic group of, 101–10,
167nn4–5; striking trash workers in, 93*f*;
trash-worker headquarters in, 93. *See also*
community-based trash collection
youth, 60–63, 88; cleaning and moral citizenship of, 74–76, 78–81; formal organizations
of, 63, 64, 72, 164nn1–2; and gender, 76,
81, 166n19; impact of SAPS on, 60, 67,
70–74; politics of garbage and, 40–44, 60;
as social category, 166n23. *See also* Set/Setal
movement